Acknowledgments

Photos courtesy of Miss Young's private collection

Send all inquiries to:

THOMAS MORE PUBLISHING
200 East Bethany Drive
Allen, Texas 75002-3804

Telephone: 877-275-4725 / 972-390-6300

Fax: 800-688-8356 / 972-390-6560

E-mail: **cservice@rcl-enterprises.com**

Website: **www.ThomasMore.com**

Printed in the United States of America

Library of Congress Catalog Number 00-109224

ISBN 0-88347-467-0

1 2 3 4 5   04 03 02 01 00

The Authorized Biography of Loretta Young

Forever Young

The Life,
Loves and
Enduring Faith
of a Hollywood
Legend

Joan Wester Anderson

To Linda,
who never
lost faith

CONTENTS

~

Foreword

≈

*Our human connections are guided by God, and ultimately
all of us are linked through His love. Thus, we have all
already met, not as actress and fan but as His children,
and we can never be lost to each other.*

—LORETTA YOUNG

Sometime in 1998, I received a call from Linda Lewis of The
Entertainment Group, a video production company then in
California. She and her husband, Christopher, were doing a
series on angels and miracles. Could they come to my house to
interview me? This request wasn't unusual—I had written several
best-selling books on these themes during the '90s, and was
frequently featured on radio and television shows. I invited
Linda and Christopher to come whenever convenient.

A few weeks later they arrived, a friendly, obviously talented
couple whom I liked right away. We went to work and by the end
of the day, had enough tape for their project. As Linda and I
were straightening the living room and chatting, she mentioned
that her husband was Loretta Young's son.

"Loretta Young, the actress?" I was astonished.

"The very same," Linda acknowledged.

Wow. How well I remembered her from my younger days,
not only in movies, but sweeping through a door each week on
her television show, wearing a beautiful gown. "She did the kind
of work you could trust," I mused to Linda. "The scripts were not
only wholesome, but usually had a moral principle involved.

And of course, she was so beautiful." Linda assured me that "Mom" still was. I gave her one of my books for Loretta.

Time passed, and Linda and I occasionally talked on the phone—we had developed a friendship that we wanted to maintain. The angel/miracle videos had been released, and she and Christopher were on to other work. Loretta, I learned, had enjoyed the book I'd sent, and had read a few more in the series. Then one evening, Linda had played the videos for Loretta.

"Linda, I like that woman, and her books." Loretta had pointed to my image on the screen. "I wonder if she would write my life story."

Linda was startled. For the past thirty years, biographers had requested meetings with Loretta, but she had turned most down; she had authorized only one work, and this had never been published. Nor had she granted extensive interviews to magazines. Now she was apparently ready to chronicle her remarkable life, and had selected a writer based on nothing more than a few quick camera shots. Or so it seemed.

When Linda phoned in February 1999, I was, as always, happy to chat. My delight turned to disbelief when she told me why she was calling. "You can't be serious," I protested. "Why, Loretta could have any author she chose. Why me? I've never written a biography. Lists and records and research and. . . ."

"Mom believes she has experienced many little blessings and wonders in her life," Linda pointed out. "These are what she wants to talk about. Who but a miracle-writer would understand?"

"But . . ."

"Both of you are Catholics too, sharing the same views."

"But . . ."

"Think it over," Linda went on. "Take all the time you need. But remember, she is 86. . . ."

Thanks, Linda. Yet she was right—I should at least consider the idea, even though I had done my best to avoid Hollywood, both the place and much of its product. However, now and then one found a little glow there, a fragile flicker of decency and beauty. Loretta had lighted many such candles during her years as an actress, and an "earth angel." Perhaps sharing the stories of her life—her moments of rapture and anguish, her mistakes, her discoveries—might inspire those who today were attempting to live ethical lives in the midst of complex conditions. Not so much a biography as a faith journey. . . .

My husband reminded me that I had never written about angels either, until the first book in the series. If God was truly calling me to this project, He would supply the necessary tools. I prayed for the wisdom to know if this was, indeed, His request. I learned later that Loretta was also praying, asking for the same reassurance. Linda prayed too—just because she's Linda.

Eventually, I went to Palm Springs to stay with Loretta in her lovely home, to see if we would be compatible. I met a gracious, down-to-earth and unexpectedly witty woman who, other than the fact that she did not wish to own a fax or computer ("Dear, even turning on the VCR scares me"), couldn't have been a more charming writing partner. We tooled around town in her massive Chevy Caprice station wagon, clipping a trash can now and then ("Can you believe?" she asked me, "that when I went to trade this car in on another just like it, they told me it hasn't been made for years?"). We shopped for clothes at an outlet mall (she was a born bargain-hunter), went out to dinner, laughed and prayed together. Her life was a hotel lobby, with her huge and varied collection of friends the jewels of her existence—and she wouldn't have changed anything for the world.

We worked too. Loretta was initially leery about going "on the record" with certain facts. "You can talk about any of this after my death," she assured me. "But as to including it in the book. . . ."

"If your life sounds perfect, what can readers learn from it? Of what use is faith?" I argued. She agreed, and yet. . . . It was an unsettled point, but I trusted we would resolve it eventually. In the meantime, I went home to write, research and interview, mailing her copies of chapters to proofread as they took shape. We sent each other little gifts, chatted on the phone, and laughed about her almost-indecipherable handwriting. At one point, she told me that whatever happened with the book, she regarded our collaboration a success because we had made a friend of each other. I agreed completely.

One day in late May, 2000, Loretta unexpectedly asked if I would come back to Palm Springs. "I'm not feeling very well right now," she said, "and you and I have a few more details to discuss."

I heard the smile in her voice, and my spirit lifted. I knew without a doubt that she had decided to leave her story completely in my hands. Our visit never took place, however, for her physical condition worsened, and she went into the hospital a few weeks later. I waited for her to rally, as she had done so many times before. But it was not to be.

Loretta Young died on my birthday, August 12, 2000. It was now her birthday too, her grand, sweeping entrance into eternity. She had fought the good fight, she had finished the race. And it remained only for others to know her as we did.

In every book, there is the same question: where to start? "Before I formed you in your mother's womb, I knew you," God reminds us. And so we begin even before the beginning—at a moment when, as Gretchen Young, Loretta's life hung in the balance. May you be blessed with her story, and may *Forever Young* bring you the reassurance that God can work in anyone's life, that He will never leave us or forsake us, and that when we are at our weakest, that is when He loves us the most.

PART ONE

⁓

Welcome to the World

"Push, Gladys!" someone was commanding her. "You can do it. The baby's almost here!" I can't, she told herself, longing for rest. But the pains kept coming. How could she raise this new child, Gladys wondered hazily. Would she have enough time for it, enough love? A logical question, given their circumstances. And God didn't always work the way she hoped He would. . . .

⁓

She had grown up with people remarking on her beauty— especially her huge eyes and high cheekbones—but Gladys Royal had not yet found the man with whom she wanted to spend her life. In the early 1900s, there were few careers open to her other than wife and mother. Her own mother had died of appendicitis when Gladys, the eldest of three daughters, was about nine. The family was living in the South at that time, and Gladys' father, a traveling real estate broker, put the three girls into a Catholic boarding school, although they were Methodists, so that they would be raised as "ladies." When Gladys was eleven, she asked her father if she could become a Catholic.

"Oh, no, Gladys," her father had answered. "That's much too serious a decision for you to make at your age. Wait until after you graduate from high school."

The girls had spent vacations with their southern relatives, and saw their father only sporadically as they grew up. By high school graduation, Gladys was determined to take her time and choose a man who would always be at her side.

When handsome Earl Young came into her life in 1907, Gladys appeared to have been struck by lightning. The fact that he had an artificial leg (the real one amputated when he was a child) mattered to her not one whit. Her innate common sense may have abandoned her at that point—no one will ever know—but she married her Prince Charming shortly after their first meeting and against her father's wishes. The newlyweds were both nineteen.

Earl Young worked as an auditor for the Denver, Rio Grande and Western Railroad, which required traveling. This was fine with Gladys, and during their first year together, she and Earl lived in Denver. All, however, was not bliss. Gladys suspected almost from the beginning that her young husband was not being faithful to her. Distraught, she sought counsel from a priest at the nearby Catholic church, and once again, her interest in Catholicism blossomed. Always intrigued by the Mass, the sacraments and commandments, the comforting rituals—"It gives me a sense of belonging to a huge, worldwide family," she once explained—she began taking instructions. She was so enthusiastic that Earl decided to accompany her. In 1908, at the christening of their first child, Polly Ann, they were baptized too.

But cracks in the marriage continued, despite Earl's newfound religion. "Earl was not a mean man," Gladys once observed, "but he was weak, and much too handsome for his own good." A *second daughter, Betty Jane, was born in Salida, Colorado, on the way to Earl's new job assignment in Salt Lake City, but her arrival did nothing to bridge her parents' growing estrangement.*

Gladys went to church frequently. Shouldn't her precious Catholic faith be an oasis during the hard times? But with Earl's outside amusements continuing, the situation was getting worse, and she, always a capable, courageous person, was running out of resources. Even her health was affected, and one day she visited a physician to complain of persistent flu-like symptoms.

"You're not sick, Mrs. Young," the doctor said, as he finished the exam. "You're just pregnant again."

Pregnant. The word, usually so joyous, dropped like a stone in her stomach. Not now, God, she heard herself praying. Not when everything is so awful. . . .

The doctor had noticed her reaction. He sat back casually on his chair. "You know," he began quietly, "there's no need for you to have babies this regularly. Maybe you'd like to skip this one, and wait for a better time for your next."

Gladys looked up, confused. "How . . . ?"

The doctor shrugged. "There are ways."

He was offering her an abortion, Gladys suddenly realized, an answer to her dilemma. And no one, not even Earl, would have to know. She thought about the constant worry over finances, of Earl's ever-growing displeasure with her and their failing marriage—what kind of strain would yet another child place on their relationship? She wasn't ready! It was too much. . . .

Then she thought of the Catholic faith she'd pledged to uphold on her Baptism day. Abortion was forbidden to Catholics, she knew, because the Church believed that every life, no matter how tiny or humble, had been sent by the Father. And who was wise enough to thwart the Father's plan?

Gladys rose. "I-I can't do it," she told the doctor. "I'm going to have the baby."

He shrugged. Gladys understood his reaction. She was probably insane, she told herself.

On the way home, she stopped to see her parish priest. He offered more comfort than her doctor had, and a suggestion as well. "Why don't you give this baby to Christ's mother?" he suggested gently.

"What do you mean, Father?" she asked.

"I mean, put the child in Mary's hands. You can trust her, you know. She's a mother too. Let her watch over this baby, and ask her for help whenever you need it."

Gladys had never thought of such a thing. But it could be done, couldn't it? On the way home, she consecrated the tiny being within her to the woman who had carried her Lord. It might not have made sense to most people. But sometimes faith demanded risks. . . .

Someone was still yelling at her. "Push, keep pushing!" And then . . . and then, the newborn's cry. "It's a healthy girl, Mrs. Young." Another girl, brought into this household of females . . . But an exquisitely beautiful girl, Gladys realized, as the midwife placed her in her mother's arms.

More suffering lay ahead. Gladys would bear a son in a few years, and Earl would abandon her shortly afterwards, leaving her penniless and exhausted. She and the four children would travel a difficult road before security and happiness finally found them. But life would be good again. And the child she might have stopped from being born, the child consecrated to Mary whom she now held in her arms, would be a major part of that success.

Right now, however, the future was hidden from Gladys' eyes. She knew only, with a sudden fierce passion, that she loved this daughter as deeply as the others, and she would leave the details to heaven. She bent over the infant. "Hello, little Gretchen," she whispered. "Welcome to the world."

Part 1 photo—Baby Gretchen with her mother, Gladys (photo on page 11).

The Early Years

Keep your face to the sunshine,
and you cannot see the shadows.

—*HELEN KELLER*

Gladys checked the table, set for the evening meal. So many chairs. . . . But she should be glad that there would be a crowd in the dining room tonight. It meant her boarding house was full, and nothing could be more reassuring to the young woman.

She and the children had come a long way in the past four years, she mused as she straightened a napkin. She had left Earl several times, and during one of their estrangements, she had taken the children and moved to Los Angeles. For a while, Gladys, the three little girls and baby Jack had lived with her sister and brother-in-law, Carlene and Ernest Traxler, and their daughters. Then Earl had shown up again, with a new job in Los Angeles, begging for another reconciliation. Gladys could not deny her loneliness and her love for him, so the family rented a small house next door to the Traxlers on Vine Street, a dirt road lined with pepper trees.

During that time, four-year-old Gretchen had her first taste of "show business." Uncle Ernest Traxler was an assistant production manager at Lasky Studios (which would eventually become Paramount Studios), across the street. One day the director of *The Primrose Ring* needed four fairies to fly around in a garden scene. "Where can we find some short people right away?" he asked Ernest.

Ernest thought. There were always a lot of "short people" in the Young and Traxler yards. He went across the street, and pulled the smallest children out of the sandbox: Gretch, her brother Jackie and Ernest's younger daughters. "At the studio, they put some tulle around our waists, little wings on our backs and hoisted us up in the air on harnesses," Loretta explained. The other children screamed in terror (since movies were silent, no one paid any attention to them), but she thought it was phenomenal. "I was flying, and I never wanted to come down!"

When the day was over, each of the children received five dollars. Jackie and Loretta ran home, and gave the money to Mama. Ten dollars could go a long way in 1917, and Gladys was delighted.

But shortly thereafter, Gladys caught Earl with the maid he had hired to help her. It was apparently the final straw. "Earl," Gladys had faced him firmly, "I don't want anything bad to happen to you. But I wish I never had to see you again!"

Earl walked out the front door on his way to work. "Gladys," he'd said over his shoulder, "you never will."

Earl had not been seen since—by Gladys or anyone else.

The Traxlers were quick to offer comfort, but financial help was harder to come by. Once the shock of being abandoned began to subside, Gladys determined to care for her family by herself. But how? She summoned up her courage, and went to the local Catholic bishop for advice. "What can you do to earn a living?" he asked.

Gladys had pondered that same question. "I was raised in a convent," she pointed out, "so I know how to cook and clean and sew." (And move furniture, she might have added; ever since she was small, she had delighted in giving the convent rooms a new look by changing chairs and accessories around.) "I'm thinking of opening a boarding house."

The Bishop was intrigued with this young woman's resolve. It would not have been possible or prudent to use church funds to finance her, but he came from a wealthy family, and decided to make a personal investment. He would lend Gladys one thousand dollars, which would allow her to rent a large house, and hire some servants to help her run it. He would also co-sign on a loan for furniture. He drew up legal papers, which Gladys gratefully signed.

Gladys found a suitable house on Ninth and Green Street, where the Catholic Chancery office stands today. It was a good location, right across from Cathedral Chapel school, where her children could attend. She decided to rent primarily to families, not only because there would be children for hers to play with, but because they tended to be more reliable. Her first family was a lawyer, his wife and their three children. Since the boarding house was near Lasky Studios, actors and technicians also requested rooms. Gladys' timing would prove to be fortunate, because the silent movie industry was captivating people all over America. Hollywood would soon turn from a small town into a capital of glamour and fantasy, attracting workers who needed places to live.

For the children, life in the boarding house was a delight. "Every family had their own bedroom, except us kids," Loretta said. "We kind of slept all over the place; wherever there was room, on couches or floors, we all piled in." A perpetual pajama party. Occasionally, the Young girls and their cousins would get movie parts too. In the classic Rudolph Valentino movie, *The Sheik,* they all played Arab street urchins, doused each day with dark liquid makeup. Every evening, Valentino would stop at the children's tent, and give them rides on his big white horse.

For Gladys, however, there was far more work than fun, and even when she could sit down, she'd be sewing to keep up with the children's clothing needs. There were times when her boarders gave her advances on the rent, so she could continue to buy supplies, and she knew her family was never very far from homelessness. Right now, however, as dinnertime approached, she surveyed her domain with a feeling she hardly recognized. Not happiness—no, it was still too soon in her healing process for that. But hope—yes, that was it. For the first time in many years, there was no humiliation, no grief nibbling around the edges of her life. Now she was limited only by how much she prayed, and how hard she worked.

Mae Murray, the star of *The Primrose Ring,* had been charmed by Gretch's enthusiasm while "flying." (Gladys had also gone to school with Mae's husband.) Since Mae had no children, she later asked Gladys if Gretchen could come and stay with her. "For how long?" Gladys asked, thinking Mae meant an overnight or two.

"Well, for as long as she wants. Forever, if you agree. I could give her a lot, you know." This was not as unusual a request as it might seem. In that era, children in working-class families, which was most of the population, were often passed among relatives due to financial straits, or sent to farm kin to help with harvests or other work. Typically, formal education ended at eighth grade, and only the fortunate went on to high school or college. Although Gladys knew that the offer would provide far more material benefits for Gretch than she could, she would not consider any permanent arrangement. (Nor did she believe the Virgin Mary, Gretch's "official" guardian, would approve.) "You may take her home with you, if one of the other girls here can go with her," she told Mae. "But when they want to come back, you must bring them."

Mae agreed. Gretch seemed to like her, and perhaps she hoped she could win the little girl over once she moved into more luxurious surroundings. Gretch agreed too, as long as her cousin and best friend, Carlene Traxler, would come with her. To the five-year-olds, it all seemed like a glorious adventure.

The girls were awed at the sight of "Maetsie's" lavish house, even more stunned at the beautifully-decorated room they were to share, along with their own bathroom! Mae hired a German governess to care for them when she was working, and arranged for dancing lessons for Gretch—a dream come true. There was also a closet filled with beautiful new clothes. To two younger daughters used to hand-me-downs, it was heaven. And they were always welcome to play at the studio, while Maetsie made movies there. If the girls got homesick, Mae's driver would take them to the boarding house, where they would spend some time in the security of their families before going back. "Maetsie spoiled us rotten," Loretta said. "It was like a game to us. We had our families plus this marvelous escapade."

During those days, Gretch realized how grand a movie star's life could be, and she chose it as her goal. Later, in first grade at Cathedral Chapel school, she would assure her teacher, Sister Marina, that she didn't have to learn to spell, "because I'm going to be a movie star, Sister, and they have secretaries to spell for them."

Sister Marina wasn't convinced. But she was impressed that, each week, Gretchen would contribute a nickel of her ten-cent allowance to the "pagan babies fund." One day Gretch went to Sister Marina. "I've been giving money for a long time," she complained. "When am I going to get one?"

"One what?" Sister asked.

"One baby!" Gretch answered.

Sister laughed and hugged Gretch. "No, honey, you aren't buying a baby. The nickels go to the baby's mother, so the baby will have enough to eat, and grow up strong, and learn to love God like you and I do."

Gretch was crushed. "No baby?"

Sister hugged her again. "Why don't you offer up your disappointment to Our Lord as a little gift to Him, maybe for all the times you've disappointed Him?"

Gretch continued to give her nickel every week. It was the beginning of a lifelong commitment to help those in need.

⌒

The girls spent over a year with Mae, and then, inexplicably, one morning Gretch awakened, and said, "Carlene, I want to go home."

"Me too," said Carlene. The two of them went to break the news to Mae.

"Well," Mae sighed, "I promised your mothers. . . ." She kissed each one, and made them pledge to come and visit. The timing was probably perfect, for shortly afterwards, Mae and her husband moved to the East Coast. Everyone kept in touch for a while, but years would pass before Loretta and Mae encountered each other again.

While Loretta and Carlene were enjoying luxury living with Mae Murray, little Jackie Young had also found a second family. Two houses away from his home lived the Boutieres, a mother, two daughters and a son. One of the daughters had married a lawyer named Lindley, and the couple moved into the family home. Eventually, Mr. Lindley became Gladys' lawyer, and he and his wife met her offspring. The Lindleys could not have children, so they enjoyed all the Youngs. But from the start, Jackie was their favorite. If he was ever in trouble at home or simply wished to get away from the crush of sisters and girl cousins, Jackie would run two houses down, crawl through a hole in the fence and hide in the Boutiere grape arbor. Shortly, Mrs. Lindley would be out to bring him a cookie, or an invitation to stay for dinner.

Gradually, Jackie spent more time with the Lindleys than he did at home, and had to be fetched for meals or bedtime. When Gladys announced plans to rent a larger boarding house several blocks away, the Lindleys were distraught. The distance was too far for three-year-old Jackie to travel back and forth by himself. What were they going to do without him?

As Mae Murray had done with Gretch, the Lindleys offered to adopt Jackie. Gladys was just as adamantly opposed this time. "I couldn't let him go," she explained. "He can stay with you whenever he wishes—I know you'll take good care of him. But he has to feel that he can come home any time he wants to."

That was how the two families left it, and the arrangement seemed to work. "Jackie would come home for a few weeks now and then, and after a while he'd get up and say, 'I'm going back to stay with Mama and Papa Bear'," Loretta recalled. "They were wonderful people, and wonderful to him."

A year passed, and although Gretch had returned home, the periods between visits from Jackie were growing longer. It was time to think about his education, and Gladys approached the Lindleys. She was considering yet another move, and perhaps he should return home permanently. The Lindleys were upset, and so was Jackie. Belatedly, Gladys realized that she had been too lenient about her son's attachment to this nice couple. To forcibly remove him might cause more problems than leaving the agreement as it was.

Boarding House Life

If you don't feel poor, you're not.

—LORETTA YOUNG

During these years, Gladys remained loyal to her adopted faith, taking the children to Sunday Mass, teaching them to pray at an early age, and presenting them with firm examples of right and wrong. One involved a boarder, Peggy Girth, who saved pennies in a giant bowl in her room. Gretchen was fascinated with the bowl, and apparently her dime a week (minus the pagan baby contribution) wasn't stretching far enough. One day she helped herself to a fistful of pennies from the bowl. "I walked the six blocks to the drugstore, bought an Eskimo Pie and had enough time to eat it on the way back before I reached home." How easy! The next day Gretch did the same thing. And the next day too.

Soon, however, Gladys summoned all the boarding house children to a meeting. Official encounters with Mrs. Young were always grave, because it meant someone had done something seriously wrong. "Miss Girth is missing many pennies," Gladys stated, eyeing each child in turn. "I think someone here must be responsible for that."

The children looked at each other, puzzled. Gretchen's heart started to pound.

"You don't need to confess now," Gladys went on. "But I expect whoever has been stealing to come to me privately, and let me know."

It was the first time Gretchen was conscious of doing something really wrong, and the feeling hurt more than she had expected. Worse was the thought of grieving her beloved mother. She wouldn't confess, she decided. The whole thing would blow over.

But that night, when Gladys was tucking in each child, she lingered a bit near Gretchen. "Don't you have something you'd like to tell me?" she murmured.

Tears rolled down Gretchen's cheeks. Gladys kissed her. "We'll talk about it tomorrow," she promised.

The next day Gretchen went to her mother immediately after breakfast. Gladys opened her purse and took out some bills. "First I want you to go to Miss Girth and give her this money, and tell her you are sorry and you won't steal from her or anyone again," Gladys said firmly. Gretchen nodded. "And then you will have to work this money off for me. For the next four days, I want you to wash and iron all the napkins we use."

All the napkins? Gretchen wasn't very good at arithmetic yet, but there were 20 people living in the boarding house, all using napkins at breakfast and dinner, times four days. . . . She lost count, and started to cry again. "I said I was sorry," she sobbed. "Why do I have to do all that work too?"

Gladys smiled. "It's good to feel sorry," she said. "But when we do wrong, we have to do more than that. We have to make amends to the people we hurt, do something to humble ourselves, just a little. Do you understand?"

Gretchen did. And, as her surprised mother pointed out a few days later, she did a better job on the napkins than the maid did.

As Gretch learned about life, so did Gladys. Her first boarding house had been a success primarily because it was located in an area of Los Angeles that had once been run-down, but was on its way back—thus enabling her to attract responsible boarders. She followed the same principle with her second house, and was now on to a third (Harvard and Washington). Gladys' skills, however, did not include handling money. She once proudly confided to Polly Ann that she had taken in $1,000 that month. "Mama, that's wonderful!" her eldest enthused.

"Of course," Gladys pointed out, "I spent $1,100."

While this was not quite the road to riches, Gladys was unconcerned with her bank balance. The boarding-house lifestyle was providing her children with a safe home in a family atmosphere, and she would worry about debts later. Occasionally, she could even squeeze a treat out of the budget. Once, Polly Ann came down with scarlet fever, then a life-threatening and contagious disease. "The garage at this boarding house had a second floor containing a playroom, storage space, even maids' rooms, so Polly Ann was quarantined there," Loretta recalled. "When Pol was feeling better, she'd come to the window and wave at all of us, and we'd yell back and forth or send things up and down in a basket." When Gretch got sick, however, she had different symptoms and no one realized that she too had contracted scarlet fever.

Gladys put Gretch in her bed, thinking she'd be better in a day or two. The children came in and out on visits, and even Peggy Girth appeared on a rather odd errand. (Despite the penny mishap, Miss Girth had moved with the Youngs from one boarding house to another.)

Peggy was a dance teacher, and she asked Gretch if she could fit a tunic on her. "I'm making it for me, honey, but I want to see how it's going to look."

"It'll be way too tight for you, Miss Girth—I'm a lot smaller."

"I know, but I like them tight. . . ."

Gretch was too tired and feverish to be suspicious, and it wasn't until she was presented with the tunic a week later on her eighth birthday that she realized just what it meant. "Dancing lessons, Mama? Really?"

"Not back at George Belcher's studio, dear." George Belcher, the father of dancer Marge Champion, was considered the best instructor in Hollywood, and Loretta had been in his class while living with Mae Murray. "He's too expensive. But we thought Miss Girth could teach you."

"Oh, Mama! I love you!" It was her best birthday to date. With the acquisition of the tunic, Gretch could move up from the oil cloth and newspaper costumes she usually constructed for the "shows" she and her sister Betty regularly produced for the boarders. (Fortunately for all of them, no one living in the house ever contracted Gretch's scarlet fever.)

About this time, Gladys also filed for divorce from Earl, on grounds of desertion. She still kept in touch with her mother-in-law, who claimed she had no knowledge of her son's whereabouts.

It was while living at the Harvard house that Gretch first exhibited signs of learning difficulties, particularly in reading and writing. "I can't tell the b's from the d's," she complained to her mother. "And some of the other letters are upside down." There was nothing wrong with Gretch's vision, so Gladys was at a loss to explain the situation, especially since the older girls learned very quickly in school. But discussions with the nuns brought no solutions. Gretch was a good girl, they all emphasized, but definitely a slow learner.

"Good," however, was a relative term. For, by the age of nine, Gretch, Carlene and their older siblings had started smoking, stealing Camel cigarettes from Uncle Traxler's bureau drawers every day after school. The group would hide in the garage playroom, and crack the window just slightly to let the clouds of smoke disappear. One day, Gladys' former mother-in-law, Grandma Young, had come to visit, and was doing dishes in the kitchen. She saw the billows, assumed the garage was on fire, and ran screaming out onto the lawn. Hearing her, the children clambered down the garage stairs, wearing virtuous expressions. "You kids are going to get in trouble someday if you keep smoking," Grandma Young yelled.

"Us? Smoking?" Gretch could always master the most innocent of looks.

Grandma wasn't impressed "I can smell it from here."

~

Gretch continued to smoke secretly until she was about thirteen. Then she smoked openly on the movie set, as did almost everyone else. "Why do you do that?" Gladys asked her one day.

"Well, Mama, it makes me feel older," Loretta explained.

"Hmmm." Gladys was at a loss. No one knew the health risks of smoking in those days, and since it didn't seem to be immoral—Gladys' standard for all behavior—she said nothing more. Loretta's habit, which was to last over fifty years, had begun.

~

By now, Gladys had enrolled her three daughters at the Ramona Convent boarding school in Alhambra, about a two-hour drive from their home. Such an arrangement, she believed, would give their education some stability. Gretch missed her old life, especially since she and her sisters were only home once a month. But she and Carlene continued a habit started years ago: going to the Saturday silent movies at the Deluxe Theater whenever they could. "By the time I had slowly sounded out a few words, the letters would be off the screen, so Carlene read all the subtitles to me, and I concentrated on watching what the actresses did."

And they added another adventure: shoplifting. Gretch had kept her tearful promise never to steal from Miss Girth again, but there had been other victims. "I only stole money from people I liked," Loretta pointed out, but since she had many friends, those who didn't watch their loose change closely were fair game (not to mention Uncle Ernest's Camels). However, when Gretch and Carlene were about nine, they decided to expand their horizons, and see what was available in merchandise.

"We could try the dime store," Gretch suggested one Saturday. The two were wearing light jackets with wide sleeves, and as they entered, Carlene ran her sleeve carefully along one of the open display counters. Thread and ribbons disappeared inside the sleeve like magic. The two girls eyed each other and smothered their laughter—it was so easy! They walked casually out the door.

"Let's see what we got!" Carlene was excited as they examined their booty. All sewing stuff, nothing valuable, but it was free! The girls ran home and found a box, into which they stashed the stolen merchandise. They hid the box under Carlene's bed. Gladys and Aunt Carly would never find it.

That could have been the beginning of a life of crime, Loretta admitted later with a smile. For the next several Saturdays, the girls continued their pattern, running their sleeves along the side of a counter, gathering whatever would fall inside, and taking it home to hide in the box. "It was ridiculous because we didn't need the things, we didn't use them or sell them or even give them away," she said. "If you had asked us why we were doing this, we wouldn't have known. Thrill seeking, I guess, just to see how it felt."

They didn't have long to wait. One particular Saturday, Gretch was engrossed in stealing when she felt a heavy hand on her shoulder. Shocked, she looked up, at the stern face of a woman. "Girls," the woman said in a tone that brooked no nonsense, "follow me."

Terrified, Gretch and Carlene walked behind the woman through the entire length of the store, as the customers' eyes followed them. They walked up the open flight of stairs, to the second floor where a door said 'Manager.' "Sit there," the woman pointed to a bench, and she went inside the door.

It wouldn't have occurred to either child to run—they were in a panic. Gretch was so frightened that she thought she would be sick. What if the manager called the police? What if he called her mother? She didn't know which would be worse. Carlene was more stoic, at least on the outside, but tears were gathering in her eyes.

Finally, the woman came out and escorted the girls in to the manager. "You were stealing from me, and our store detective saw you—is that right?" he asked bluntly.

Neither girl had ever heard of a store detective. But they both nodded slowly.

"Is this the first time?" he asked.

"No," admitted Gretch—who could steal but apparently not lie. "We've been putting things in a box at home."

"What kind of things?"

The girls described the trinkets. They both began to cry. "Please don't tell our mothers," Loretta sobbed.

The manager sighed. "I'll make a deal with you," he said. "If you two will promise that you'll never steal anything from anybody again, I won't tell your mothers. Think about it . . . will you promise?"

Oh, yes, they would promise. And as they walked out of the store, Loretta said, it was a turning point for her. "We never brought him the box—he didn't ask for it, and we were too afraid to go back. But he kept his word, and I kept mine." God was very kind to send someone to her with just the right mix of firmness and mercy, at a time when she might have begun a bad habit.

Loretta also had a positive habit: making and keeping friends. There was Carlene, of course, and Josephine (Josie) Saenz, the daughter of a doctor who was Counsel General to Panama. Josie was actually Polly Ann's friend, but since the girls all knew each other's pals, Josie and Gretch saw a lot of each other. At Ramona she also met Jane Sharp, and the two became fast friends. Because Gretch's academic achievements had continued to be lackluster, Jane was a godsend. She became protective of Gretch's inability to read, and helped her sound out the letters. The nuns were baffled, but also sympathetic. One day a substitute teacher announced that "the best behaved child can give out the spelling words today for the test." Loretta was immersed in her daydreams, not listening until the nun selected her.

Loretta was alarmed. "Sister," she whispered, "I can't read the spelling words!"

"Oh." The substitute frowned. Jane and the others who had heard, nodded vigorously. It was common knowledge. Gretch was popular and participated in all the school plays, but she could barely spell or read. "Well," the teacher decided, "you just stand close to me." Gretch did, and the substitute whispered each word to her, which Gretch then announced to the class.

She also continued along her self-appointed path to fame. "I used to love it when the nuns at Ramona would say, 'Gretchen, you're going to be working at the studio tomorrow, so your mother will pick you up tonight.'" She was usually cast as an extra, but occasionally had a dramatic scene, which she always played to the hilt. Instinctively, she had learned to stand out by simply doing something different than the rest—leaning right instead of left, running faster than others in a crowd scene, any piece of business that attracted attention. Her paychecks went right to Gladys, who continued to repay the Bishop's loan, and marvel at how God was working everything out in their lives.

The Family Grows

The family is one of nature's masterpieces.

—George Santayana

In 1923, Gladys did something very uncharacteristic—she married George Belzer, one of her boarders, who was a non-Catholic divorcee. Since Gladys was also divorced, the marriage was a civil one, unsanctioned by the church. Why she would make a move so contrary to her own belief system was a mystery, but Gladys never explained if she decided something was no one else's business.

Ten-year-old Loretta and her older sisters liked Mr. Belzer very much. Shortly after he'd moved into the boarding house, he had declared to everyone that he hated dogs, and had then been caught by the children feeding a stray and calling him a "cute little mutt" . . . so everyone called him "Mutt," which he handled good-naturedly. He was gentle and quiet in this family of charming extroverts, and also a bank examiner, good with funds. He took over the hopeless muddle that was Gladys' "budget," and obligingly tried to teach his stepdaughters a little about expenditures and compound interest. None showed the slightest curiosity. But they were all thrilled when Gladys and George announced a year or so after the wedding that there was to be another baby in the clan.

By now the family had moved again, this time to what was called a bungalow court—eight bungalows housing eight families. Gladys used one for her family, and rented out the other seven. Hardly missing a beat, she gave birth to Georgiana in 1925. Georgiana became everyone's daughter. Her sisters were thrilled with her, and so was her father. Gladys had cautioned George against getting too involved with or disciplining her children, but Georgie belonged to both of them. So, in an era when men barely recognized a diaper, George was delighted to co-parent.

Georgie was just a toddler when a girl living in a front bungalow came down with St. Vitus Dance, a dreaded disease whose symptoms involved startling involuntary movements. One morning at the breakfast table, Gretch and Betty were giggling and imitating the afflicted girl. "Stop it, that's cruel!" Gladys scolded them. "You could get it too!" Only a few days later, Gretch had the same symptoms.

There was no cure for St. Vitus Dance. Rest seemed to be the only option, in order to let the nerves calm down. So, as in the days of her scarlet fever bout, Gretch was put in her mother's bed, and told to lie as quietly as she could. Despite her efforts, her limbs would flail out at the most unexpected times.

"It was terrible," Loretta recalled later in life. "I felt awful, and since reading was such a struggle for me, and visitors weren't allowed, and meals had to be brought to me, there was no way to pass the time. My mother had red-and-white checked curtains on the windows, and I remember counting each square at least a thousand times." She had made her confirmation recently, and had selected the name, "Michaela," in honor of Michael the Archangel. He stood for strength and courage, but now Gretch felt frailer than ever before.

One day she reached for a holy card which a priest had given her on her First Communion Day. The card had a picture of Jesus on it, and underneath, the caption read, "Remember, He only sees the trying."

He only sees the trying. "There, in that lonely room, I began to think about that, and what it really meant." She thought about her stealing, her inability to read, the times she was selfish or vain or defensive. . . . "I began to comprehend, in my child's mind, that He already knew I was weak, but all He cared about was how hard I tried. I think, during those weeks, I really learned about prayer. And it has stayed with me ever since."

Ultimately, Gladys called in a specialist, who decided to remove Gretch's tonsils. After the operation, her symptoms disappeared, so it was assumed that this had been the source of her infection. "I'm just sorry it took so long to make you better," the doctor told her.

But Loretta admitted later in life that she wasn't sorry. "We don't always see God's plan at the time," she said. "But I think I was meant to have that quiet period with Him, just before my life began to dramatically change."

Boarding school had been an adventure. But Gretch missed her sisters after they graduated, so Gladys allowed her to come home, and finish grade school at St. Thomas. She was one of three girls in class, along with twelve or thirteen boys, and immediately developed a mad crush on Marty Hiss. Despite her flirting, Marty paid no attention to her. On graduation day, as the eighth-graders lined up in the schoolyard, Gretch and Marty were side by side. The pastor went down the line, asking each child what he or she was going to be in life. As always, Gretch replied, "I'm going to be a movie star."

Marty was next. "I'm going to be a priest," he announced.

A priest! Gretch was a woman scorned. "You'll never make it, Marty!" she whispered furiously. She saw him just a few times at summer parties, and then lost touch. But not forever. . . .

After graduation, Loretta enrolled in Catholic Girls' High School, her sisters' alma mater. At this point, however, the older girls were both under contract to studios, Betty having dropped out of high school and changed her name to Sally Blane when Paramount signed her. It was just a matter of time, Loretta believed, before she would be "discovered" too. (She and Sally had tried out for numerous stage productions in their handmade costumes, but had never won a role.) Once on a movie set, formal schooling would be unnecessary because she would be provided with a tutor. "In those days all you had to do was be pretty and obey your director, because everyone in the movie industry was simply experimenting," Loretta explained. Although she was proud of her beautiful sisters, she knew they didn't have the driving desire to be a star, as she did. But now she was at that awkward age—too old for child roles, too young and thin to play adults.

And too young to drive, too. She was complaining about that one day when Joe Benjamin, a professional boxer and one of Polly Ann's beaus, overheard her. "I'll teach you," he volunteered. It was probably a great way to score points with beautiful Polly.

"You will?" Loretta was incredulous. Joe had a big Cadillac, and she was only thirteen. (In those days, drivers didn't need licenses.) Eagerly, she followed Joe outside to the car, slipped behind the wheel, and listened carefully as he gave instructions. Then she turned on the engine, eased the car out onto the empty street and drove around the block!

"Not one mistake, kid. You did great!" Joe praised her as they approached the house. "Now, can you pull it into your driveway?"

"Sure, Joe." Confidently, Loretta turned the steering wheel, and pushed down on the clutch. Or was it the accelerator? The car gathered speed, and instead of gliding up the driveway, she crashed into the porch of the house next door.

The neighbors ran out, yelling and pointing at the splintered wood. Loretta was horrified. All Joe said was, "We're sorry, folks. I'll have everything fixed."

He did but, not surprisingly, that was the end of her driving lessons. It would be another two years before Loretta got her first car, a Buick coupe, black with a tan top, which she drove for six or seven years before selling it to one of the boarding house maids.

~

Loretta never became a skilled driver. Friends remember her cruising down the center turn lane on the Los Angeles freeways, delighted that no other drivers seemed to be using it. Friend Jack Sacco says she was the worst driver he ever knew.

"One Sunday she offered to drive us to church. I was silently strapped in as she wove and bobbed our way to Good Shepherd,"

Jack recalls. "After Mass, she pulled out of the church parking lot and almost crashed into several vehicles. They screeched to a halt, and she looked around, wondering what the commotion was all about. A block later, she sent two taxis swerving through an intersection in an attempt to avoid her.

"Stop the car!" I yelled.

"What's wrong?," she asked, laughing. "Why are all those people honking?"

Jack drove the rest of the way.

Leaving Gretch Behind

This time, like all times, is a very good one,
if we but know what to do with it.

—RALPH WALDO EMERSON

One day director Mervyn LeRoy phoned the house, looking for Polly Ann. "She's not here," Gretch informed him. "She's on location, doubling for Dolores Costello." ("Doubling" was doing anything too dangerous for the star to do. Polly Ann also doubled frequently for Joan Crawford.)

"Too bad," Leroy said. "There's a nice little part for her in a picture Colleen Moore is doing, *Naughty But Nice*. But we need her tomorrow."

Gretch's heart leaped. "W-would I do?" she asked.

LeRoy laughed. "I don't know. Who are you, and what do you look like?"

"I'm Polly's sister, Gretchen, and I guess I'm not bad-looking. . . ."

"Fine. Stop by any time today and we'll talk about it."

Today? First National Studios was at least three streetcar rides away, and she had never traveled there by herself. "I can't go with you today, dear," Gladys informed her excited daughter. "But if you want to be in movies, you'll have to learn to get around by yourself."

Mervyn LeRoy was not only a top director, but a prominent and respected member of Hollywood society. When he immediately cast Gretch in the part, it validated her as someone with possibilities.

Colleen Moore, the star, was also enchanted with Gretch. Colleen had noticed her among the child extras on a previous set, and after *Naughty But Nice* was finished, she prevailed upon the studio to give the young girl a screen test. Gretch photographed beautifully, but her front teeth protruded. Colleen suggested that the studio moguls provide her with a dentist. They agreed, because they had decided to put Gretch under contract.

The studio dentist was summoned, and decided to pull Gretch's two front teeth the following day, replacing them with false ones that slanted backwards. Gretch casually mentioned it that evening to Gladys. "What?" Gladys was shocked. These movie people might have authority over her daughter's work, but not her teeth! Gladys disliked going to the studio ("most of the people there have no manners at all!" she would huff), but she accompanied Gretch to the studio the next day, and lodged a vigorous objection. They would take this thirteen-year-old as she was. They did.

Mervyn LeRoy has been credited with changing Gretch's name, but Colleen Moore also had a hand in it. Neither thought that "Gretchen" was an "actress name," but Leroy always said he selected "Loretta." Colleen claimed that "Laurita" was her first choice (Colleen collected dolls, and her favorite was named "Laurita"), but because it sounded foreign, "Loretta" became the compromise. Whatever the truth, Gretch learned of her name change by reading it in the newspaper a few weeks after she began working on the picture. "It took me years to learn to like it," she said.

During that first year, Loretta learned far more than how to act. One morning she missed one of her streetcars, and arrived at the studio an hour late. "I dashed onto the set, but the director, George FitzMorris, called me up in front of everyone. 'I want to tell you something, young lady,' he said. 'Don't you ever, ever, EVER be late again, on my set or anyone else's! You were supposed to stand right behind Miss Moore in that scene, and we couldn't shoot her close without you. You have kept this entire set waiting. Inexcusable!' "

Loretta felt the tears gathering.

"No crying!" FitzMorris commanded. "Just remember what I said!"

Despite her immaturity and her transportation problems, she finally received a break—a loan to Metro Goldwyn Mayer and a test for the leading role opposite Lon Chaney, in *Laugh, Clown, Laugh.* Despite her thin, as yet undeveloped figure, her beauty was becoming apparent; and her luminous gray-blue eyes, radiant skin and high cheekbones won her the role of the tightrope-walker over sixty other girls. (Later, Loretta described herself somewhat differently: "A screenful of big eyes and buck teeth!")

The director, Herbert Brenon, was rumored to be hard to please. It was an understatement. Loretta, now fourteen, had never experienced treatment like his. "It started right away," she recalled. "He criticized me in front of everyone, told me I was stupid and useless." Brenon mocked her acting ("Who ever told you you had talent?") and kept threatening to fire her, if she could not master the techniques he had in mind. Once, she was supposed to walk across a foot-high tightrope, when he signaled the camera and yelled at her to start. The camera rolled, but Loretta lost her balance on the rope, and stumbled off. Furious, Brenon threw a heavy chair at her. Fortunately, it missed, for it probably would have broken her back.

Often, after his tirades, Loretta left the set in tears. But she wept alone in her dressing room, determined not to be unprofessional. Her mother had always assured her that she didn't have to make movies, but if she chose this life, she shouldn't quit when things got difficult. "If you give up on something when you're 12 or 13," Gladys would remind her, "it's going to be easier to walk away from more important things when you're twenty or thirty."

Loretta didn't want to tell Gladys how miserable she was. Nor did Polly Ann and Sally know, mistaking her reticence for a "high and mighty" act. They teased, and one of them hung a cutout star on Gretch's bedroom door, then waited for the inevitable explosion. But although feeling persecuted from all sides, Loretta decided not to react. After a while, the sisters felt sheepish, and took down the star without comment.

Loretta's co-star had noticed her difficulties. Lon Chaney was already famous as the "Man of 1,000 Faces" due to at least 150 characters he created, most involving elaborate makeup. Although he often played monsters (the Hunchback of Notre Dame and the Phantom of the Opera were perhaps his most well known roles), Chaney was a kind man, and extremely popular with the public. Now he intervened on Loretta's behalf.

"If it were not for his compassion, I would not have continued working in the motion picture business," Loretta said. "The treatment I was receiving from the director was so traumatic that I could no longer cope." Chaney, apparently, had a few private words with Brenon, and from then on, the situation changed. Chaney himself whispered (and sometimes interpreted) all of the director's suggestions to Loretta, and because she liked and trusted him, she was able to respond. Brenon ceased his abuse and the movie stayed on schedule. Chaney also remained on the set when Loretta was working with others in the cast, in case she needed protection or encouragement. Just like a guardian angel, Loretta always thought.

"He indeed saved my career, but he also taught me how to cope with a difficult personality without getting an ulcer or a nervous breakdown," she remembered. "I shall be beholden to that sensitive, sweet man until I die."

Yet damage had been done. Although Herbert Brenon later assured Loretta that his treatment of her hadn't been personal, but necessary in order to get a good performance out of her, Loretta's faith in herself, her goals and judgment, had been badly shaken. She had not realized how truly ugly and harsh the world could be, especially the world of Hollywood, how many things went on behind the scenes that no one should have to see or hear. It was the beginning of her two lives: the warm and secure Gretch-world, where she could be who she really was, and the public persona of Loretta, the star. For the next few years, she would wear a veneer of cool assurance that actually covered deep feelings of anxiety and apprehension. *He only sees the trying,* she would remind herself when doubt and failure loomed. "I had to pretend I had confidence," she admitted. "I knew I couldn't be a star without it."

PART TWO

The Perfect Godmother

My family attended Church of the Good Shepherd in Beverly Hills when I was growing up. They had decided to ask Loretta Young to be my godmother. She was that rare breed in Hollywood, a Catholic who wore her moral spirit on her shoulder and never compromised her principles. They felt she would be a fine role model for me.

As a Confirmation gift, Loretta gave me a little statue of the Blessed Mother holding baby Jesus, set on a jade base. The whole thing wasn't more than four inches high. The statue has sat next to my bed since I was eleven, and I kept it there as I grew. Sometimes I took it along when I traveled. It's been next to my bed my whole life.

I saw Loretta frequently as I grew up. No matter what the occasion, she was impeccably dressed (often wearing a hat), dignified yet funny. I teased her sometimes about her retainer brace. Here she was, so glamorous, yet carrying it in her purse, and slipping it in or out (I know she lost several in restaurants). As I became successful as an actress, she would write me notes, saying how proud of me she was, commenting on my performance in this movie or that play.

When she married Jean Louis, I sent her a gift, along with a note. I was so thrilled for her, I wrote. Even at eighty years old, she was still a romantic, and I was inspired by her. So many older people wouldn't want to remarry, but there she was, ready for a new chapter. She loved the comment and told me that I was right—life hadn't finished with her yet.

She was the perfect godmother, and I'll miss her.

*—**Marlo Thomas,***
Actress

Part 2 photo—Loretta and Spencer Tracy doing a scene from *A Man's Castle* (photo on preceding page).

Becoming Loretta

*Lord, help me to remember that nothing is going to
happen today that You and I together can't handle.*

—ANONYMOUS

By 1929, Loretta was carving out a place in the industry, doing
five or six pictures each year, and earning $250 a week at a time
when the Great Depression loomed, and the average family
income was about $50 per month. When she wasn't in front of
the camera, she watched other actresses work, learning about
hair, clothes and makeup. (Being allergic to mascara, she heated
wax for her lashes over a candle and, years later, would develop
a line of "warm" cosmetics.)

It was an era of great change, since new technology had
finally brought forth the much-anticipated "talkies." However,
many stars who had succeeded in silent pictures discovered to
their consternation that their voices could not make the
transition. For a time, it looked as if Loretta would fall into that
category too. The directors of First National, her studio, thought
her voice was too low. But then-president Al Rockett disagreed.
He told the directors that if they dropped Loretta, he would put
her under personal contract himself. Since Al's brother, Ray
Rockett, was an agent, it seemed a perfectly possible scenario.

And why should the Rocketts have the benefit of an actress that First National was training? The board renewed Loretta's contract after all. (Interestingly, the American Institute of Voice Teachers eventually voted hers the finest female speaking voice on the "talking pictures" screen—three years in a row.)

Loretta was in the first "talkie" that First National made, titled *The Squall,* originally a play. It was shot at night to minimize background noise, since there was not yet anything resembling a soundproof stage. "Myrna Loy played the part of the gypsy, and she was fascinating," Loretta said. "I was the ingenue, and I was boring." Whether boring or not, her voice had passed the test.

To introduce "talkies" to the public, many of the movie studios also produced musicals, and Loretta had at least two parts requiring her to sing and dance. Miss Girth must have been proud of her protege, as Loretta sailed easily through the roles. At least, that's the way it looked on the screen. Real life, however, was somewhat different.

For instance, the work hours were incredibly long. This was before the days of labor unions or protection for minors, and "even though being an actress meant years of getting up at 5 A.M., it was never natural for me," Loretta, a late-riser, recalled. "They used to save all my close-ups until late in the afternoon, when my face finally came to life." Loretta and other young actors had tutors on the set, and were technically finished when their tutors were, at five o'clock. In reality, however, especially if a picture was behind schedule, children were instructed to dress in their street clothes at quitting time, and appear to be going home as their tutors left. Then the kids would race back to the dressing room, pull on their costumes and work far into the night.

"In those days, everyone was under contract to the studio— the writers, directors and actors," explains Jack Valenti, chairman and CEO of the Motion Picture Association. "They were like serfs; they had to do assigned movies for their own studio, or go out on loan to another, or risk suspension." Contract actors worked six days a week and took role after role, so there were no real breaks to relax and revive. On the positive side, hopefuls were given years to hone their craft, "practicing" in smaller roles until they became ready for starring ventures. Loretta was not consistently on this treadmill, but she soon would be. (The contract situation would continue until 1943, when actress Olivia de Havilland sued her studio over her suspension, and won.)

Loretta often commented that "if you knew Mama, you'd know me," but most observers disagree. While the women were similar in many ways, Gladys rarely demanded from herself the high degree of achievement that her daughter did. Now, as Loretta's career evolved, so did her self-imposed perfectionism. Every seam on a dress, every line of dialogue, every lift of her lashes had to be, not merely acceptable, but flawless. She practiced endlessly, memorizing complete scenes in order to compensate for her reading difficulties. Doing less might indicate that she was ungrateful or worse, unworthy of this amazing opportunity.

The other situation that bothered the Young girls was the unspoken understanding that actresses were "available" to any man who was interested in them. If a woman was not cooperative, her career could be brought to a halt. Loretta's sister Sally had a dramatic example of that when, at sixteen and under contract to Paramount, one of the bigwigs there asked her to come and live with him. "I wouldn't like that," Sally retorted. "And my mother wouldn't like it. And most of all, Our Lord wouldn't like it!" Furious, she stalked out of his office. Six months later, her contract was dropped. (Sally didn't tell Loretta about this experience until years later; she didn't want to scare her kid sister out of the business.)

Since 1922, industry leaders had "talked the talk" about ethics by supporting an organization to enforce self-censorship (hopefully avoiding potential government regulations). Former postmaster-general Will Hays had been put in charge, thus the original name "Hays Office." The first formal Motion Pictures

Production Code came after a series of off-screen scandals. By the time Joseph Breen assumed the helm of the organization, profanity, explicit violence, unpunished criminal activity, and even married couples in bed together was strictly prohibited on the silver screen. Later, the Catholic Legion of Decency set up a movie rating system, and people in the pews signed pledges to boycott immoral films. As a result of what was known as the "Fatty Arbuckle scandal," a "morality clause" was inserted into stars' contracts, which could be used to void legal agreements with anyone involved in a personal scandal:

> *The artist agrees to conduct himself with due regard to public convention and morals, and agrees that he will not do or commit any act or thing that will tend to degrade him in public or bring him into public hatred, contempt, scorn or ridicule, or that will tend to shock, insult or offend the community or ridicule public morals or decency or prejudice the product or the motion picture industry in general.*

Some stars could get away with semi-sordid behavior; an actress who frequently played "bad" girls on the screen might be excused for being a cut-up in her personal life. But those who portrayed noble characters were expected to live virtuous private lives as well. Violations of the morals clause could, and sometimes did, lead to the end of a star's career. (*Note:* In 1921, Roscoe "Fatty" Arbuckle, a popular Hollywood comedian, was accused of raping and murdering one of two prostitutes, who had crashed a Hollywood party he was attending. Lurid newspaper headlines heralded the charges around the country. When it was discovered that the woman had died of a ruptured bladder and there was no evidence to suggest Arbuckle had anything to do with it, charges were inexplicably reduced to manslaughter, and Arbuckle stood trial. The first jury was hung; so too the second. By now, it seemed apparent that there had been a rush to judgment, and the third jury acquitted Arbuckle in six minutes, five of which were spent writing a statement of apology.)

However, Arbuckle found himself blacklisted by the movie industry, and deeply in debt due to lawyers' fees. He worked as a director, using an alias, for almost ten years, and finally was permitted back into films. He died soon afterwards at age 46 from heart failure, or as a colleague charged, from "a broken heart."

"It should be noted, however, that Loretta's royal demeanor was actually her best defense against the exploitative Hollywood system," notes author Joe Morella in an earlier book about her.* "Loretta had never been available for executive 'parties' . . . and her most effective strategy was to remain aloof and unapproachable. She is one of the few screen beauties who has never been accused, even by her most hateful critics, of taking the casting couch approach to success."

Loretta believed that being underage was a good defense too. By the time she was established, word had gotten around that she was not "getable." Or," she shrugged, "it's possible I just didn't appeal to any of the moguls." (Which is hard to believe.) "I must say that I never had a man make a pass at me that I hadn't wanted him to, first . . . so I never quite believed all those stories about being 'chased around the desk.'" However, Loretta was extremely susceptible to the male species—she fell in love with almost every one of her leading men. Later, she would point out that, for her, such a situation was almost necessary, in order to be convincing in her romantic roles: "We are in intimate daily contact with the most emotionally appealing men in the world . . . and it is nonsense to pretend that we do not fall in love with them. We do," she told a fan magazine. "We aren't committing ourselves to anything, of course. It's just a pleasant, romantic glamorous kind of flirtation." But having grown up without a father or brothers, in a rather sheltered environment, Loretta understood little about men. And she seemed more attracted to older men than to those her own age. One wonders if this was an unconscious search for the security of a father in her life.

---

* *Loretta Young, An Extraordinary Life,* Joe Morella & Edward Z. Epstein, Delacorte 1986, p. 113).

As a hopeful precaution, Gladys turned the Young home into a constant open house during weekends and vacations, so she could get to know her daughters' friends, and keep them under her watchful eye. There were no drugs, no teenage beer parties, no fear of strangers in the Roaring Twenties, just high energy and fun. By now, high-schooler Josie Saenz was dating a college man, Duke Morrison (later to be renamed John Wayne), and they and Jane Sharp were almost members of the family. So were Joan Crawford, Carole Lombard, Sue Carol (Alan Ladd's future wife), Arthur Lake and many others. Joan Crawford was several years older than Polly Ann but had changed her official birth date to make herself appear younger; she was always irritated when Loretta tagged along to dances and parties with the older group, since Loretta attracted most of the men! It was natural that many of their friends were involved in the entertainment business. As time passed, a sub-group of Catholic pals would emerge from the larger group, jokingly referred to as the "Catholic mafia."

One of Loretta's first official "dates" was arranged for her through Corrine Griffith, whose husband ran First National Studios. Corrine invited Loretta to travel with them to San Francisco, to attend a football game on Saturday, and a formal dinner on Saturday night. Bill Goetz, a young man who worked for the studio, would be Loretta's escort. Since the Griffiths and another couple would chaperone, Gladys gave her consent.

"Bill and I already knew each other—we had probably met at the studio," Loretta said. "The football game was fun, and then we went back to the hotel to change for dinner." Loretta had brought a short, black creation designed by Irene. (Gladys had found the soon-to-be-famous designer working in a small Hollywood shop, and paid very little for the garment.) When Bill Goetz met her at her hotel room door, however, he took a quick look at it.

"I'd like to get you some flowers," he smiled.

In the backyard of the Young home in Salt Lake City, Gretchen Young (to become film star Loretta Young) is held in the arms of sister Polly Ann as Sally looks on.

Loretta's first role as a fairy (she's last on the right), age 4.

One of Loretta's first publicity shots (age 13) and another still publicity shot at about the same time.

The beautiful Young sisters: (left to right) Loretta, 16; Polly Ann, 20; Sally, 18.

Loretta Young and Lon Chaney. The pair appeared in *Laugh Clown Laugh,* her first starring role.

Loretta right before her ill-fated marriage to Grant Withers in 1930. After the divorce, all reference to the marriage was removed from her official biography.

John and Josie Wayne's wedding. The wedding was held at the Young home, and Loretta was maid of honor (right).

A garden party at the Bel Air home: (left to right) Polly Ann, Sally, Gladys. Loretta is standing.

Actor Jimmy Stewart and Loretta were an item for awhile.

The four Young sisters in the movie *Alexander Graham Bell,* the only movie they all appeared in. Back row (left to right) Georgie and Sally; first row, Polly Ann and Loretta.

Still portrait from the movie *Shanghai,* about 1935.

Loretta and Tyrone Power made several movies together and also dated.

Judy, age 2,
Loretta's daughter
with Clark Gable.

Another of
Judy around
the same time.

A still from the movie, *The Men in Her Life,* released in 1941.

Tom Lewis wooed and wed Loretta in 1940.

Christmas 1946 at the Carolwood house, Christopher (left) and Peter, on Loretta's lap. Judy is seated with her mother.

Judy visiting Mom
on the set of *The
Farmer's Daughter.*

Loretta and Rosalind Russell
embrace after Loretta won the
Best Actress Award for *The
Farmer's Daughter,* 1948.

"Oh, you don't have to . . ." Loretta began, but Bill took her up to the lobby florist and selected a huge gardenia corsage. "Isn't this kind of big?" she asked.

"It'll look great," Bill reassured her.

As soon as Loretta entered the room, she realized Bill's motive. For all the women were in long formal gowns, the men, including Bill, in tuxedos, and Loretta's simple dress was completely inappropriate for the occasion. Loretta was horrified. But Bill proudly steered her to their table, and Corrine came to meet them. Slipping off two of her four strands of pearls, she draped them around Loretta's bare neckline. "You look beautiful, my dear," she whispered.

It was an exquisite evening, but perhaps the best part was the memory of Bill and Corrine's kindness. "Even at that age, I knew how thoughtful Bill had been, to try to save me embarrassment," she said. It was the beginning of another strong friendship (and another lesson in proper fashion and accessories).

In addition to entertaining her daughters' friends, on Thursday nights Gladys always invited a priest for dinner, preferably a Jesuit because of their superb education in theology. She wanted her daughters to be exposed to the finer points of the Catholic faith and one of her favorite guests was Father John Ward, who taught at a nearby school. Rather than conducting religious education classes around the Young table, Father Ward became more of a surrogate parent. He was unflappable, refused to give anyone "star treatment" and, as everyone agreed, much cheaper than a psychiatrist. Once Loretta, in a flippant mood, asked him if kissing was a sin.

Expecting a long lecture, she was nonplussed when he simply retorted, "Gretchen, the way you probably kiss, it is."

On another occasion, Loretta had been invited to a studio party, and she didn't want to go. "I'll be so-o-o bored," she complained at the dinner table.

Father Ward folded his napkin. "Did it ever occur to you that whenever you're bored, it may be because you're boring?" he asked.

It hadn't. Loretta thought about it. "What should I do?" she asked.

"Pick out someone at the party who you assume is especially bor-r-ring," Father suggested with a smile. "Focus all your attention and charm on him or her. See what happens."

Loretta was intrigued. That night at the party she saw someone she'd met while filming. The man had always seemed a complete dullard but, remembering Father Ward's counsel, she approached him and began a conversation. The man was initially taken aback—why would this lovely little starlet be seeking him out?—but could not help but respond to her genuine regard.

"And do you know, Father," Loretta reported later, "he was absolutely the nicest, most entertaining person—we talked all night!" Much later, Loretta would write in notes she took at a retreat: "The longer I live, the more fortunate I realize I have been, to be able to live and work with all kinds of people, attractive, honest, clever, educated, in short, my fellowmen. And in all of them, regardless of their good or bad qualities, one finds their primary purpose in life is the pursuit of happiness. Since my pursuit is exactly the same, I find that I can love even the most unattractive among us. I thank God that I can cut through that outer shell." Perhaps her ability to do so stemmed from her early awareness that taking interest in others was the surest way to stay interesting.

Remarkably, there did not seem to be much professional rivalry between the three Young sisters. Loretta was under contract, so she worked more frequently and was earning the largest salary. Sally was also busy, but bounced from one studio to another. The girls shared a communal wardrobe, and the first one out in the morning was the best dressed. They tossed their salaries in a common pot, and Gladys gave them money if and when they needed it. Sally and Polly (who shared a room) still regarded their younger sister as an occasional pain, and dubbed her "Gretch the Wretch." But these were petty quarrels. Beneath the surface, their loyalty ran deep. Once, both Polly Ann and

Loretta had been invited to a studio party, and were permitted to have gowns made. Loretta selected a rather flashy model, which both her mother and Polly Ann loathed.

"Gretch, you'd look much nicer in a dress like Pol's," Gladys cautioned. But Loretta was her usual headstrong self.

The gowns were delivered late on the day of the party, and as soon as the girls tried them on, Loretta realized her mother and sister had been right. "This looks terrible," she moaned. "I can't go."

Polly Ann slipped hers—another classic Irene creation—off. "Here, we can switch," she handed it to Loretta.

"Pol! I can't wear yours. It wouldn't be fair!"

Polly Ann smiled. "Gretch, haven't you figured it out yet? Everyone's going to notice you tonight, not me. You have to look great."

Loretta did wear her sister's dress. "And that," she said many years later, "is the kind of person Polly Ann was."

Another time, Polly was invited on a sightseeing trip to Europe and Africa with two antique dealers, friends of Gladys'. Her fare and expenses would have to be paid by Loretta since she was the primary breadwinner. "Do you have any objections to spending all this money on Pol?" Gladys asked her.

Loretta had none at all, and was delighted for her sister's opportunity. "That kind of attitude made life very simple," she explained. "'You take my stuff, and I'll take yours.' Money itself never really meant much to us. At that point, we were just glad to be alive, and there was enough work for everyone who wanted it. What more could we ask?"

Another benefactor of this philosophy was Gladys' father, Robert Royal, who had become a dentist and now lived in Seattle. He had been widowed a second time and, due to Gladys' influence, had become a Catholic. Occasionally, he would spend Christmas with the Youngs, and everyone loved him. "Grandpa Royal sent Mama ten dollars a month all through those first years in the boarding homes, and she used it to buy material for our dresses," Loretta said. "As we got older, we looked forward to those precious letters.

It was the only way any of us could have gone out on dates." (Polly Ann met her future husband while wearing a "Grandpa dress").

As Dr. Royal aged, he married for a third time. His wife, Elizabeth, seemed a bit peculiar, but every family has its share of eccentrics, so Gladys was not particularly concerned—until she received a letter from Elizabeth, claiming that Grandpa had become poverty-stricken. Now that the granddaughters were working, why were they not sending him any help?

Gladys was upset at the thought of her father being in need. "Mama, send him whatever you want," Loretta urged. "We can afford it, can't we?" So every month for about nine years, Gladys took money from the family "community fund" and sent it to her father.

At age 94, still visiting his office every day to oversee the six young dentists working for him, Dr. Royal suddenly died, ostensibly from natural causes. But when Gladys and Polly Ann arrived for the funeral, they discovered that "natural causes" was stretching the diagnosis a bit. Apparently, he had fallen asleep in the bathtub and, attempting to awaken him, Elizabeth had repeatedly pounded his head against the tub—so hard that it had caused a skull fracture. "Is that what killed him?" Gladys asked the attending physician.

"I'm afraid so," he nodded.

The women were horrified, especially since arrangements had been made for Elizabeth to be taken care of by nuns at a nearby convent. Should they warn the sisters? They decided to keep mum—and discovered later that the sisters knew all about everything, as sisters usually do.

The surprises had not ended. Gladys still needed to clean out the Royals' apartment. Elizabeth had stacked boxes everywhere, and as Gladys went through them, she was shocked. There were all the envelopes she had sent her father over the years—with the money still inside! Either he hadn't needed it, or hadn't known she was sending it. When Gladys and Polly Ann arrived back in California, they had plenty to tell the rest of the family—who didn't know whether to cry, or laugh.

Grant Withers

What you don't know intrigues you more than what you do know.
I believed all those love stories—the hero was the hero—because that's
what I grew up with. I loved the romance and the roses, but when it
came down to a more realistic life, I would back away.

—LORETTA YOUNG

At the end of summer, 1929, Loretta was cast opposite Grant
Withers in a movie titled *Second Floor Mystery*. Grant was a
charming, handsome party boy. He had married and fathered a
child before he was 20, and was now 25, divorced and a heavy
drinker. Although today he is little more than a footnote in
Hollywood history, Withers was then a rising matinee idol, and
considered by most actresses as a "catch."

Loretta had already fallen in and out of "love" with former
co-stars Douglas Fairbanks, Ronald Coleman, John Barrymore
and others. But Grant loved her back—which was certainly a
welcome new experience—and immediately began to woo her.
The family was concerned about it; Grant was certainly too old

for someone as naïve as Gretch, who could not be counted upon to recognize the difference between passion and love. Nor was Grant free to marry in the Church. Gladys could only hope that her daughter's current school-girl crush would end as abruptly this time as it had on earlier occasions.

Instead, two weeks after her 17th birthday, on January 26, 1930, the pair eloped. "Grant told me he would die if I didn't marry him, and I was dumb enough to believe him. So we hired a little airplane to fly to Yuma, Arizona, where we could be married." (In Arizona, the legal age for a woman to marry without parental permission was 16.) "When we took off, I remember thinking, 'Well, since we're not getting married in the Catholic Church, I'm not really getting married at all.' That was how I justified it that day."

The newlyweds flew home to a storm of publicity. When Loretta looked down at the ground, her heart sank. Members of the press were milling around and as the plane landed, she saw Mutt coming toward her, looking stern.

"Gretchen, your mother wants to see you Right Now!" Mutt announced, as the press surrounded them.

"Oh." Loretta turned ashen. "Okay. Come on, Grant."

Gladys was waiting in the living room, as pale as Loretta. "We'll go upstairs," she said stiffly. Loretta followed her into the bedroom.

Gladys sat down and began to cry. It was the first time Loretta had ever seen her mother weep. "What have I done that would make you do something like this?" Gladys sobbed. "Don't you realize how serious this is?"

"Mama, please don't cry. I guess I didn't think. . . ."

"It's my fault," Gladys went on. "I set a bad example for you, marrying George out of the church. Now you've gone and done the same thing."

"Mama. . . ."

"Loretta!" It was Grant calling up the stairs. "Let's go home."

Home. . . . It wasn't this house, with Mama and her sisters, anymore. No, now she was going to live in an apartment with a man, someone she barely knew and already suspected that she didn't love. Her own thoughts echoed her mother's. Why had she done this? What was she trying to prove? Slowly she rose, and went down the stairs where her husband was waiting.

Loretta called her mother daily, but Gladys refused to come to the phone. Gladys did, however, take steps toward getting the marriage annulled by a civil court. Polly Ann, with whom Loretta was working on the set each day, wouldn't speak to her either. "Right or wrong, Gretch, Mama is *right!*" Polly Ann declared, with the inexplicable logic Gladys inspired in all her children. "You hurt her, and that's enough for me!"

The press seemed disappointed in Loretta too. They felt her wholesome image had been compromised. "You have class," one told her. "This made you look cheap."

Perhaps the most stinging rebuke came from Father Ward. "You have chosen a very public profession, Loretta," he told her, "one through which you will be able to exert influence on others, for better or worse. This week I've already spoken with two sixteen-year-old girls, who each wanted to elope. 'If Loretta Young can do it, why can't I?' they asked."

"But Father," Loretta protested, "that's not my responsibility."

"Loretta, what does the Bible say? Rather than give bad example, you should have a stone tied around your neck and be thrown into the sea. Extreme, yes, but if you're not going to live according to your faith, you should at least get out of the movie business. You have to decide, Loretta. Where are you going— Heaven or hell? There are rules for each, and you get to choose."

Father Ward understood something that Loretta, as yet, was only starting to comprehend: sin is never a solitary act. It always has societal consequences. The thief raises the price tag on goods and services for everyone. The reckless driver strews accidents in his wake; the unfaithful spouse damages entire families. And when a young role model professes to believe in certain religious teachings, then blithely casts them aside, those who admire her become disillusioned, even cynical. How long would it take to rebuild their faith?

Father's statement shook Loretta to her very core. Years from now she would still be measuring her behavior on that basis: am I causing scandal? God would always love her, she knew. But if she continued along this path, perhaps she would one day love someone or something more than Him. That way lay the ruin of her soul.

Eventually, Gladys relented; she began speaking to Loretta again, and abandoned her quest to have the marriage annulled. By now, however, there was trouble in Paradise. Loretta was working exhausting hours, and tiring of Grant's drinking, gambling and hunting with "the boys," including his good pal, John Wayne. Having snared his bride, Grant was reverting back to his usual behavior. Romance—at least with him—was not all Loretta had expected it to be. Perhaps she had been more in love with love than with her husband. "I was playing at being married," she admitted. "As an actress, I sometimes didn't know where play acting ended and reality began." The day that he was sent away on a tour, she ran home to Mama. "I don't want to be married anymore," she announced.

"Well, tell Grant about it, not me." Gladys was determined not to bail her daughter out of this latest situation

When Grant phoned that evening, Loretta summoned her courage and announced her decision. And although her astonished husband attempted to talk her out of it when he returned, Loretta had made up her mind, and nothing more could be said. Although they were working together in another movie, ironically titled *Too Young to Marry,* the couple went through a civil divorce, and Loretta was again able to reconcile with her church. Further, she suspected that God had been guiding her all along. For if she had married Grant in a Catholic ceremony, and then divorced him, she would never have been free to marry again. At least, at seventeen, she hadn't made an irrevocable error. Grant was not her white knight after all, but hopefully, Mr. Right was still out there waiting for her.

"I'm sorry to have made my mother unhappy and Grant unhappy," she told reporters at the time. Everyone soon forgot about it—everyone but Loretta. If she did have an influence on viewers, she was going to take it seriously. "That was probably another turning point for me," she said. "After that, I never wanted to play evil people in movies, or wear immodest costumes or do drape art" (revealing photography shots). Her perfectionist tendencies solidified. She would do her absolute best not only at work, but also in life.

We Can Make You a Star!

I have found that if you love life, life loves you back.

—Arthur Rubinstein

By 1931, Loretta was reaping the happy benefits of her professional self-discipline. She had eight pictures scheduled, and rated the "star treatment"—a hairdresser, makeup artist, wardrobe consultant and others in attendance. She had a portable dressing room, which rolled around from set to set, and a studio driver, who drove her own car to and from her home. The studio was faithfully "merchandising" her, with photographs and carefully staged interviews. For the next almost-thirty years, there would rarely be a month when a story or cover photo of Loretta would not be seen somewhere. "Today, stars go on talk shows," Loretta explained. "Then it was print—movie and fashion magazines, newspaper columnists, and fan clubs." Studio publicists invented tales of romance between stars to keep audiences intrigued and interested, but few resembled reality. Once, exasperated with some misleading publicity, Loretta fumed, "The reason why people are always hearing about me being engaged is because Hollywood reporters assume you're engaged after the second date!" She gave very few personal interviews.

She did, however, date Howard Hughes for a time, and he showered her with marvelous jewelry and threw her a huge eighteenth birthday party. But Hughes was the jealous type. At one point Loretta and Gladys went to New York on a promotion trip, and on the train, befriended a young serviceman. As they were arriving in New York, Gladys impulsively asked him to come along to the theater that evening with them and Howard Hughes. The young man gasped. "Ma'am, there wouldn't be any way I could get a ticket at such short notice," he told Gladys.

"Howard Hughes can do anything," Gladys assured him. "He's even taking me to Vermont tomorrow to show me some wonderful antiques."

Hughes was not happy about the uninvited guest. He sulked all evening at the theater. When the women returned to their hotel, Loretta had made a decision. "Mama, I'm going to break off with Howard tomorrow and return his jewelry," she declared. "His behavior tonight was ridiculous."

"Do it some other night," Gladys urged. "I want to see those antiques!"

But Loretta prevailed. As usual, she refused to discuss the break-up with the press. It made her uncomfortable to criticize others, and her private life was her own business.

Still, the gossip columnists were usually benevolent where Loretta was concerned. She was easy to like because she genuinely enjoyed people, and she had a fragile, vulnerable quality that inspired protectiveness in others. Loretta had strong opinions and wasn't afraid to voice them, but if she was wrong, she admitted it. Such pleasantness also allowed her to remain friends with the leading men whose hearts she broke—or who broke hers. It was impossible not to run into Grant, Howard, and others at social affairs, but none ever seemed to make life awkward for her.

Gladys had finally selected a dentist to take care of Loretta's protruding front teeth. Since there would be no extractions, the dentist arranged for rubber bands to hold everything in place. Unless the camera was actually rolling, Loretta did her next several movies with braces on her teeth. And she would wear (and lose) plenty of retainers along the way. The braces were finally affordable because Loretta's salary had leaped to $1,000 per week (super salaries were $6,000–10,000 per week). But as the Depression deepened, Warners cut everyone's salaries in what was promised to be a "temporary" move, and she was now earning $800. Still self-taught, she continued to absorb information like a sponge, and disciplined herself to be on time and always prepared. Her shaky self-confidence had taken a giant leap forward when she was directed by Frank Capra, a highly respected director. "Acting is what you think," he told her. "Don't be afraid to trust your instincts." *Zoo in Budapest, Midnight Mary* (her unusual role as a gangster's girl in this picture turned out to be one of her favorites) and *The House of Rothschild* all showcased her deepening talent.

Loretta was not, however, receiving every role that she wanted. When Warner Brothers decided to do *Berkeley Square,* and cast Leslie Howard as the lead, Loretta asked to be tested for the female starring role (she had always had a huge crush on Leslie Howard). Typically, she prayed that God would give her the part, and felt certain she would get it. Instead, the studio cast a British actress named Heather Angel. Loretta was terribly disappointed. "I assumed they must like Heather better than me, and was plunged into doubt again," she said. "But when you put God into the mix, things always work out." *Berkeley Square* was a flop, and Loretta ended up thanking God for not giving her the part. She always maintained that she was more grateful to Him for the prayers He didn't answer, than the ones He did.

It was heady treatment for an eighteen-year-old, but her older sisters made sure she didn't start to believe her own press clippings. One evening at the dinner table, Loretta was complaining about both her heavy workload and her current part, which she felt was far too small. "It's a nothing role," she declared.

Sally threw her napkin on the table. "Gretch, you make me sick! I'd give anything to play a part with George Arliss!" she said, and stomped out of the room.

It was true, Loretta had to admit. Despite being considered the beauty of the family, Polly Ann had never really cared about making movies. But Sally knew the business well enough to be proud of her younger sister, yet irritated at her attitude. Loretta would remember to be more grateful for her opportunities.

Gladys

*Mrs. Belzer was a beautiful woman, wonderfully sweet
and seemingly vague, with an impeccable taste in
antique furniture. The girls all worshiped her.*

—*DAVID NIVEN,* THE MOON'S A BALLOON

With Polly Ann at Metro, Sally freelancing, Loretta at Warners
and Georgiana in school, Gladys now had some time for her own
pursuits. She had already taken several art and interior design
classes, because people kept asking her to help them do their
houses, and she felt she didn't have enough formal training.
Now, with Loretta's financial help, she bought a lot for $5,000,
and hired a famous architect, Garret Van Pelt, to build on it. The
finished product, the Bel Air mansion, was a luxurious and
elegant testimony to Loretta's growing stardom, and Gladys'
talent. The Youngs all moved there, along with assorted guests who
were always welcome to use the bungalow built alongside the
swimming pool. "We loved the house but our new lifestyle had

come so gradually that it seemed perfectly natural, and we took it in stride as we did everything," Loretta recalled.

After Gladys had practiced a bit at Bel Air, trying out different styles of furniture and wallpaper, she decided to rent another house, refurbish it and rent it out. "Houses in Beverly Hills were cheap then, about $8,000 or $10,000, with little or no down payment required," Loretta said. "Mama was no businesswoman, and neither she nor I realized that instead of signing papers to rent these houses, we were actually buying them." Since the rent from each house paid the mortgage, it was some time before the women realized their error. Gladys' timing, however unintentional, was fortunate, since the success of talking pictures was bringing more people to Hollywood, people who had money to spend, but no time or talent to choose fabrics, wallpaper, and accessories. Leased houses in move-in condition appealed to them. Soon Gladys was visiting antique auctions and estate sales, looking for special pieces for friends as well as tenants, and storing her "finds" in rented garages around town. As word spread, she rented homes to producer Jerry Wald, Lauren Bacall and Humphrey Bogart, Bob and Dolores Hope and the Waynes. (After John and Josie divorced, Gladys did homes for John and his second, and third wives!)

The only problem was her bookkeeping, or lack thereof. Gladys loved the challenge of making something beautiful. Whether it was also profitable didn't seem to matter. Mutt despaired of her "system," which was nothing more than notes scribbled on small pieces of paper. Each night when she returned home, he would empty her purse and her pockets, gather the scraps together and try to make sense out of them.

"What is this $300?" he'd ask, holding up a memo. "Did you buy something or sell something?"

Gladys would frown. "Did I write down anything else?" she'd ask.

"No."

"Hmmm. I think that might have been the hall table I sold to that woman in Beverly Hills. It cost $400, but she only wanted to spend three."

"So you sold it for less than you paid?"

"Well, it looked so nice there. . . ."

Nor did Gladys send bills. "They'll eventually remember to pay me," she would assure her increasingly-incredulous husband.

"But how will they know how much to send?"

"How do I know how much to charge?"

"She'd buy something for six thousand, and try to sell it for seven," Loretta remembered. "But if a client couldn't pay that, she'd sell it for six. 'Well, honey, what can you afford?' was the way she priced things."

To Gladys it all seemed logical. She was rarely cheated, and although she often forgot whether she had left merchandise on consignment or had intended to sell it, her clients kept track for her. True, as she acquired more property, she often leased a dwelling for the same or even less than she'd spent to refurbish it. But she was doing what she loved, her family and her clients were happy, and what could possibly be a problem? "Never work for money," she told her daughters, "because you'll be miserable. You'll get selfish, and you won't want to help anyone else." Loretta never saw Gladys go to bed without an armload of decorating magazines and spiritual books—her two greatest interests.

Of course, Georgiana was the light of her life. The youngest daughter was becoming tall and beautiful, and loved to play dress-up like her big sisters. The girls frequently brought cast-off costumes from their studios for Georgie to use. At one point, Loretta had a nun's habit made for her. Georgie was enthralled with it, and wore it so often that several neighbors asked Gladys if one of her daughters had joined a convent.

But all was not idyllic. Although Gladys and Mutt maintained a friendly demeanor, it was mostly for Georgiana's sake. Theirs had never been a truly happy union, and Mutt had turned out to be unfaithful to Gladys, just as Earl was. When she discovered Mutt with a friend of hers—an eerily familiar scene—Gladys insisted that he leave. Mutt agreed. He settled nearby in an apartment in Westwood, and stayed bonded to the household, attending all family functions with ease, and visiting Georgiana frequently. He also continued to handle everyone's business accounts. (Ironically, years later, Mutt converted to Catholicism due in part, he admitted, to Gladys' influence.)

Gladys was tight-lipped about it all, and refused to reveal her feelings. But she must have wondered why every male in her life—her father, her husbands, even her son—had ended up leaving her. Was it her fault, or just an especially heavy cross to carry? Being Gladys, however, there was no time for tears. She covered any pain she might have felt with her customary antidotes: work and prayer.

By 1933, Loretta's seven-year contract with Warners was ending. Producer Daryll Zanuck was leaving Warners, and planning to open a new company, Twentieth Century Pictures, headed by Joseph Schenck. Bill Goetz, her one-time escort in San Francisco, would be the third partner. The men wanted her aboard. Loretta liked and trusted both Schenck and Goetz, but she had no use for Zanuck. "He just didn't like women," she said, "and he was far more interested in making pictures about men. I didn't see any reason to go with him." But Zanuck wooed her with promises of star treatment, and a real vacation every year (not just a trip to the hospital to rest for a few days—which stars typically considered "a break"). The salary offer—$1,700 per week—which more than doubled what she had been making at Warners finally turned the tide. Because she was still under age, Gladys had to co-sign the contract. "Thank heavens, that's the last time I'll ever have to step inside a studio," she told Loretta when she returned. "That man Zanuck doesn't even know enough to stand up when a lady walks into the room! Picture people have no manners, or morals either!"

"Mama, I agree with you," Loretta answered. "But they have talent, and I can put up with almost anything for that. And just think! I'm going to have a real vacation!"

Before Loretta could plan one, however, she was scheduled to be maid of honor in a special wedding, standing in for Polly Ann who was in Europe. John "Duke" Wayne had finally persuaded Josie Saenz's father that he was good enough to marry Josie. However, not even for her would Duke consider converting to Catholicism, so their wedding would not be held in a Catholic church. Instead, they had a large, formal ceremony in the gardens of the Bel Air house, arranged by Gladys and Loretta, and attended not only by Hollywood friends, but many members of the social set to whom the Saenz family belonged. Josie looked radiant. But Duke was no longer the struggling law student she had fallen in love with some seven years ago. Ironically, in order to win her, he had developed a career that would make a stable and faithful marriage very difficult to maintain.

After the wedding, Sally went to film in Europe, and Loretta longed to vacation with her before she began officially working for Twentieth. But once again, a film offer came along that was too good to resist. It was titled *Man's Castle*.

Spencer Tracy

The reason a man or woman remembers that "lost love" is because it was lost, and never fulfilled; thus it always stays in that romantic bittersweet stage of promise and mystery.

—LORETTA YOUNG

In the early '30s, it seemed almost impossible that movies and theater would ever meet. Broadway actors looked down on screen people as "hacks," and had no desire to subvert their art to be like them. But movies were attended by far more people than plays, so Hollywood was where the money was. If one was up against it financially, California was the place to go.

So decided Spencer Tracy, whose career had started in summer stock and then the Broadway stage in the early '20s. Brash, arrogant, Irish Catholic, and already a heavy drinker, Tracy had married a fellow stage actress, Louise Treadwell, in 1923. A year later, Louise had given birth to a baby boy, Johnny, and the couple had subsequently learned that Johnny was profoundly deaf. When the news came, Spencer fell apart. Consumed with both guilt—had his genes or drinking been responsible?—and a desire to make as much money as possible to find a cure for his son, he began to accept movie roles. For a while, he commuted between New York and Hollywood, enduring false starts, minor parts and a growing animosity toward the movie industry. Finally, in 1931, he, Louise and Johnny moved permanently west.

Gradually, Spencer's income increased, and his brother Carroll came out from the family home in Milwaukee to become his business manager. The couple also had a daughter Louise, nicknamed Susie, whose hearing was perfectly normal. But Spencer and Louise were drifting apart. In 1933, he moved to a hotel and issued a statement saying he and Louise would continue to "work on our ten-year marriage." A month later, he met Loretta.

She was 20, and he was 33. They had both been cast in *Man's Castle*. It was his first leading role; she had been in over forty films by now. But as Loretta and Spencer went to work on the movie, it was obvious to onlookers that they were making a personal connection as well.

On the second Saturday after filming began, Loretta brought Spencer home for dinner. Everyone liked him immediately. But a few days later, Loretta's agent phoned Gladys. He had seen a newspaper blurb about Loretta and Spence on a date, and was concerned.

"Gretch, be very careful," Gladys warned her. "Mr. Thompson told me that he doubted you know this, but the word around town is that Spence is an alcoholic."

"Oh no, Mom. He must have meant Lee Tracy, not Spence." (Lee Tracy was an actor well-known for his drinking.)

"Well, that's good. But did you know Spence is a Catholic and married? Don't fall in love with him!"

"Oh, Mama. . . . I think I already have!"

It was true. Tracy had a way of focusing all his attention on Loretta, and seemed to find absolute joy in her presence. For

Loretta, it was a time of romance unlike anything she had ever experienced. The pair occasionally dated others, in an attempt to apply brakes to what was becoming an intense association. (It's doubtful Spencer saw much of his wife during this time). The fan magazines provided monthly updates—in one issue, Loretta and Spence were rumored to be splitting up; in the next, they would have happily reconciled. Actually, they were simply struggling to stay chaste, deal with burdened consciences and decide what to do.

"Tracy's . . . relationship with Loretta was steeped in the kind of innocence that appealed to his Irish heart and soul," observes Edward Funk, a friend of the family. "At age thirty-three, he was recapturing a sense of first love, the kind where you play ping-pong at your girl's house with her sisters, and on Sunday afternoons, you sit down at her mother's table for roast beef dinner in good conscience, because you've yet to sleep with her daughter. Couples in love, practicing restraint, and not "going all the way" was fairly conventional behavior, fitting the mores of that time. As frustrating as this must have been for a man of Spencer's worldly experience, he must have yearned for Loretta all the more, idealizing her beyond measure. . . ."

Despite her personal life, Loretta never lost sight of her career goals. She had been receiving good reviews, and when the picture with Spencer was finished, she could hardly wait to read the critics. *Man's Castle* was the best she'd ever done, she believed, and she wondered if anyone else had noticed. As the first review circulated on the set of her current picture, she had to keep herself from literally ripping it out of the hands of other actors. Finally, breathless, she scanned it. "After praising the director and writers, the reviewer complimented Spencer for another paragraph or two," she recalled. The last line held the sole mention of Loretta: "Miss Young is beautiful, as always."

Although not an insult, Loretta felt the words like a slap across the face. She must be awful, when an expert couldn't find anything nice to say about her ability, only her looks. Everyone knew how important critics were. After she muffed her lines for the third time, Loretta received permission to leave her new set.

"Of course, I phoned Father Ward and told him I was coming over," she said. Father met her at the door of his residence holding the usual box of tissue. (Being a "free psychiatrist" for the Young women had taught him to be prepared.) In between sobs, Loretta poured out her tale of sorrow. Father listened patiently until the tears had dried on her flushed cheeks.

"Now then, Loretta," he settled back in his chair, "let me ask you something. Do bad reviews make you work any better?"

Loretta thought. "No," she said finally, "because by the time I read the review I'm into another role, and I can't do anything about that one."

Father nodded. "Do the good reviews make you work any better?"

"No," she answered, "because I'm always trying my hardest. And each script is different."

"Good! Now I don't know if you're smart enough to accept this advice, but I'm going to give it to you anyway: Don't read reviews, Loretta. Good or bad. Just do the very best you can with each role, and leave the rest to God."

It was excellent advice. From that moment on, she abandoned the idea of keeping scrapbooks, because they would emphasize the past too much. Today was the only day she could do anything about.

Of course, Father Ward could have pointed out that once again, her off-screen behavior was raising some eyebrows. But this time, he refrained. Loretta had to grow, and part of that involved making her own choices.

And, like Scarlett O'Hara, she was going to think about those choices "tomorrow." For the Academy Awards were coming up. Although Spence still hated Hollywood and worked only for the money, he had agreed to escort Loretta. They would be going with Duke and Josie Wayne. "Everyone was supposed to come to our house for supper first, but Spence didn't arrive," Loretta recalled. She called his apartment. No answer. The three went ahead and had dinner, then Loretta phoned again. Still no answer. "We went to the Awards, and I didn't hear from Spence. Not the next day or the next. . . . Since there were no accidents reported, I had no idea what could possibly have happened to him."

It was one of the longest weeks she had ever spent. She called his apartment every day, and finally, at the end of the week, his brother Carroll answered. "Oh, Loretta," he said matter-of-factly, "Spence has been drinking. He's been on a bender all week, and probably won't be okay for several more days. I'm sorry you didn't know."

Loretta was astonished. She had never seen Spencer drunk. Just a few weeks ago she had met him and little Johnny at the polo field, and had been touched by Spence's gentleness with his son. And hadn't he always been tender and protective with her? "I rarely drank, so I was pretty dumb about those things," she said. About ten days after the Academy Awards, Spencer finally phoned, full of apologies. He was so very sorry. It would never happen again. Loretta forgave him.

They became even closer, almost inseparable. But Loretta was starting to feel ashamed about being cast as a real life "other woman." The two began to go to Confession every Saturday evening before going out for dinner. Maybe the graces flowing from this Sacrament of forgiveness would help them sort things out.

One evening, Loretta went to a priest who was known to be gentle, avoiding another in a confessional across the church who had a "tough" reputation. Inside the soft darkness of the confessional, Loretta admitted that she was dating a married man. The priest told her he would not give her absolution unless she broke it off that very night. "You know that after the first misstep, the second gets easier," he said. "You have to say good-bye right now, before that happens."

Loretta was shocked. "W-We're going out to dinner after this," she protested. "He's here going to confession too. We can't stop seeing each other, Father—we just can't."

The priest, however, was adamant. Loretta left the confessional almost in tears. *Whose sins you shall retain, they are retained.* . . . Never had she been denied the comfort of mercy. But church rules were clear. In order for forgiveness to be given by God, one must possess a firm purpose of amendment, that is, a decision not to repeat the sin. (The fact that people would give in to temptation again was a testament to God's eternal love and acceptance of His children, but not a license to do so).

Spencer was nowhere to be seen. As she walked disconsolately down the aisle, she noted that there was no line outside the "tough priest's" box. Could he be any harder to talk to than the priest she had just left?

She entered his box and told him what had happened. "Is it true?" she asked. "Can I be denied absolution because of this?"

Rather than thunder at her as his reputation might have suggested, Father listened gravely. When she had finished, he spoke the words of absolution that she had been longing to hear. "Keep coming back to me," he advised. "And pray for the grace to break off this relationship, as you know you must. The sooner, the better."

"Yes, Father." As she left, she saw Spence kneeling in a pew, head buried in his hands, looking as dejected as she felt. She was very much in love with him, in a far different way than she had experienced with Grant Withers, or any of the men on whom she'd had crushes. This was different. Yet, who did she love the best—Spencer, or God?

Months of turmoil passed. Spencer continued to disappear for days at a time, only to return with an enormous hangover and a plea to Loretta for forgiveness. "I am sure the pressure and the soul-searching had something to do with it," she recalled, "but gradually we faced the fact that there was nothing we could do." The Church would not allow Spencer to divorce Louise and re-marry Loretta within it. And as for Loretta—she had had one illicit marriage, and the pain of being estranged from God had been too intense.

One day, Loretta made her decision. Rather than tell Spence in person, she would send him a letter. Slowly she took sheets of paper, and her ever-present dictionary (to be sure these important words were spelled correctly), sat down at her small bedroom desk, and began to write:

> *My darling,*
>
> *I think you know that the time to separate has come. I have just been to Father Ward and he assures me that, after everything we've been through, if we can be just friends, that will be all right. But if it's going to lead either of us down the wrong path, we can't spend any more time together.*
>
> *I'm quite willing to be friends. Just to look at you would be enough for me, since I love everything about you. And if you can do that with me, then we can continue to see each other. Otherwise, we can't, since it won't lead anyplace. I want to eventually get married and I know I will never again marry out of the church, and I know that you won't either. So if you can agree to this, call me. Otherwise, don't.*
>
> *Somehow I hope you don't.*
>
> *Me.*

Spencer never called. Loretta issued a quiet statement to the press (October 24, 1934), explaining that since she and Spencer could not hope to marry because of their religion, they had agreed not to see each other. It was widely accepted that Spencer had loved her dearly, and was devastated at the end of their relationship. He went home to Louise, who, it was said, never mentioned the situation.

Loretta would act with Spencer again, and occasionally see him socially but always in the company of others. Spencer would go on to an illustrious acting career of his own. Although he and Louise eventually lived separate lives, they never divorced. Louise devoted herself to the cause of curing deafness, and in 1942 the John Tracy Clinic was opened, ultimately housed at the University of Southern California. About that time, Spencer met Katherine Hepburn, and she became his lifelong partner. His drinking bouts grew more severe, and unlike his sensitivity with Loretta, he was frequently abusive to Katherine, but she tolerated it all. "Acting was easy for him," she remarked years after his death. "Life was the problem."

In 1967, Loretta was in New York as word circulated during the filming of *Guess Who's Coming to Dinner* that Spencer was gravely ill. Gladys phoned Loretta. "I understand Spencer is in a bad way," she said. "Do you think he's made his peace with God?" After his long relationship with Katherine, Gladys assumed such might not be the case. As always, she was more interested in the state of a person's soul than his accomplishments or possessions.

"Mama, I haven't talked to Spence in years. I just don't know."

"Well, do you think I should get a priest to see him?"

"How about Monsignor Devlin?" He was the pastor of St. Victor's church, in whose parish Spencer was currently living.

"I'll try," Gladys promised. The next day Gladys reported that Spence had expressed a wish to see a priest, and Monsignor had been dispatched to offer the last rites of the Catholic Church.

Spencer died at home. The next time Loretta attended Mass at St. Victor's, she spoke to the pastor. "Everything was taken care of," he reassured her. "Spencer is at peace now."

Peace. She felt a wave of gratitude. What a good decision Spencer had made decades ago, not to phone her after receiving her note. Perhaps he had simply tossed it away; perhaps his feelings for her had never been as deep as hers for him, and he was tiring of her moral standards. Whatever his reaction, he had made it easier for both of them to make the only decision they could.

Years later, a friend phoned. "Loretta, remember Susan Tracy? She would like to see you. May I bring her over to tea?"

Loretta readily agreed. She had never met Susan, and was curious. When the guests arrived, Loretta was introduced to a beautiful little gray-haired lady. Surely not Spence's daughter, surely not so many years had passed. . . . Susan had never married, she explained. "Taking care of my mother, and Johnny—this was really what I was here for," she said. Loretta was charmed.

After tea, Susan reached for her purse and extracted a letter. "I don't know whether I should be doing this or not," she said uncertainly. "I have something that belongs to you."

"Where did you get it?" Loretta asked, surprised.

"I found it among my father's things after he died, along with two letters from Johnny, written from camp. There was a rubber band around all three. I read the letter, but no one else has. I was going to burn it, but. . . . Lately, I've felt I should give it to you."

She handed the letter to Loretta. Folded and yellowed, it was addressed to Mr. Spencer Tracy, and looked familiar. Slowly

Loretta opened it. "My darling, I think you know that the time to separate has come . . ." it began, in her own handwriting. Her eyes slipped down to the signature. "Me."

Memories flooded her. It seemed as if she was back in her childhood bedroom, writing and rewriting. She could see her desk, feel her heart breaking in two. But . . . "Susan—how did you know that this letter was from me? My name isn't anywhere on it."

Susan smiled. "Ms. Young, there were only two women in my father's life. My mother, and you."

The women exchanged a tender look. "He must have been very proud of you." Loretta could say no more.

PART THREE

~

My Angel

By the age of eight, I was cutting out pictures of dresses I thought would be suitable for Miss Young, that beautiful lady on television. In my daydreams, I was a costume designer; Miss Young would wear one of my creations to a fabulous party, and of course I would be invited too.

Real life was a bit different. My dad was a good person but an alcoholic; my mother was what I now know to be a classic manic depressive. I don't know which was worse—the terrible fights when my dad was drinking or the days that stretched into weeks when my mother was depressed or on the warpath. So when I retreated to my room, I got out my scrapbook and dreamed about my favorite actress. What was she doing now? What was she wearing? I saw Loretta, not as a mother figure but as this marvelous person who seemed to be saying, "Come have fun with me" or "Watch, and maybe we will learn something together." She was Catholic too, like me. Her life seemed like a fairy tale come true, so I thought that things would just have to be better for me too someday. She kept me going.

I hauled my box of prized possessions—scrapbooks, newspaper articles and photos—away to college. It accompanied me to each apartment and finally, to my house with my second husband in Centerville, Ohio. Over the years I accumulated copies of almost all her movies, over 2,000 magazines, lobby cards, loose clippings, three binders of photos. . . . Except for another fan, Salvadore Iglesias, I think I have the world's largest LY memorabilia collection. When her Internet site went up, I was able to help with photos and information, and meet other fans.

It was then, after all those years, that Loretta and I began a correspondence. In one of my letters, I mentioned that I had left the church before the church left me. In a July 1999 letter to me, she wrote that she would "run the risk of barging in where angels fear to tread." She was concerned about what eternity would be for me—heaven or hell. "The joy, the peace, the true happiness one enjoys when one is living life His way is indescribable." She told me that our Lord was "simply waiting there, with open arms, for you to come running into them. Trust Him."

When I read those words, I knew she was not just being gracious, she genuinely cared about me, a virtual stranger to her. As of August 1, 1999, I am a member of St. Henry's Catholic Church in Dayton, Ohio. And although I have a long way to go, spiritually speaking, I hope someday to meet my "angel" in heaven.

Diana Schafer
Centerville, Ohio

Part 3 photo—Judy, at the Carolwood house,
age 11 (photo on preceding page).

Call of the Wild

Loretta Young represents great movie history. There are few whose body of work is as rich as hers, or as deserving of full-scale attention.

—ROBERT OSBORNE, THE HOLLYWOOD REPORTER

It was Hollywood's "Golden Age," and like her mother, Loretta found relief from her personal problems in work. If it is true, as G. K. Chesterton once quipped, that "anything worth doing is worth doing badly," such sentiment was lost on Loretta. Her schedule of films for Twentieth Century was formidable, and she pushed herself to play every scene perfectly. When she wasn't on-screen, she was learning other aspects of the industry, everything from lighting to new makeup techniques to photography angles (it is estimated that she posed for over 125,000 photographs). Eventually, she planned to accompany her family on the long-awaited sabbatical to Europe. But the trip would again be postponed, for in January 1935, Daryll Zanuck committed her to *Call of the Wild*, opposite Clark Gable.

Location pictures were rare in Hollywood, due to the added expense and variable weather, which could strand a movie company for days or even weeks. But this picture, adapted from Jack London's classic novel, had to be filmed outdoors. The base of Mount Baker in Bellingham, Washington, was selected.

Although Clark and Loretta had never met, she certainly knew about him. With a background in stage work, he had had some difficulty breaking into films until his role in *It Happened One Night,* 1934's huge box office hit. Although married to his second wife, some seventeen years older than he, Clark was already considered a romantic idol, and swooning female fans followed him from location to location. His leading ladies usually fell in love with him.

Loretta and Clark met on the train going up to Bellingham for their expected ten-day film project, and she was not immune to his charms. Initially, the making of the picture consumed most of her attention and energy, especially as storms began to move in. There were over one hundred people in the cast and crew, and the snow became so high, the wind so fierce, that everyone spent most of the time shoveling. If there was a romance blossoming between Clark and Loretta, as some members of the crew believed, it seemed just a way of passing the time.

"We were living in summer quarters because the main winter lodge had burned down earlier," Loretta said. "Not enough heat, not enough rooms, no recreation areas. For meals, the cast and crew had to walk outside hanging on a rope suspended from one pole to another, for about half a city block, in the freezing cold." The ten days stretched into weeks, much of it idle, as people waited for the weather to clear, and tried to keep warm. At one point, Loretta rebelled and insisted on going into Seattle to have dinner with her grandfather Royal, and spend a night in a decent hotel, with good food and hot water. "The minute Clark Gable and Jack Oakie heard I was taking off, they insisted on going too," she said. "The production manager gave us a car and driver, and strict orders to call him the minute we got settled so he could contact us if necessary. We felt as though we had been let out of jail."

After a treacherous drive, Loretta's grandfather welcomed them with delight. He made reservations at the best hotel, took everyone to dinner and "charmed the men as much as he had always charmed me, with his southern sense of humor," Loretta said. But the trio's vacation was short-lived. The following morning the headwaiter brought a message to their table: they were to return to location. If the weather was still bad, they would work on a covered set.

"We complained loudly, but Grandpa reminded us that we were lucky to have jobs. He sent us on our way with his blessings. As it turned out, we didn't work anyplace the next day, as it was too cold even on the covered set to do anything but shiver."

The weather never did clear enough to finish all the work scheduled for location in Washington. Nor was director William Wellman reportedly happy with Clark, who was unprepared for takes and "tending not to business but monkey business," Wellman complained. After a few more futile weeks, everyone gave up, came home and finished shooting on the back lot of the studio. Clark was delighted and shocked a few months later when he won the best actor Oscar for *It Happened One Night* (recently voted the 9th funniest film in movie history by the American Film Institute.) Soon he left his second wife and moved into a hotel. He and Loretta were not seen together on the party circuit, and the gossip died down.

Now behind schedule, Loretta immediately reported to Paramount Studios for *The Crusades,* a religious film directed by the already-legendary Cecil B. DeMille. Known as "the master of spectacles" because of his financially successful and visually stunning extravaganzas, DeMille too—although short and bald—was larger than life. His staff quivered at his every movement. By the time Loretta finally turned up, production had completely bogged down. DeMille, whom she had not previously met, looked at her and said, "Well, Miss Young, I don't know whether to kiss you or kill you."

"I'd suggest you kiss me—a better beginning for both of us," Loretta laughed. No longer a novice, she was obviously feeling more confident. She sat down with him to discuss some details involving the film. "DeMille prided himself on his knowledge of many different religions," she recalled. "And sometime during that conversation, he mentioned Mary's Immaculate Conception. I realized right away that he meant the Virgin Birth, the fact that Mary was a virgin when she gave birth to Christ. So, probably showing off, I corrected him: 'Forgive me, but I think you mean the Virgin Birth'."

"No," he responded firmly. "I mean the Immaculate Conception."

"Well, let me put it this way," Loretta said. "The Catholic Church teaches that Mary was conceived in her mother's womb without original sin on her soul. That's known as the Immaculate Conception. The Virgin Birth means that Christ was born of a virgin. They're not the same." People within earshot of the debate paled. One did not contradict the great DeMille.

DeMille stared at her for a moment. Then, "Bring me a Catholic encyclopedia!" he commanded one of his entourage. Someone found the book and rushed it to DeMille. He looked up the particular section, read it, closed the book and set it down. "Oh. Well. Now, about your costumes. . . ."

"From that moment on, we became great friends," Loretta said. "Mutual respect is very satisfying."

Loretta didn't like the movie. "A Crusade was not a holy war," she said. "It was a terrible war, just like every other." But she found humor in the unlikeliest places. "One day, two girl extras were hanging around outside my dressing room. It was hot, but DeMille kept working. Eventually, one of them muttered to the other, 'I wonder when that old bald-headed son-of-a-bitch is going to call lunch.'"

Suddenly, over the loudspeaker came DeMille's voice. "WILL THE YOUNG LADY SITTING OUTSIDE MISS YOUNG'S DRESSING ROOM STAND UP AND REPEAT THE REMARK SHE JUST MADE?"

Dead silence descended upon the set. Mortified, the girl remained sitting. Poor kid! Loretta poked her head out her dressing room door. "Honey," she whispered, "you'd better do what he says. Otherwise, he'll never let up on you."

Trembling, the girl stood. In a whisper, as all watched, she repeated, "I-I wonder when that old bald-headed s-son . . . ah . . . is going to call lunch. . . ."

There was a long, hushed pause. Then, "LUNCH! BACK IN A HOUR!" DeMille bellowed. He never mentioned the episode again.

By now, Polly Ann had married Carter Hermann, a convert to Catholicism and a kind, wise, generous and loyal man who all the Young women would lean on. Sally was engaged to Norman Foster, a motion picture director. Georgie was absorbed in school. David Niven, an attractive young would-be actor, had arrived from England and been invited by Sally and one of her friends to take up temporary residence in the Bel Air pool house while attempting to break into films. He was astonished as he met the family—they were the most beautiful girls he had ever seen, "and their beauty came from within, because each was filled with concern for others, and kindness and generosity." The girls regarded him as a big brother, and would sneak him onto sound stages so he could view the movie business firsthand; they also alerted him to casting calls (he usually lost out to either Ray Milland or Fred McMurray) and helped him buy an elderly Auburn car for ninety dollars. Niven's "temporary" stay in the pool house stretched on for months, but finally he was put under contract at Metro Goldwyn Mayer, and was able to move to a real apartment. He would make several movies with Loretta, and stayed friends with all the Youngs for the rest of his life.

With things somewhat settled at home, and *The Crusades* finished, it seemed like an opportune time for Loretta and Gladys to sneak in their European trip. They went to England and attended a royal luncheon. (Gladys sat next to the King of Spain.) They visited Wimbleton and went on to Paris where actor Charles Boyer showed them around. Reporters followed them everywhere, and word floated back to America that Loretta was enjoying a well-earned rest.

The European trip ended in August. Immediately upon arriving home, Loretta went to bed on what was explained as "doctor's orders." She was not to be disturbed. Her next scheduled film, *Ramona*—Twentieth Century's first western to be shot in color—was postponed. Rumors began to fly: Had she been in an accident in Europe, left disfigured? Was it a terminal illness? Was she penniless, mentally ill?

Twentieth Century attempted to handle the press but phone calls, mail and fans sending money to "bail out" their darling became overwhelming. Dorothy Manners, a top fan magazine writer and reporter for Hearst newspapers, and one of Loretta's favorites, was granted an exclusive interview at the Young home.

Loretta was lying in bed, swathed in heavy comforters, when Dorothy and her writer-husband arrived for their allotted twenty minutes. The starlet looked healthy, Dorothy would inform her readers in *Photoplay Magazine*. But according to the family physician, Walter Halloran, Loretta had an internal condition that had sapped her energy for some time, and an operation was the only remedy. She had been put on bed rest to build her strength for the surgery, to be done sometime after Christmas. "Both Dorothy and her husband seemed satisfied I was ill, and not maimed, nor off my rocker in any way," Loretta said. If Dorothy had doubts, she never voiced them publicly. Her report did much to quell the rumors.

On October 8, 1935, Sally and Norman were married in a private ceremony at the Bel Air home. Loretta was still in her upstairs bedroom, but her door was opened so she could hear the music. In late November, she reported for work on the set of *Ramona* (the studio ended up holding the role for her). Loretta looked her usual radiant, size six self, and ready for a role requiring dancing and filming on location. "No one, press or otherwise, ever confronted me directly about my absence," she said, "not until at least fifty years later."

Judy

Whoever welcomes a child such as this for My sake, welcomes Me.
—MARK 9:37

The past months, however, had all been an elaborate fabrication. Loretta was actually facing one of the toughest situations any unmarried girl could, especially given the moral climate of the time. It had begun in January, when she met Clark Gable. She had been wildly infatuated with him—even more in "love" than she usually was, and no doubt more vulnerable, due to her recent breakup with Spencer. It is obvious by looking at their love scenes in the movie, that Clark returned her interest. The fact that he had been baptized a Catholic, despite his current illicit marriage, attracted her too. Perhaps she would be the one to place him—permanently—on a spiritual path.

However, as always, Loretta had maintained her moral principles. There had been no affair, as gossip mongers would assume, instead, only one night when her iron will slipped. It would have been a casual event to many, especially in Hollywood, but she was ashamed. As in her elopement, she had again failed to live up to her own principles. She vowed not to let it happen again.

But shortly after starting work on *The Crusades,* Loretta realized she was expecting a child.

One can only speculate on the depths of her shock and despair. She had been building a blessed life, lacking only an abiding love to make it all complete. But now her dream seemed an unending nightmare.

What was she to do? Although abortion was illegal, it was quite common in Hollywood, usually arranged by the studios. (Some stars had so many that when they eventually tried to conceive, it was impossible). But such an escape was not for her. Not only did the Catholic Church forbid it, it repulsed her very soul. She would not compound one problem by adding another. Yet she had violated the morals clause in her contract, and if anyone, ANYONE involved in the movie business discovered her secret, it would mean immediate dismissal from the studio, and the end of her hard-earned career and the financial support she was providing for her family. Devastated, Loretta went to the person who had always understood her best, Gladys.

"In those days, unmarried pregnant women were sometimes thrown out of their homes in disgrace," Loretta said. "But Mama was not angry, the way she had been when I married Grant. She comforted me, and talked to Clark about it." Yet although women were definitely held to a higher standard of behavior than men in that era, Clark's contract had a morals clause too, and his burgeoning career would also be in jeopardy if people knew he fathered an illegitimate baby. Further, Loretta refused to take his phone calls; she was terrified of exposure should anyone see him hanging around the Young house. And although Clark may have wanted a role in his child's life, he apparently wasn't interested in marrying Loretta. Ultimately,

Gladys realized that she and her daughter would be handling this alone.

After Loretta finished *The Crusades*, the two women left for a much-ballyhooed "vacation" tour of Europe. (A few acquaintances claimed to have seen Loretta in Europe, looking a bit heavier than usual, but since she was always trying to gain weight, no one took much notice.) When she returned unobtrusively in August and cancelled *Ramona*, Gladys reported her daughter's "illness" to the press. Loretta spent the rest of her pregnancy incognito, most of it at a nearby house that Gladys owned. Dutifully she ate the right foods, and took walks at night. "Mama or my sisters would go with me, someone driving while I walked, so I could jump in the car at a moment's notice," Loretta said. One night, Gladys was walking alongside Loretta when she tripped and fell. "After that, Mama rode too."

It was a lonely, heartbreaking time for Loretta. She had looked forward to having a baby, but the scenario had also included a loving husband whose enthusiasm for parenthood would match hers, not this dark and lonely journey. Her optimism and sense of fun faded, and according to one sister, she grew uncommunicative, keeping her feelings to herself.

On November 6, 1935, at the house, Loretta gave birth to a baby girl, whom she named Judy. In another country, Clark received an unsigned telegram, stating only that the baby had arrived safely, and she was blonde and beautiful. No one in the Young household ever admitted sending the message, but Loretta always believed it was Polly Ann's husband Carter, already stepping into a patriarchal role.

Judy would be cared for at the house by a nurse for a few months, so Loretta could visit and feed her on her way to and from the studio. The baby would spend the next year or so in a foundling home, until she could join the Young household in a hopefully-casual way. Hadn't Loretta considered putting Judy up for adoption, as many unwed mothers did? "Oh, I couldn't," she was definite. "Judy was my baby, I loved her, and I knew I'd have enough angels around me, my mother and sisters, so that we could take care of her properly and give her a good life."

Wouldn't a two-parent household provide more stability? Not necessarily, Loretta believed. In this time of economic hardships, with many adoptive babies available, there was no guarantee a child would be placed in a home better than the one she'd left. "And anyway," Loretta pointed out, "I didn't have a father, and I got along fine. I believed that Judy would too." She went back to work, and re-entered her social life with enthusiasm. Nothing further was ever mentioned about the "operation" she had been anticipating.

And if she wept a little, late at night, no one ever knew.

On Suspension

One can never consent to creep,
when one feels an impulse to soar.

—HELEN KELLER

Along with her personal difficulties, professional trouble was brewing with Daryll Zanuck. As head of Twentieth Century, he had taken only Loretta and Constance Bennett with him when his company merged with the Fox Company in mid-1935. He now wished to renew Loretta's contract, which still had two years left. Loretta refused. She had turned down several assignments because she hated the roles he gave her, which were mediocre, she felt, and did little to push her toward leading lady stardom. "I can only do the kind of scripts I like, otherwise, I'm not very good," she told him one day. He ignored her. At one point, he assigned a script written for Cary Grant and Jean Harlow to Loretta instead (Jean was unavailable). Loretta protested, to no avail. Later, a reviewer wrote, "I saw a movie last night starring Cary Grant and Loretta Young, *Born to be Bad*. And it is!"

Things came to a head when Loretta refused to do *Lloyds of London*. She was furious that her friend, Don Ameche, had been dropped from the film in favor of a better-looking young man, Tyrone Power, and disliked the script. The film was slated to be Zanuck's prestige movie, and he threatened to fire her.

"Go ahead!" Loretta lost her temper. "I'd be delighted to leave!" She stormed out of his office, then ran across the street to the Good Shepherd Church and slipped into a pew. The church was empty and dark, and her heart pounded even harder. *Oh God, what am I going to do? Why did I argue with him— he can see to it that I never work again! And there's the house in Bel Air, and Judy and Mama and Georgie and even Grandma Young to take care of . . . and what could I do if I left the movies? . . . I don't have any other talents. . . . I can't even read. . . .* Breathless, she stopped for a moment. She and God had not been on very close terms lately. She had confessed her sins, but had He truly forgiven her? Did she have the right to ask Him for anything?

Suddenly, she caught a hint of movement ahead of her, across the pews. She had thought she was alone, but there had been another figure praying in front of the altar, someone who now was coming down the aisle. Quickly, Loretta put her tear-streaked face into her hands, then peeked through her fingers. She saw ladies' shoes going past, and curiosity got the best of her. The woman was actress Irene Dunne, one of Loretta's idols. A practicing Catholic woman, probably up against many difficult situations in this crazy business, yet somehow managing to make movies without compromising her professional or personal standards.

If Irene can do it, you can do it, God seemed to be telling her. *But the strength you need is here, not at the bargaining table with Daryll Zanuck or anyone else.* Loretta was calmer now. What were the odds that she would bump into the perfect role model just when she needed some courage—unless God had arranged it, unless He was somehow telling her that, despite her failings, He loved her just the way she was? She had her answer. She would stick to her principles.

Loretta was currently dating Eddie Sutherland, a director at Paramount. He was aware of her problem with Zanuck. "You know, he can destroy you," Eddie commented one night. "And although an agent is supposed to protect you against these kinds of things, yours is just too nice. You need Myron Selznick."

By most accounts, Selznick was the toughest and best agent in the industry. He represented Carole Lombard, Constance Bennett, Merle Oberon, Joan Bennett . . . most of the top female stars. His brother was David Selznick, a brash and audacious risk-taker who had formed his own studio to produce *King Kong*, and was soon to make *Gone with the Wind*. David was married to Louis B. Mayer's daughter Irene, and was a bitter rival of Zanuck's.

Loretta objected vehemently. "I can't stand Myron Selznick! He's so crude."

One evening at a party, as she explained to Eddie, she had been wearing a topaz cross. Myron had been drunk. "Loretta," he had leered as she danced past him, "why do you insist upon being so damn Catholic?"

Furious, she had said the first thing that popped into her head. "For the same reason that you insist upon being so damn Jewish!"

Unexpectedly, Myron had roared with laughter. "The kid's got spunk!" he told a friend.

Now, Eddie laughed. "I don't care whether you love him or hate him," he told Loretta. "He's probably the only person who can help you, and I'm bringing him to your house tomorrow at nine A.M. Be ready—please."

The two men arrived at precisely nine the following morning. Myron looked around. "Got anything to drink?" were his first words.

Typical Myron, Loretta fumed. Their house had a bar, but since the girls rarely drank, the selection was meager. She rummaged, and found a bottle of sherry. "That'll do," said Myron, and poured his first glass. "Now . . . what's our story?"

Grudgingly, Loretta filled him in: she had two years left on her contract with Twentieth Century Fox, and could foresee Zanuck offering her more of the same lackluster roles. If she refused, her popularity would eventually wane—fans had plenty of other stars to follow. If she accepted the parts, most would make her look like a second-rate understudy, not the polished professional she had worked so hard to become. "I don't want to work for Zanuck anymore," she told Myron. "He knows nothing about developing a woman's career."

Myron seemed to understand. He dialed Twentieth Century Fox. Mr. Zanuck was in conference and couldn't be disturbed. "Tell him I'm here at Loretta Young's house," Myron told the secretary, and hung up.

The phone rang almost immediately. It was Daryll Zanuck.

Was this going to work? Loretta was incredulous. "You've been nasty to her," Myron was saying. "No, I'm not her agent but I am a friend of hers. . . . Okay, we'll be there." He hung up, and turned to Loretta. "We have a meeting with him tomorrow," he said. "I don't know if anything will work, but we can try."

"Do I have to go?" Loretta asked.

"Of course," Myron said, and walked out the door. He had consumed the entire bottle of sherry, Loretta noticed. It hadn't seemed to affect him at all.

The next day was a pitched battle, the likes of which Loretta had rarely seen.

"The two men fought. I'd try to interject something, and Myron would tell me to be quiet. Then they'd fight again. Finally, we left." Loretta was not doing *Lloyds of London*. But, as punishment, she would go off salary again, this time for ten weeks, and the weeks would be added on to the end of the two years left on her contract.

"Did we win or lose?" she asked Myron.

"A little of both." He shrugged. "But don't worry about it. And if you get short of money during this ten weeks, just let me know and I'll lend you whatever you need."

Loretta was dumbfounded. Such a kind gesture, from someone she'd detested for so long. She had judged too hastily, she realized. Myron Selznick might well turn out to be one of those special angels God was always sending her.

Cecil B. DeMille also offered some help during this time, inviting her to appear on his popular radio show, titled *Lux Theater*. Each week, with a full orchestra and a live audience, DeMille presented condensed versions of both old and current movies to an estimated 50 million listeners. Sometimes, the stars he hired played their original roles; at other times, they were cast in parts new to them. (Many also did commercials for Lux Soap.) It was great publicity for the studios, inexpensive for networks, and exciting and fun for the stars, despite the fact that perfectionist DeMille expected a full week's work out of everyone. Loretta debuted on November 10, 1936. The show would prove to be a godsend for her during the rocky time that lay ahead.

Her ongoing conflict with Zanuck was eventually settled during another acrimonious meeting after her ten-week suspension, and it was Loretta who had to give in. Daryll Zanuck held all the legal cards, and Myron Selznick was unable to do anything to help her. She would work for Daryll, on the movies of his choice, or she would continue on suspension—forever.

A New Member of the Family

*Love does not consist in gazing at each other, but
looking outward together in the same direction.*

—ANTOINE DE SAINT-EXUPÉRY

Several years before, Josie Wayne and Loretta had developed a
holiday tradition. Every Christmas they would help a particular
charity. One season, they had selected an orphanage, Nazareth
House, in the San Fernando Valley. The women bought or
begged presents from all the merchants they did business with—
several hundred gifts—wrapped them all, bought a tree and
trimmings and brought everything to Nazareth House.

"We had a ball," Loretta recalled, "but it wasn't until thirteen
years later that I realized it was a gift from heaven for me."

About that time she received a letter. "One Christmas Eve,"
it began, "in the orphanage where I lived, I peeked through the
window of the playroom, and watched excitedly as two angels
trimmed a tree. I could only see the legs of one—she was on a
ladder and hidden from view—but I remember she was wearing
silk stockings. It was a magical moment for me."

Many years later, the boy had asked a nun who the ladies
were, and when he discovered "Silk Stockings" was Loretta
Young, he had decided, finally, to write to her. "I want you to

know that I have prayed for you two angels every day since that Christmas Eve," he finished. "And prayer has made a difference in my life. I am now a Catholic priest."

Since that Christmas, Loretta had continued to keep in touch with the sisters at Nazareth. And in June, 1937, columnist Louella Parsons published a major scoop: popular actress Loretta Young had become an adoptive mother. Although adoptions by single or divorced women were prohibited in California, Loretta had somehow managed to bypass the law, and was now the proud parent of two preschool girls. Loretta told the press that the girls had been put into a Catholic orphanage, Nazareth House, and the nun in charge had alerted her that they needed a home. Eventually, the story continued, the aunt and uncle of the older girl, Jane, decided to raise her. Loretta returned Jane, and kept Judy, who was almost two. (There is little evidence that "Jane" ever existed.)

At this point, Polly Ann and Sally each had an infant, and Loretta was godmother to Josie and John Wayne's first son, Michael. But marriage (and children) were still eluding Loretta. "With me, marriage has got to be for life," she often told reporters. "I won't marry until I meet the man I can't live without." Now, however, her delight in Judy seemed to make life almost complete. Photos of these two exquisite faces, cheek to cheek, sold thousands of fan magazines.

Gossip, of course, abounded. To anyone who could count, Loretta's three-month "illness" in 1935 corresponded to the latter stage of pregnancy. Was baby Judy Loretta's biological child? Even though the little girl was said to be twenty-three months old, her birth date could have been altered to make her seem older than she actually was. Could she be Clark Gable's daughter? Had "Saint Loretta" fallen from grace?

Loretta refused to acknowledge or comment on Judy's adoption or paternity. If reporters hinted, she simply gave them a cool look, then changed the subject. "It was a rumor then, it's a rumor now and it will always be a rumor" became her stock answer and gradually, the more blatant snooping subsided. By unspoken agreement the Hollywood community, which had most certainly guessed the truth, decided to let two of their favorite stars get on with their lives.

"Judy slipped into our household with the greatest of ease," Loretta recalled. "Polly and Sally still lived nearby, and Georgie, Mama and I were still at the Bel Air house. Being a parent changed nothing in my life except it brought me more joy." She was fortunate, also, to find good caretakers for Judy. "Parsada Carver was her first nanny, a woman who had worked for our family as a cook. Parsada was wonderful, very spiritual, and loved reading Bible stories to Judy." Gladys was delighted with her granddaughter too.

Loretta was still working out her two final years with Zanuck, and was again assigned to a movie with Tyrone Power. They did three together in 1937 and began to date. According to some, it was Zanuck who eventually broke them up—Tyrone was a handsome newcomer, attracting many female movie-goers, and it wouldn't do to have him married too early in his career (although he did marry within a year or two.) Loretta claimed they were never more than friends, and they remained so for many years.

Not too long after the adoption, Loretta met William Buckner, the nephew of the chairman of the board of the New York Life Insurance Company. William was a financier, dealing in stocks and bonds, and "an entirely different personality from the men I knew," she said. "He was Catholic, had never been married, was a member of high society—and loved Judy!" Further, he was apparently wealthy in his own right, so Loretta needn't wonder if he loved her for anything other than herself. Her family liked him too, and offered him the use of the Bel Air pool house, David Niven's former home. It was almost too good to be true. As they dated throughout the next few months, Loretta felt herself falling into that familiar and warm abyss—love. When Bill asked her to marry him, she immediately accepted.

However, there were warning rumbles. Word had it that Bill was involved in some less-than-forthright business deals. Loretta refused to believe it of him, but because he had a month-long European business trip coming up, she suggested they delay setting their wedding date until he returned.

"We wrote back and forth almost every day," she said, "and Judy scribbled little notes to him too." But when Bill stepped off the boat in New York in December,1938, federal agents arrested him. "LORETTA YOUNG'S FIANCÉ ACCUSED OF FRAUD!" read the headlines. Loretta was stunned.

In Bill's luggage, along with proof of the accusations, the agents found cables and letters from Loretta. Columnist Walter Winchell managed to read the love letters, but wrote that they were so tender he had begged they not be published in their entirety. The press, sympathetic to Loretta, agreed, and used only snippets. No one, however, could initially make sense of the scraps of notepaper with scribbles, also found in the luggage— were they some kind of code? Eventually the investigators realized that they were the "letters" from little Judy, which Bill had also kept.

Over objections from prosecutors, Bill was given permission to go to California, and called Loretta immediately. "I want to see you and straighten out some things, but I don't want to embarrass you. Should I come?"

She already sensed the ultimate truth, but she had to hear it from Bill himself. "Yes."

Bill arrived at the guest house, got dressed up, as did Loretta, and the two walked into Ciro's that night to face everyone down. "You could hear the crowd inhaling in unison," Loretta said. "But we made no statements to anyone, but each other."

"Is it true?" she asked after the waiter had taken their order.

"I'm afraid it is," Bill admitted quietly. "I got in over my head, and because I did it through the mail, I committed a crime. You're going to be asked if I ever asked you for money, or to introduce me to your friends who had money."

"I will be honest. No, you did not."

But it didn't matter. Bill went on trial, was found guilty and sentenced to several years in jail. It was assumed in Hollywood that Loretta had been set up, and marriage proposed only so that she could not testify against her husband, should the need arise. That was not accurate; Bill might have begun with an intention to borrow money from her, but by all accounts, he truly loved her. Yet another broken romance in a growing string of heartache was making Loretta doubt her judgment about men even more. God, why? she often asked Him during her prayer time. No answer seemed to come.

At long last, Loretta's final movie with Fox was announced: *The Story of Alexander Graham Bell*. It would bring her past her two-year deadline, but she did still owe those ten weeks of suspension. Most directors wouldn't have enforced them, but "Daryll had to have his last drop of blood," Loretta said. "I was so happy to be getting away from him that I didn't care." And this movie would be more fun because for the first time, all four Young sisters had been cast in it, along with Don Ameche, Henry Fonda and Charles Coburn.

Georgiana, in particular, needed something nice to happen to her. She had appeared in small parts in a few earlier movies, but her self-image was suffering now that she was fourteen and almost six feet tall. Loretta had found her one day, crying on her bed. "Honey, what's the matter?" she'd asked in alarm.

"Oh, Gretch, I'm so tall. Taller than almost everyone in the world!"

"No, Georgie, you're gorgeous!" She was, but being "different" is a teenager's worst nightmare.

The film was the last major role for Polly Ann and for Sally. From now on, the two older girls would work only if a part was small and compatible with their busy family lives. Georgiana would not make any subsequent movies. However, when this, her final film was shown in Mexico, a young man would fall in love with her face on the screen, and life would never be the same for her again.

Ironically, before production on *Bell* had ended, and despite their troubled relationship, Daryll Zanuck asked Loretta to renew her contract with Fox, offering her a five-year contract for two million dollars—an enormous amount considering the low rate of income tax in those days. The Hollywood community was shocked when she turned it down. Assuming that she was holding out for more money, columnists chastised her for her greed. Myron Selznick, now Loretta's agent, was also surprised, but he knew the real reason: her difficulties with Zanuck. "I just wanted to freelance at this stage," Loretta said. "The work pace had become exhausting, and as a free agent, I would be able to pick and choose my material more carefully, and wait for better parts." She again emphatically rejected Zanuck's offer.

Strangely, around that same time, Earl Young suddenly reappeared, contacting a priest at the family's parish, St. Paul the Apostle. "I don't want to disturb the girls or their mother," he reportedly told the priest, "but I have had amnesia and recently discovered that I have been married with several children all these years, and my second wife died in 1934." Earl needed a new artificial limb, and knew his daughters were employed. Could they provide it for him?

The priest verified Earl's identity, contacted Gladys and she called her offspring together. Everyone was furious, especially Loretta. "Not a dime!" she told her mother. "Not after what he did to you! And as for that claim of amnesia after twenty-three years. . . ."

"Nevertheless, he is your father, and you must take care of him," Gladys said calmly.

"Why?"

"Because you are supposed to honor your father and your mother. Do I really have to say anymore?"

The family had been sending money to Earl's mother, Grandma Young, for many years, so Gladys suggested they just add more. Then they could avoid any communication with Earl.

Reluctantly, Loretta agreed. None of the girls were willing to meet their father, but during the next several years Jack did make contact a few times, mostly out of curiosity. He didn't tell Gladys, for fear of hurting her feelings, but Gladys never seemed to hold a grudge against her charming ne'er-do-well. She simply did not want to see or talk to him. Nor would she tolerate her children saying anything against him in her presence. She never had.

Eventually Earl's health collapsed, and he began seeing the same physician, Walter Holleran, who had treated the Youngs since the children were small. When Earl was admitted to the hospital, he asked Dr. Holleran to get in touch with his daughters so he could see them again.

"No, Mr. Young, I'm not going to call them," Dr. Holleran said. "You've caused them enough pain. The girls know you're here, and if they want to come, they will." Dr. Holleran could have added that, since Earl was currently living with yet another woman who was not his wife, this would also open old wounds for everyone.

No one but Jack visited. When Earl died in June, 1948, the Young family again paid all the expenses. "I felt no real remorse or sadness then," said Loretta. "But I'm sorry that I sat in judgment of him, and I think now that we should have gone to see him. He could have died knowing he had been forgiven—it would have brought him a little happiness at the end." It was a tragic finale to a sorry life, one that obviously had a deep lifelong impact on all Earl's children.

It turned out that Earl did have children with another wife, and although the Youngs never met them, Loretta would occasionally be contacted by someone who claimed to be her half-brother's son or grandson-in-law or some such. "I suppose it could be true," she pointed out. "Our extended family was confusing, to say the least."

~

After *Bell* was finished, the Young sisters did some personal appearances to publicize the movie's release. They and the rest of the cast went up to San Francisco, where they appeared in a parade, and were presented with the keys to the city. One day, dressed in their movie costumes, the four sisters were doing a photo shoot in the Bel Air house. Jimmy Townsend, one of Myron Selznick's assistants, came to get Loretta. "There's someone here to see you," he announced.

Loretta was ready for a break. She went into the living room, and met Tom Lewis, the head of the radio department of Young and Rubicam advertising agency in New York. Tom produced and created shows, and had recently launched the Screen Guild Theatre radio show; performers' salaries would be donated to the Motion Picture Relief Fund, for the building of a hospital and retirement home for those in the industry. (The idea had been developed by Jean Hersholt, Mary Pickford, and a relatively unknown actor named Ronald Reagan.) Tom's first show had featured Jack Benny, Joan Crawford, and Judy Garland, and had been a smash hit. Now he was wondering if Loretta would accept a part in an upcoming show.

By now, Loretta had done several Lux radio programs for Cecil B. DeMille, and had also guested on the Hallmark Hall of Fame. She liked radio, and she liked Tom too. She watched as his automobile wound down the driveway and out into the street. Jimmy Townsend noted her interest. "What did you think of Mr. Lewis?" he asked.

"He's very attractive. . . ." she murmured.

"Should I ask him for lunch tomorrow?" Jimmy persisted.

"That might be nice," Loretta answered, and went upstairs to take off her period costume. She was no longer the wife of Alexander Graham Bell, she reflected. Just an ordinary woman, who'd be pleased with an ordinary man.

PART FOUR

~

Moral Quality

I was a Catholic boy of 17, just starting college, when I met Judy Lewis. She was a high school junior, and we attended the same church, Good Shepherd. I wanted to take Judy out on dates, but her parents, Loretta and Tom Lewis, made me hang around their house and "court" her, until they got to know me. The '50s were an idyllic time to be a teenager. Society was decent and safe, and we guys respected our girlfriends. We understood that they would remain virgins—that's just the way it was. Still, Judy's parents grilled me.

I enjoyed visiting the Lewis house—there was always something going on. Loretta and a producer at her studio, Dore

Schary, constantly argued politics, and she'd tell me what they said to each other. Once, she let me read a script for her new movie, The Accused, *and asked me what leading man she should pick. (She didn't choose my favorite.) Her guests were fascinating. I remember a Baroness von Gutenberg from Germany who stayed with them. The Baroness had met Hitler, and she said that when she looked into his eyes, she believed he was possessed by the devil. It was heady stuff for a kid like me.*

Judy and I did date, but eventually she fell for my cousin, Jack Haley, Jr. I finished college, went into the Air Force, and when I finally returned to Beverly Hills, I had a wife and three little red-headed babies. Loretta saw us at Good Shepherd one Sunday, and invited me over. "We have to talk about your future, Bobby," she said.

I was thrilled. Loretta knew so many people. Maybe she was going to recommend me for a job in the movie industry. But she didn't.

"I would not help someone I like get into this business," she told me. "Not today, when the moral quality of everything is going down."

Then she looked at me. "God didn't give you red hair for nothing, Bobby Dornan," she said. "You belong in politics!"

And she was right.

Robert Dornan
Political talk show host,
and former Congressman

Part 4 photo—Christmas 1946 at the Carolwood house.
Christopher (left) Peter, on Loretta's lap, and Judy.
(photo on preceding page)

Tom Lewis

There's a rhythm to life.
What we do has eternal consequences,
and you've got to have faith
that whatever job you're given, it matters.

—*Touched By An Angel*

It might have been attraction at first sight, but Tom and Loretta didn't start dating immediately. The timing certainly wasn't right. Loretta was going out with James Stewart and was, of course, madly in love with him. She had been hoping Jimmy would ask her to marry him, but he never did. "We just weren't on the same wave length," she said. "Jimmy got the woman who was right for him." He and his wife Gloria were married for over forty years, and remained good friends of Loretta's until their deaths.

Tom had a romantic interest too, actress Glenda Farrell. And he lived in New York, a continent away. But he returned to direct Loretta's first Screen Guild appearance, which starred Fred Astaire, Herbert Marshall and herself, and everything went fine until the Saturday night before the Sunday show. Tom called for a final rehearsal at 8 A.M. Sunday morning. Loretta sent word that she would not be there.

"She has to be there," Tom told her agent.

"She says it's impossible," the agent answered. "She has to go to Mass."

Tom laughed. "I have to go to Mass too. Tell her I'll pick her up at 6:30 A.M."

He did, and Loretta couldn't help being impressed. However, as they left church, Sister Marina, Loretta's first-grade teacher, bumped into them and eyed Tom. "Is he the Catholic husband I've been asking God to send you?" she demanded. Several people turned around to look.

"Sister, let me give you a kiss," a blushing Loretta put her arms around the nun.

To no avail. "He'd better not be like that Withers fellow. . . ." Sister went on. By now, Tom was trying hard not to laugh. It was one of the few times he'd ever see Loretta speechless.

The two kept in touch. She did a few more radio shows, he shuttled from coast to coast and escorted her to various parties. Everyone in her crowd thought Tom was The One, and her family was equally enthused, especially Gladys. He was eligible, attractive, successful, twelve years older than she (again, the father figure?) and best of all, a practicing Catholic. What else could Loretta possibly want?

Perhaps carried away in the collective wave of approval, Loretta initially accepted Tom's proposal. Women at that time were conditioned for marriage, and despite her career, she very much wanted to be a wife and mother. However, in the winter of 1940, she broke the engagement. "I saw some warning signs," she said, "and I was hesitant about them." Tom seemed self-centered and bossy, and that worried her. Admittedly, she was sometimes self-centered and bossy. . . . Were their two strong personalities a dire mix, heralding a grim future, she wondered? Or was it just one of those compromises that people make when they marry, realizing that no one is perfect? Although they shared the same Catholic bond, it too was sometimes a point of dissension. "Her training seemed to have stressed the legalistic aspect—hell and purgatory," Tom once pointed out, "while mine concentrated on the Christian community, God's love and forgiveness."

Loretta had made many mistakes in her choice of men, and no longer had confidence in her own instincts. And she must consider Judy—whoever she married would have to accept her daughter as his. Tom seemed enchanted with Judy, but would his feelings last? It should be noted that Loretta had not entrusted Tom with the secret of Judy's birth, which probably speaks volumes about her insecurity in the relationship. Would Tom continue to love her if he knew?

Another dilemma was the puzzling lack of movie offers coming in since she had turned down Daryll Zanuck's contract in favor of freelancing. At first, she had been glad for the respite. The radio shows created far less pressure, and she enjoyed them. Then one day Jimmy Townsend came to her. "Loretta, I've been looking around and the scuttlebutt is—and I think it's right— that you're being blacklisted, and you're not going to get another movie job."

Loretta was astounded. "But why?"

Jimmy had a theory. She had had the colossal nerve to go against a studio boss, Zanuck, who had regarded it as a snub. Retribution from the "suits" had been swift.

"It was all very subtle," Loretta explained. "The Hollywood producers were a 'good old boy' network—they had dinner together, met for steambaths and sports. . . . It would be very easy for Daryll to simply say, 'No one here is planning on using

Loretta Young in anything, is he?' and the word would be passed." She had seen it happen to others. Jimmy was right. She had stepped out of her "place," and despite the fact that 3,000 independent theater owners had just voted her their most popular star, she was being officially shunned. Was she a has-been, at 27?

Loretta fought panic, and tried to be logical. There was one silver lining in her situation—she was probably financially secure. During these past years of high earnings, instead of squandering her money (or spending it ahead of time and going into debt to her studio, as many stars did), her mother had invested it in property. It was doubtful as to what their actual worth was—they had never figured it out. And everything seemed to be heavily mortgaged. But the family would certainly not be penniless.

If her career had ended, what would she do for the rest of her life? Was she being guided to forsake Hollywood, marry Tom, and become a housewife and mother? In many ways, the idea appealed to her. Despite her caution, she loved Tom, and she had been working non-stop for over a decade. And yet . . . acting was as much a part of her as her eyes, her ears. Could she be a whole person while letting her talent go unused?

Myron Selznick, however, was livid when Jimmy discussed the situation with him. "Over my dead body are they going to blacklist her!" he shouted. Instead, he phoned Harry Cohn, the president of Columbia pictures, a second-rate studio at that time.

"Harry, I'm going to do you a big favor," Myron announced grandly. "You know I'm asking $100,000 per picture for most of my stars." ($100,000 was considered the top of the line in those days). "But you can have Loretta Young for $50,000 if you come up with a good script for her."

Harry Cohen was well aware not only of the blacklist, but of Loretta's popularity. And Myron was offering him a good financial deal. He sighed. "I always had a crush on her anyway," he told Myron. Not too long after that conversation, Harry sent Loretta a script for *The Doctor Takes A Wife*, with Ray Milland as her co-star. It broke the blacklist, and she could work again.

She resolved her doubts about Tom too. Rather than approach the subject of Judy directly, Loretta reportedly asked Tom if there was "anything you want to know about me?" Tom assured her that he had no questions, at least, none that he wanted to pursue. It was, according to Gladys, the perfect answer. And so, on July 31, 1940, Loretta married Tom Lewis in what was intended to be a small and intimate Mass at the chapel of St. Paul's Church in Westwood. Georgie was her maid of honor, her brother Jack gave her away, she wore a lavender tulle gown designed by Irene—and thousands of fans unexpectedly showed up to clog the streets, sit on rooftops, wave, cheer, and wish her well.

The couple honeymooned in Mexico. Friends arranged activities and escorts for them, and they assumed they would be unrecognized. However, their anonymity was not to be. Everywhere they went, people followed them. One afternoon, they attended a bullfight, and the matador threw his toreador hat to Loretta.

"It is in your honor," those around them explained. So Loretta took off her corsage, and threw it to the matador. A stampede ensued, everyone now recognizing Loretta and trying to get close to her. Police threw up a blockade and got them safely out of the stadium.

Neither she nor Tom had expected all this interest, and Tom's reaction was less than enthusiastic, especially when fans shoved him aside or worse, called him "Mr. Young." He complained to Loretta, and she was relieved when they returned home.

Since Loretta and Tom's lives were rooted on different coasts, they decided to establish a home in each place. Gladys had been assigned to find and decorate a house for them to use when they were in the Beverly Hills area. ("Put a lot of brown in it, Mama," Loretta reportedly suggested. "Tom likes brown.") Gladys did, but the house on Camden Street was not ready when the honeymooners returned. Gladys and Georgie went to live in another house, while Tom, Loretta and Judy used the Bel Air mansion temporarily. Tom was unhappy about this; he wanted to begin their new life in a new house, not one already filled with memories he couldn't share. But for the moment, there was no other solution.

Loretta also decided to turn the management of her finances over to Tom, as most wives in that era did. After all, he was not only her husband but also a businessman, certainly more knowledgeable about money management than she. It proved to be her first major marital mistake.

Tom called an initial meeting with Gladys and Mutt, who had continued as the family's accountant after his divorce from Gladys. When Tom saw the accounts, he was shocked. Loretta had only $5,000 in the bank. How could this be? Where had all her money gone? True, there were mortgages on about fifteen houses—six that Loretta had kept for herself, the others she'd given to her mother—but the rents weren't covering the loan payments. There were expensive furniture and antiques belonging to Gladys stored in garages around the city, intermingled accounts, debts, back taxes . . . a financial quagmire. Tom came home, and vented to Loretta.

"Tom," she laughed, "you don't understand. I'm as surprised as you are to discover I'm not rolling in cash, but I've never paid any attention to what I earn, and Mama never told me to spend or not to spend."

"Loretta, nobody lives like that!"

"My family does. So far it's worked out very well. We've had everything we needed, and that's due to Mama. . . ."

But it was to no avail. Tom was furious, and one day she overheard him on the phone. "You're damn right I'm going to look into this!" he shouted, and slammed down the receiver.

"Who were you talking to?" Loretta asked.

"Your mother," he answered grimly.

"My mother?" Loretta was appalled. "Don't you ever talk to Mama like that!" The two strong egos were already clashing.

"I understand now why Tom was concerned," Loretta said. "He thought he was marrying a rich movie star, and then found out there was no cash flow." She tried to persuade him that houses in this developing area were a good investment, but Tom turned a deaf ear. During the next year, he and his advisers liquidated everything but the newly purchased Camden home, selling the Youngs' beloved Bel Air mansion for $50,000. (The next owner sold it just a few years later for over $1 million.) Tom also sold Loretta's classic 16-cylinder Cadillac Town Car, one of only five produced that year—for $900.

One lamentable fallout from Tom's actions was a rift with Gladys, who regarded his actions as a criticism of her. Hurt and dismayed, she refused to speak to Tom and, instead, went to Europe to look for antiques, and let the dust settle between her and her new son-in-law. Loretta believed that a wife should support her husband in all matters, but now she found herself unwillingly on Tom's "side," against her own mother. It would be an entire year before Gladys would finally accept Loretta's invitation to dinner, and resume her relationship with Tom as if nothing had ever happened. This was, again, typical of both Gladys and Loretta—if an issue could not be settled, it was ignored.

Nonetheless, Loretta was severely jolted by Tom's unexpected and high-handed attitude about her financial affairs.

She had believed he loved "Gretchen," the part of her that was real, her own person whatever her occupation. Now, a troubling inner voice prodded her: had Tom actually wanted Loretta Young the actress, and the wealth and status that accompanied that role? She would never feel as assured in his love again.

Life in New York

*How wonderful it is that nobody need wait a single
moment before starting to improve the world.*

—ANNE FRANK

Before leaving for Europe, Gladys did finish the Camden house,
turning it into what friend Ray Milland called "a miniature
estate." Every square inch was utilized, down to a lily pond
outside the master bedroom window. Loretta, Tom and Judy also
settled in New York, where a friend was leaving town, and had
offered the newlyweds the use of his apartment. It was a wrench,
saying good-bye to the family, with whom Loretta had lived all
her life except for her brief marriage to Grant. And once again,
as their train pulled into Grand Central Station, Loretta was
mobbed by thousands of screaming fans. Five-year-old Judy
developed a fear of crowds, which continues to this day.

Now that she was married, Loretta decided to do only two
pictures annually. A picture took ten weeks to make, so two
would obligate her less than half the year. She had just been cast

as a ballerina in *The Men in Her Life,* so while Tom went to the office, Loretta enrolled in dance class at the American Ballet Company in New York (even though a double would perform the most difficult steps in her routines). She moved the furniture out of the apartment drawing room, and installed practice bars and mirrors, so she could rehearse there with her partner and her double. Other dancers in the cast—as well as friends—began to use the practice room as a sort of party place, and Loretta welcomed them all. It was just like the "revolving door" household of her childhood, except that Mama wasn't there.

During Easter week, Josie Wayne came to visit. Her marriage to John was becoming increasingly shaky, despite their shared love for their four young children, and she needed to get away. Traditionally, St. Patrick's Cathedral hosted a speaker during the afternoon of Good Friday. The women decided to attend. The speaker was then-Monsignor Fulton J. Sheen.

Monsignor Sheen was a professor of philosophy at Catholic University in Washington, D.C., and already a prolific author (he would ultimately publish ninety books, and write two syndicated columns). He was well known around the country, since he spoke each Sunday afternoon on NBC's radio broadcast of the Catholic Hour. (Sheen was the program's regular speaker from 1930 to 1950; at his peak, the show pulled thousands of fan letters each week, about one-third from Protestants.) He was building a reputation as a brilliant teacher, staunch anti-Communist and charitable giver—he lived frugally and donated all his income to missionaries. Sheen had also converted many people to Catholicism, notably Louis Budenz, former managing editor of the Communist *Daily Worker.*

Loretta and Josie were mesmerized by Monsignor Sheen. He talked from noon to three o'clock on the Passion and Death of Jesus, without ever looking at a note. He also discussed the importance of developing a devotion to the Blessed Mother.

"Any Catholic worth his salt ought to be saying the rosary every day," he declared.

On the way home, the women were discussing what they had heard. "I'm going to say the rosary every day from now on," Loretta announced. "Aren't you?"

"No," Josie answered.

"Why not?"

Josie frowned. "I don't like to make promises I may not be able to keep."

She had to be crazy, Loretta thought affectionately. What could be hard about saying the rosary?

When they returned to the Lewis apartment, Tom had news. Monsignor Sheen's assistant had phoned; apparently, Sheen had recognized Loretta at the church, and was inviting her, Tom and Josie for dinner at his residence. "It was a marvelous evening," Loretta recalled. "He was just as wonderful a conversationalist as he had been in church that afternoon." It was the beginning of a long and close relationship.

(For the next ten years Loretta tried saying a rosary every day, but too often, she forgot. Obviously, she wasn't a "Catholic worth her salt." Much later, she shared her predicament with her "free psychiatrist," Father Ward, who pointed out logically that God had never said she had to recite a daily rosary, and that her scrupulous conscience had been working overtime. "That's just your idea, and you're mad because you can't accomplish it all by yourself." Far better, he pointed out, to start a regular prayer habit by concentrating on God, with attention and meaning.)

While in New York, Loretta also met Clare Boothe Luce, the wife of Henry Luce, publisher of *Time* Magazine. In addition to being a congresswoman and future ambassador to Italy, Clare had written several successful Broadway plays, and was another of Monsignor Sheen's converts. Loretta looked forward to dinner parties when Clare was on the guest list, because she loved to listen to this brilliant and sophisticated woman discussing points of theology with Monsignor. Soon Irene Dunne got to know Clare too, and the women enjoyed their time together.

In late 1941, Loretta and Tom went on a second honeymoon to Hawaii. Rear Admiral Isaac C. Kidd was a fan of Loretta's and happily volunteered to show the couple around the battleship he commanded, the USS Arizona. Two months later, he and 1,176 other crewmen died when the Arizona sank during the bombing of Pearl Harbor. The Second World War had begun.

War Years

America in the forties was a nation of railroad tracks and trains.
Railroad stations in small towns and cities were crowded with
men in uniform, their wives and sweethearts giving a last
embrace before the trains departed for a distant port. . . .

—TOM BROKAW, THE GREATEST GENERATION

Hollywood was as affected by the war as any other community. Movie-makers switched focus, and scripts began to concentrate on military matters. Off-screen, stars enlisted or came out in droves to entertain troops, as patriotism ran high. Tom enlisted, and because of his experience developing radio shows, the special services division of the War Department asked him to create the Armed Forces Radio Service, broadcast to the men in the military to keep morale high. Tom was also to arrange troop entertainment, which he did with great expertise. He began with the rank of major, and proceeded to colonel, with headquarters in Hollywood and another office in Washington D.C.

Since Loretta didn't sing or dance professionally or tell jokes, she couldn't actually "entertain." Her preferred job was to visit hospitals and induction centers, and talk to servicemen.

119

"The only thing I asked was to please let me go alone, except for a nurse to show me the way," she said. "If a colonel accompanied me, it only made the soldiers ill at ease. But if a nice, friendly-looking woman approached, only wanting to sit and talk for a while, it was just what they needed." Although she took part in patriotic radio programs, went on a bond-selling tour and appeared in a huge fund-raising rally in Madison Square Garden, Loretta enjoyed this personal contact the most.

On one occasion, a B-26 Marauder gunner, Clarence (Cy) Cyford, spotted Loretta visiting an air strip, and asked her to autograph the nose of his plane. He found an empty ammunition crate for her to stand on, and she wrote her name in chalk, promising to pray for each crew flying the plane. A painter traced her signature, to keep it permanent.

~

In May, 1944, after several missions, the "Loretta Young" started out on a bombing run from the field at Great Dunmov, England. It lost an engine on take-off. Carrying a full load of bombs, the crew could not continue, and the frantic pilot radioed the next airport, in Boreham. But Boreham was also launching planes, and the "Loretta Young's" pilot was denied permission to land.

However, there was no other option, and finally the controller gave clearance for the wounded plane to come in on the short runway—an almost impossible feat, given the weight of a full bomb load. At touchdown, the pilot blew both tires on the main landing gear, collapsed the nose wheel, then the left wheel, and finally skidded to a halt off the end of the runway. It was the "Loretta Young's" last mission. Damaged beyond repair, the plane was stripped and taken to the scrap yard. But her namesake must have been doing some special praying that day, because each member of the crew walked away from the crash unharmed.

~

In addition to her war work, Loretta continued to make two movies a year, but again, she was not happy with the scripts Myron Selznick was bringing her. "I loved Myron, but as everyone knew, his primary interest for his clients was money. He and I had often discussed what I wanted to do with my career, and more *Doctor Takes a Wife* scripts weren't it." Myron couldn't understand why Loretta wasn't happy, since she was now away from Daryll Zanuck, and earning $100,000 per movie. What else did this woman want?

Loretta's perspective was different. She wanted roles that would inspire people to make their lives better, or bring them hope during these difficult days. "If you don't care about what kind of parts I get," she told Myron, "then find me someone who does."

Myron was dumbfounded. He was the kingpin in Hollywood, and everyone knew it. When one was privileged enough to be his client, one never left. "You mean, you actually want me to find you a new agent?"

"If you can't get me better parts."

Myron smiled. This was a new wrinkle. But if that's what she wanted, he would do it. He interviewed several, and chose three for Loretta to review. She selected Bert Allenberg, who remained her agent until her movie career ended.

Things were changing in the family, too. Georgie, 17, was now six feet tall, and depressed about it. So when Gladys snagged two important decorating jobs in New York, she brought Georgie with her. "Mama introduced her to Carmel Snow, the editor of one of the top fashion magazines," Loretta recalled. "The woman took one look at Georgie, and within months my beautiful sister appeared on the cover of four fashion magazines." Georgie worked all the time, absorbing praise like a sponge as the feature model for *Town and Country, Harper's Bazaar, Vogue,* and other industry leaders. About nine months later, when Gladys announced it was time to go home, Georgie was willing to leave. "I think she learned what she needed to learn," Loretta surmised. "Being tall or short has nothing to do with what kind of person you are. Kindness, compassion—that's what counts."

Judy was also blossoming, from a beautiful toddler into a stunning little girl. Her only physical flaw were her protruding ears. To many, they seemed a miniature version of Clark Gable's. Judy hated them, and when she complained that children were calling her "Dumbo," Loretta arranged for a plastic surgeon to correct them. Judy also bore a strong resemblance to her Aunt Sally, which grew even more striking as she got older. Tongues again wagged, but as always Loretta refused to lend credibility to the gossip by addressing it. She had enough pressure, including the recent beginning of migraine headaches, which sometimes lasted as long as three days.

Loretta was still in touch with Clare Luce, who had recently read and fallen in love with C. S. Lewis' *Screwtape Letters,* the story of how Satan ingratiates himself into a human's psyche and eventually "converts" him to evil. Twentieth Century producers wanted her to write for them, so Clare suggested a movie based on the book, and the moguls agreed. Instead of Screwtape writing to his nephew, Clare suggested, there would be a mother in Paris writing to her daughter in New York.

Fine, fine, said the bigwigs, none of whom had probably read the book.

And, said Clare, she would like one clause in her contract.

Sure, anything.

There was a line in the original book, which must stay in the finished version: "We know in the long run that the Enemy (God) will always win."

No one objected. Clare wrote the screenplay and accepted a $125,000 fee.

When Twentieth's producers saw the script, however, they were shocked. Nobody had told them this was going to be "one of those crazy religious things." And it was far too intellectual for the average moviegoer. The bigwigs began the pruning process, starting with the important line that Clare had written into the contract.

You can't edit that line. Read the fine print, she told them.

Take your script, your fee and leave, they retorted.

Clare went on a retreat to one of her favorite places, a convent in Bethlehem, New York, where she knew many of the nuns. She felt guilty about keeping the fee Twentieth had paid her, even though, legally and morally, she was entitled to it. She wrestled with her conscience for a while. Maybe she should try again.

Clare called Daryll Zanuck and made him an offer: if the studio would agree to donate $25,000 to the Bethlehem convent, she'd write a screenplay he'd like. Zanuck readily agreed. A charitable gift generated better publicity than a script fee any day.

It took Clare only two weeks to pen *Come to the Stable,* a story of two nuns who want to build a hospital in thanksgiving to God. The nuns' personalities were loosely based on the sisters Clare knew in Bethlehem, and she felt the parts would be perfect for Irene Dunne, as Mother Superior, and Loretta as her assistant.

But once again, the producers at Twentieth Century reacted in unison. Not another religious thing! Put it on the shelf!

Loretta, who read the script, was heartbroken when Twentieth turned it down. "Oh, they can't—it's so good!" she told Clare.

"Not according to them." Clare didn't think she'd better try a third time.

"Then I'll make a novena, and we'll see what happens!" Loretta prayed fervently that something would work out, but nothing did. Gradually she forgot about it. But the script was not dead. . . .

~~~

Loretta also kept in regular touch with Fulton Sheen (another "free psychiatrist") in whom she had utter confidence. Be it over the phone or in person, he seemed able to guide her in the right direction. Once she told him that she was never sure whether God really heard her prayers. "Well, then, ask Him for a sign," Monsignor suggested.

"What kind of sign?"

"Something to let you know He's taking care of things. For example," Monsignor went on, "once when I was at Lourdes, I prayed for a favor I had not yet received. I actually started complaining to the Blessed Mother, saying that if she loved me as much as I loved her, she would intercede and ask God to grant the favor."

"And then?" Loretta was fascinated.

"And then I felt ashamed. I apologized, and asked, if she wasn't mad, would she send a sign: before I left the grotto gate, I wanted to meet a twelve-year-old girl dressed in white, who would stop and hand me a white rose." He looked at Loretta. "You have to be specific, you see—otherwise, you might just think it was coincidence."

"What happened?" she urged.

"Well, I was just going out through the grotto gate when I heard a child's voice call, 'Father'? It was a girl dressed in white, who handed me a white rose. 'How old are you?' I asked her."

"'Twelve'," she said."

Loretta was shocked. "I couldn't do that," she told him. "I'd be too afraid that He wouldn't answer me."

But she continued to think about it. And she was still thinking on the Sunday of Judy's First Communion. She dropped her little daughter off at school to join her classmates for the procession, left friends talking outside, and slipped into a pew in the church's dark quiet interior. It wasn't as if she needed a huge favor. Yes, she was longing for a baby, had even had some minor surgeries to hopefully help her conceive, but God would surely answer at the proper time. Her quest was larger, yet nameless. She just wanted to know that He was there with her, loving her, pleased with her. . . . "I'm not going to ask for a sign," she told God, "but if I did, I'd ask that the candle on the altar's left side wouldn't burn. But You understand, I'm not really asking."

People were starting to enter the church. A little nun came out, carrying a candle lighter. She lit both candles on the altar, and turned to go back down the stairs. Just then, the candle on the left side of the altar went out.

Loretta stared. Just a coincidence. Someone pointed the candle out to the nun, and she went back, climbed the altar stairs and re-lit it. Turning, she started away as the organ began the processional hymn. The left candle went out again.

Now Loretta had goosebumps. Quickly the nun lit the candle for the third time. The children were moving solemnly down the aisle, and the priest had come onto the altar. Once again, the flame flickered and died.

It was too late to try again. Judy would make her First Holy Communion with only one candle burning on the altar. And Loretta would understand, just a little, what "faith the size of a mustard seed" could do.

Some people's faith in God is an explosive conversion—from A to Z in but a moment. Others, perhaps most of us, must spend a lifetime plodding through the alphabet, one letter at a time. Loretta had already experienced some growth in her journey, and the candle episode was another step. But she still had a distance to go. It bothered her that she had not apparently had the faith to ask for a sign. "I started to wonder, was this the way

I did everything? Was I a lukewarm Christian, afraid to get too close to God for fear I'd be let down?" She prayed about it.

The following winter Tom and Loretta rented a house in Palm Springs, and as Lent approached, they decided to attend services every Wednesday and Friday nights. One evening they invited Rosalind Russell and her husband Fred Brisson over for dinner, and it was not until the Brissons left that Loretta realized it was Wednesday. "Oh, Tom, we probably missed everything at church!" she lamented. They decided to drive over anyway, to see if they could attend the last part of the novena.

When they arrived, the church was unlocked, but darkened and deserted. Services had ended. Loretta slipped into a middle pew, while Tom walked over to a side altar. "I did it again—forgot about You" she prayed. "I'm sorry, and I'll try to be more attentive." Then, for some reason, she remembered what had happened at Judy's First Communion. "I'm still not asking for a sign that everything's okay between You and me," she told Him. "But if I did, I'd ask . . . that the crucifix would explode into light."

Just like that, it did!

Loretta couldn't believe it. For the second time, an improbable event had occurred, just as she asked. But how? Suddenly, she realized that Tom, over at the side altar, had been attempting to light a candle, and as he'd struck a match, the entire box had ignited, thus throwing a bright reflection onto the crucifix. He was staring at the burnt box in amazement, not knowing that the timing had been perfect.

She buried her face in her hands. "All right," she whispered, "I believe You. And I won't have to ask for signs anymore." Through the years, when life became difficult and her faith faltered, she would find herself remembering this moment, and the lesson it brought: *I will never leave you nor forsake you.*

The Family Grows

A baby is God's decision that the world will go on.

—*UNKNOWN*

In 1944, Loretta was delighted to learn she was, at last, pregnant. The baby would be born in August. Since the family lived on her earnings (Tom's salary at Armed Forces Radio was quite modest), she had previously been thrilled to sign her best offer ever, a seven-year, seven-figure contract with International Pictures. Better yet, the studio was headed by Bill Goetz, whom she had loved since her early teens when he saved her from being embarrassed at the formal dance.

Loretta had finished her first and second movies for Bill. Now, with the baby's birth approaching, it was time to look for a larger house. Tom was on the East Coast, so Loretta searched with a realtor. She signed a contract on a house in Holmby Hills being sold by Benjamin "Bugsy" Siegel, a notorious criminal.

Tom didn't like the idea of owning a gangster's house, especially when he discovered that Siegel had made changes in the escrow papers, citing faucets, chandeliers, and marble flooring he now wished to remove from the house. That was illegal, but who was brave enough to challenge him? The house also had termites. Fortunately, "There was a clause in the contract setting a limit on the amount we had to pay to get the house in shape," Loretta recalled. "If we exceeded that figure—and termite removal certainly would—we could void the contract." They did, but Siegel took them to court. The lawyer put an almost-nine-months-pregnant Loretta on the stand, and asked her if it was true that she had a phobia about termites.

"I don't like any kind of bugs!" Loretta responded emphatically. The courtroom onlookers roared with laughter.

The judge ruled in the Lewises' favor, and they went house-hunting again. (Siegel, apparently, never put a "hit" out on them.) Constance Bennett's home on Carolwood Drive was available—forty-five rooms, and down the street from Walt Disney's mansion—just what Tom had in mind. On moving day, Loretta was delighted to discover that Jane Sharp and her family lived next door. The women had lost touch after Jane got married, but now they would resume their relationship without missing a beat.

At a family gathering on July 31, Loretta's long labor began, and she gave birth to Christopher Paul at six the following morning at Queen of Angels hospital. A son! Tom was as thrilled as she.

One day in the hospital, Dr. Walter Halleron, the Young family physician, came in to check her. "Loretta," he said, "there's a Franciscan nun here, Sister Mary Winifred, who wants to see you for a moment."

Loretta wanted to rest and get to know baby Christopher. (She regarded any hospital stay as a vacation.) Besides, when people wanted to "see her," it usually meant they wanted her to "do something" for them. "You told me I wasn't supposed to have any visitors," she reproached him.

"Oh, she's not a visitor," Dr. Halleron protested, "just a charming woman who needs ten minutes of your time."

"Well, okay." Loretta always had trouble refusing a nun's request.

"I'll only take eight minutes," said a voice belonging to a cheerful nun who came in and sat down at Loretta's bedside.

Because of the war, she explained, there were more dislocated families, more unmarried pregnant women alone and needy. Sister Mary Winifred wanted to start a residence for them here in Los Angeles, called St. Anne's Maternity Home for Unwed Mothers.

"I have a little house, and five nuns willing to staff it, but we need a famous name and some help to get everything off the ground," she wound down. "Will you be the president of our board of directors?"

Later Loretta noted that Sister Winifred should have been running a Fortune 500 company, so intelligent and accomplished was she. Now, though, Loretta was incredulous. "Sister, I don't know the first thing about sitting on a board," she objected.

"You don't have to know."

"But. . . ."

"Just your name and reputation will open many doors."

"Well. . . ." Loretta had met her match. "Let me think about it, Sister. Call me after I get home with the baby."

A few weeks later, Loretta hosted a tea party, and invited Dolores Hope, Josie Wayne (now divorced), and several other women. Sister Winifred came and explained her plan. From these small seeds, many blossoms would grow. Dolores Hope eventually ended up as president of Holy Name Adoption Foundation, the agency that was started as a result of the home. Josie served on Holy Name's board. Loretta agreed to become president of the board and, as promised, Sister Winifred talked a Los Angeles allergist into running the actual meetings. "He was brilliant, with a superb reputation," Loretta said. "People might assume I was in charge, but he and Sister made a great team."

At one point, Sister wanted to buy and raze two buildings, then build an office to house Dolores' burgeoning adoption agency. The whole project would cost about $50,000. It might as well have been $5 million, since there was no money in the treasury. "I suppose we could throw a fund-raising dinner dance or a fashion show," Loretta suggested to Sister one day. But such events were done all the time, and people were getting tired of them. "I know!" she said. "How about an auction?"

Sister Winifred looked blank. "We haven't anything to sell."

"We'll get donations, Sister, from movie stars and designers. Personal memorabilia. Jewelry. Stuff. Then we'll auction it off and sell it back to them! And we can invite the public too— they'll come just to see the stars." It was a good idea, the women realized, and practical for Loretta because she could handle much of it by phone. She called everyone in the Hollywood community who might have something to donate, and was warmly received.

"I remember calling Nancy Sinatra, who I had never met," Loretta says. "She was nice, and she sent a pair of Frank's diamond cufflinks." Loretta found a jeweler to do a display and another to donate pins; a furrier offered a fur jacket; each designer donated a dress; there were paintings and antiques. . . . Sister had been right—just Loretta's name (and charm) would open doors.

St Anne's received so many donations that the auction had to be held on three successive nights. Everyone had an enormously good time. But when the proceeds were tallied, Loretta was surprised and disappointed to learn that the $50,000 goal had not been reached. There was nothing more she could do. After all this work for the girls and their babies, would the project fail?

Sister Winifred didn't think so. "You know, Loretta," she said thoughtfully, a few days after the auction, "I've always believed that it's easier to raise funds to finish something than to start it. Let's go ahead with what we've got, and trust God to supply the rest of the money."

And so they did. Within months, two anonymous movie actors donated enough to complete the project, just as Sister had predicted.

On another occasion, Sister greeted Loretta by asking, "Who do you know who has money?" (Sister was rarely subtle.)

Loretta thought. "My mother is decorating a big house for some man who makes ball bearings," she said. "How much do you need?"

"Ten thousand dollars."

"Isn't that an awful lot?"

Sister shrugged. She was used to miracles.

"Let me call him," Loretta decided.

The man was Patrick Frawley, the president of Papermate Pen Company (the ball bearings were pen-sized). He had a soft, warm voice, and invited Loretta to come to his office that afternoon.

Once there, she barely started to explain when Frawley reached for his checkbook. "Would ten thousand dollars help?"

Loretta was stunned. The exact amount! Frawley wrote the check, and smiled. "I'll have to tell your mother that I finally met her charming daughter."

~

The Frawleys enjoyed making miracles for other people, because they had been given one early in their life together. Patrick's wife, Gerry, had developed tuberculosis during her first pregnancy, and had been sent to a sanitarium. Pat and his sister-in-law juggled baby care, and the whole extended family prayed for Gerry's healing. But she worsened. A year passed, then two. If she did survive, the doctors told her, she could never stress herself with another pregnancy.

During this dark period, both Pat and Gerry walked by faith, abandoning themselves completely to God. "Do what You have to do," Gerry often prayed. She knew that whenever God says "no" or "not yet," He must have a good reason for it.

Then she passed the three-year mark, and was able to go home. "Remember, no more children," the doctors cautioned her.

However, Gerry and Patrick decided that they would continue to let God be in charge. And as Loretta started a lifelong friendship with them, she discovered that the Frawleys were now the parents of nine.

~

Tom had gone to London. Loretta missed him, especially since there seemed to be a growing chasm between them. Their easy banter had diminished; he was frequently displeased with her, and she was baffled over what she could do to change. She could only hope that the situation would ease when the war ended and he could come home for good. In the meantime, she kept busy caring for the new baby, filming *Along Came Jones* with Gary Cooper, and helping to launch St. Anne's. She also did an occasional radio show. "One night we were recording two or three Christmas shows for the Armed Forces Radio Service," she said. "Spencer Tracy was narrating 'The Small One,' about the donkey that carried Mary to Bethlehem. Charles Tazewell had written that story, and happened to be at the studio that night." Loretta told him how much she loved the story.

"I wrote it between migraine headaches," Charles told her.

"I don't see how you could." Loretta recalled the distress of her own migraines.

He shrugged. "Sometimes the best things come out when I'm in the most pain."

Somehow, she could understand that. Acting was sometimes a painful process. Acting—and life. She got through it all with patience and prayer. Yet Charles, despite his sensitivity, was not a religious man.

He was looking at her. "Someday I'll write something for you," he said.

It was a kind thing for him to suggest. But Charles Tazewell was world famous, and Loretta could not imagine him taking the time to do that.

Loretta's Choice

Arrangements were being made for a movie about Elizabeth Blackwell, the first American female physician, when Loretta realized to her amazed delight that she was pregnant again. No doubt, since the movie was to be a period piece involving long dresses and bustles, she could probably get through most of it before she started to show. But her doctor disagreed. Loretta was farther along than she had thought—about four months—and she would have to bow out of the Blackwell movie. In fact, since her role in *Along Came Jones* had involved a lot of activity—bouncing along in a buckboard, jumping and running—her doctor thought it was a blessing that she hadn't suffered a miscarriage.

Loretta called Bill Goetz. "I hope you're not too disappointed—of course, it's wonderful news for us. I'm four months pregnant, and won't be able to do Elizabeth Blackwell."

Bill knew how long Loretta and Tom had waited for a baby, and now a second! "Don't worry about it," he assured her. "We'll cancel the picture."

A few days later, however, Loretta's agent, Bert Allenberg, phoned. "The chairman of the studio board and some of the others want a meeting with you," he told Loretta. For some reason, it sounded ominous.

When Loretta and Bert entered the boardroom, she sensed the tension right away. Everyone looked grim, and Bill Goetz seemed uneasy—not his usual affectionate self. The chairman got right to the point. "Loretta, you recently held us up on *Along Came Jones* until you recovered from childbirth, and now you're canceling Blackwell due to another pregnancy. It appears to us that you're far more interested in having a family than a career."

"Actually, I'm trying to have both . . ." she began, but he cut her off.

"Unless you skip this baby, and go ahead with the Blackwell picture, we'll have no choice but to cancel your contract. It's up to you."

Skip this baby? Stunned, Loretta looked at Bill, waiting for him to intervene. Bill remained silent. Unable to speak, she got up and left the room. Bert followed her.

"Bert, did they say what I think they said?" Loretta whispered.

"They said that unless you have an abortion now, they're going to cancel your contract. That's a few million dollars you aren't going to earn."

Not again! She could hardly believe she was facing this situation once more, forced to choose between a baby and her career. She thought of the years it had taken her to reach this pinnacle, and felt sick to her stomach. "I can't believe they would fire me."

"Believe it," he said grimly.

"Well, Bert, you take care of it," she told him. "I can't look at any of them again. I'm going home."

The next day Bert phoned. "Loretta, they did it. They canceled your contract. And you won't believe this. . . ."

"There's more?"

Bert reminded Loretta that instead of being paid in a lump sum when she completed a picture, she had requested that the studio pro-rate her fee and pay her each week. It had seemed easier to keep up with family expenditures if money was coming in regularly. "Well," said Bert, "according to their calculations they've overpaid you $50,000, and they're expecting you to return it."

It was the final blow. "Bert," Loretta's voice was like steel, "tell them they can hang by their thumbs waiting, because they're never going to see one dime of it!" She put down the phone, and only then, let the tears come. The bills—how was she going to handle them? What if International sued her for the overpayment? Worst was her bafflement over Bill Goetz's behavior, or lack of it. Why hadn't he defended her? (It would be years before Loretta discovered that although Bill was the titular head of International Pictures and ran the studio, the board of directors was actually in charge, and he had no real authority.)

Life was now on hold, Loretta realized. They could live for awhile on savings, maybe sell this huge house. Perhaps Tom would leave the military and find a good job. But for the next five months, she would have to sit squarely in the palm of God's hand. There was no place else to go.

A short time later, the postman delivered a package to Loretta from Charles Tazewell. Inside was a script titled *The Littlest Angel,* accompanied by a note. *"Dear Loretta, This is for you. Do anything you like with it. Love, Taze."*

It couldn't have come at a more opportune time. Loretta read the script, and was enchanted. She phoned Bert Allenberg about it, and he soon called back to say that Decca Records would do a recording of the story.

"Wonderful," she told him, "but not this weekend. I'm going to my annual retreat at Marymount."

"Enjoy it," said Bert, who could never understand why people would spend a whole weekend just praying. "It won't be this Friday—too soon."

He was wrong. Loretta was settling in at Marymount on Friday evening, when Bert phoned. He was frantic. "The script was sent to the president of Decca records for him to look at it," Bert explained. "But before he had a chance to read it, Greer Garson came in for an appointment. When he left for a moment, Greer saw the script, read it and fell in love with it. Now she wants to narrate it, and the president doesn't know it belongs to you."

"She'd be wonderful, but Taze gave it to me!" Loretta exclaimed.

"I know, but we'll need that note he wrote to you to prove it. You do still have that note, don't you?"

Oh, no! She remembered tossing it somewhere, not realizing that it was, in effect, a contract proving ownership. Given the vastness of her house, and dutiful maids discarding anything out of order, she'd never find it now.

"I was afraid of that," Bert sighed, "so to save everyone embarrassment, I've booked the studio, and arranged for Victor Young and his orchestra to do the recording with you at eight o'clock tomorrow night. There will be three records, each with two sides, which is a lot of dialogue—get there early to rehearse. We'll explain everything later, and the Decca people can check with Tazewell if they need to."

"Bert, I can't do that—I'm on a retreat that won't be over until Sunday night."

"Loretta, do you or do you not want to do the recording?" Bert was quickly running out of patience. When he used that tone of voice with her, she knew better than to argue.

Loretta left Marymount about six on Saturday evening, drove to the studio, ran through her first reading . . . and suddenly realized that this project was graced. For the practice had been absolutely flawless, and there seemed no need for another. Instead, the director decided they would try an actual recording. Musicians looked at each other. They had only rehearsed once. How could anyone be ready for a take?

But no one made the slightest mistake this time either—no stumble or missed dialogue from Loretta, nothing dropped or banged, no technical problems, not even a sour note on a violin.

When it was over, everyone sat in disbelieving silence. Such a thing had never before happened. "I-I think that's a wrap," the director announced in wonder.

Loretta was back at Marymount before ten-thirty, thrilled at having done this exquisite story with a group of such talented, extraordinary people. Later, when she listened to the finished product, she recognized a new quality in her voice. "I think it might have been because I was pregnant with Peter and had a baby son at home as well, and of course, the story is about a little boy who died," she says.

Whatever the reason, the record was a smash success. Even Greer Garson was pleased. "I was so upset when I heard you had recorded it," she told Loretta later. "But then they explained the situation to me. And really, Loretta, it couldn't have been more charming just as it was." Later, Helen Hayes recorded it. Walt Disney wanted to make it into an animated feature with Loretta narrating that too, but arrangements fell through. However, the story is still a best-selling book, especially at Christmas, and today, on the Loretta Young website, people leave messages, asking if the recording that they remember from their childhood is still available for their own children and grandchildren. Perhaps some day it will be.

On July 14, 1945, when she was eight months pregnant, Loretta, Tom and Josie Wayne were leaving for a dinner party at Claudette Colbert's house. As Loretta came downstairs, wearing a dazzling maternity gown, she felt strange. "Josie, I think my water just broke," she said.

Josie looked alarmed. "Sit down—now," she warned.

Loretta sat on a stair step. "I feel okay. Nothing hurts. Let's go to the party!"

"Is that wise?" a worried Tom asked Josie.

"Well, it could be hours yet. I suppose you can go to the hospital just as easily from Claudette's as from here. . . ." Josie was dubious, but they decided to go.

The party was great fun, and although Loretta didn't dance, she only agreed to go home at 2 A.M. because Josie told her she was getting dark circles under her eyes. ("In those days, if anyone left before 1:30, the party was considered a disaster.") She and Tom dropped Josie off, and were just getting ready for bed when Loretta felt a pain. "I think it's time to call the doctor, Tom," she said.

The doctor was furious that Loretta had gone to a party instead of coming straight to the hospital at the first sign of labor. And baby Peter Charles proved him right by being born less than two hours later.

All that day Loretta rested in a haze of contentment, as she put it, "halfway between heaven and earth." This time, the struggle and pain had ended quickly, and she knew only joy. "Some reporter once asked me what was the happiest day of my life, and I said it was that day," Loretta recalled. "I don't know why it stands out in my mind. Maybe because I had done so many things that seemed unnatural—playing other people's characters, dressing up in other people's clothes, not being myself, trying to do things that I couldn't or shouldn't be doing.

"But on this day I had done the most normal and marvelous thing in the world. I was a woman, having a baby." An especially cherished baby too, as she had laid her principles on the line for him. Kissing his downy head she knew, as she had known since the moment she faced the kingpins at International Pictures, that whatever came, her decision had been right.

~~~

One day when Peter was about four, he was scheduled for an inoculation at the doctor's office. Loretta always prepared the children for these unpleasant situations, and she was forthright with Pete. "It's going to hurt a little," she told him, "but if you are real brave and don't cry, I'll give you a treat. Let's see—we'll go to The Brown Derby for lunch, just you and me. Would you like that?"

Mom all to himself? You bet! This was a major excursion for Pete who, as the baby of the family, was always attempting to tag along. In the doctor's office, he screwed up his little face when the needle approached, and managed to not shed a tear.

"Good job!" Loretta congratulated him, and they went on to The Brown Derby. The maitre d' greeted Loretta and escorted the pair to a booth off on the side. Peter was thrilled, especially when the waiter fussed over him and gave him his own menu to "read." Smiling, Loretta glanced around the room. Suddenly, she realized that sitting directly opposite them was a table full of men, among them Bill Goetz.

Bill saw her, and nodded, and she nodded back. They had crossed paths socially during the past four years and had remained cordial, but had never discussed the meeting in the board room. Now, as the entourage got up to leave, Bill came over and slid into the booth next to her. His eyes were fixed on Peter. Finally he said under his breath, "Is this . . . the child?"

"Yes." Loretta whispered back. "Don't you think he's worth a million dollars?"

"Loretta, please don't talk about it. It made me sick."

"It made me sicker!" she retorted. Bill nodded, never taking his eyes off Peter. "I'm sorry, Bill," she relented. "I knew in my heart that it wasn't your doing."

Loretta would work for Bill again, and they would pick up their friendship where it had left off. But she never forgot the way Bill gazed at Peter that day in The Brown Derby. For she knew that although he and his wife had two much-loved daughters, he had always wanted a son to complete the family. And the Goetzs were unable to have more children.

Ironically, so were the Lewises. Despite her hopes for many more, Peter was the last baby Loretta would have.

Patrick Peyton

The family that prays together, stays together.

—Father Patrick Peyton

When Loretta and Peter came home from the hospital, her physician reminded her to stay in bed as long as she could, to nurse her new son, and ease almost-one-year-old Christopher into the role of big brother. So she was not at all amenable when Tom phoned one morning. "Loretta, I'm sending a young Irish priest over to you," he informed her. "A Father Patrick Peyton, from Notre Dame. He's got some interesting ideas."

"Tom, not now! I'm in bed by doctor's orders . . . remember?"

"He won't mind. He'll be there in a few minutes. You'll like him." Tom hung up.

Flustered, Loretta grabbed her bed jacket just as the front doorbell rang. There was no time for a more formal meeting. Father Peyton would just have to take her as she was.

The housekeeper ushered him into the room, and sat him next to the bed on a pink satin boudoir chair. "He was a very large man, and I will never forget how awkward and embarrassed he looked," Loretta recalled. "He kept turning his hat in his hands, and his mouth seemed too dry to speak." Finally, however, he began. It was like witnessing a small explosion, as the words tumbled out of his mouth.

"When I was 18, I came to America with my brother, and we both went into the seminary at Notre Dame, which we had always dreamed about, you see, and everything was wonderful, and one day the priest sent me for a doctor's exam, and it turned out I had tuberculosis, and I had to go into the hospital." He paused to draw breath. "I kept thinkin' that I wanted to be ordained the same day as my brother, but how could I if I stayed sick, and they put me in machines and told me not to worry, but there was nothing more they could do for me."

Another breath. Loretta was fascinated.

"So I was weepin' all the time, and finally a priest friend of mine visited, and said he was surprised at me. That surely if I profess to love the Blessed Mother and I believe she could ask God to give me a miracle, that I ought to pray for one. And if healing would be good for me, God would heal me, and if it wouldn't, He wouldn't. And I thought, of course! So I made a nine-day novena to the Blessed Mother and promised that if I was cured, I would spend the rest of my life promotin' the Holy Rosary. And on the ninth day of the prayers, I asked a nurse to send in a doctor, and she said none were available and what good would it do, but I insisted, and finally one came in and I wanted an examination, and they finally put me back in the machine, and turned me this way and that, and kept sayin' 'look at this!' 'look at that!' and the tuberculosis was gone. And I ended up being ordained on the same day as my brother."

"What a miraculous . . ." Loretta began.

"And so someone donated a train ticket for me to come here," Father Peyton blurted on, "to ask if you could help me get a lot of movie stars together to say the rosary on the radio on August 15th, the Feast of Mary's Assumption."

It was an amazing, and highly unlikely request. "Father Peyton," she began gently, "I don't think that's possible. For one thing, radio air time is very expensive and I don't know who would be willing to buy it."

"Oh I have the time," he assured her casually, "on the Mutual Broadcasting Network" (since gone out of business). "If I can get the people." He explained that he had been leading a Family Rosary show on a local station in Albany for the past few years, but wanted to reach more people. Mutual had recently allowed him to do a network program, on this past Mother's Day. Singer Bing Crosby, the Sullivan family of Iowa (whose five sons had gone to their death together on a battleship sunk in the Pacific) and New York's Cardinal Spellman had participated, and to everyone's surprise, the rosary recitation had been enthusiastically received. Now Father wanted to do a weekly show; he believed strongly that "A world at prayer is a world at peace."

Loretta didn't think it was likely—how many movie stars were going to be willing to pray on radio?—but she was afraid to say "no" to this earnest, energetic priest. It would be somehow like saying "no" to Christ's mother herself. Loretta had moved from one house to another, given birth to two babies, finished a movie, and become chairman of the board of St. Anne's during the past twelve months, but what was one more project? "I'll be glad to call some people and see what they think," she told him.

The "Catholic mafia" was still very much in evidence during those Hollywood years. Loretta insists she was never subjected to bigotry or bias due to her faith (she points to *Ramona*, where the actors actually had Mass on the set each day—co-star Don Ameche as server—and the crew went about their business very quietly). But others faced less rosy scenarios. Chief complaints were pictures done on location, where no arrangements were made for Catholic actors and crew to get to Mass on Sundays or keep a Friday fast. Naturally, when asked to support each other, the group closed ranks.

A month later, Loretta, Irene Dunne, Rosalind Russell, Ann Blyth, Bing Crosby, Jane Wyatt, Pat O'Brien, Ethel Barrymore, Don Ameche, and several more gathered to pray. (Said Loretta, "We had to meet early in the morning, and when I got into the car, which had picked Irene Dunne up first, I pulled out my cigarettes. Irene moaned, 'Oh please, dear, not at 7 o'clock in the morning.' It was the first I'd known that Irene was allergic to smoke." Of course, the cigarette was more necessary to Loretta than breakfast. "I sat up in front with the driver, puffing away," she admitted, "and closed the window behind us so poor Irene wouldn't be sick.")

The rosary morning was an unexpected success. The stars prayed, as did listeners at home, then Father Peyton spoke for a few moments. The presentation should not have succeeded—no one had ever heard of such a thing, and Father was universally acknowledged to be only a passable speaker, barely understood due to his thick brogue. But people seemed to be fascinated by his very presence. "Later, I saw him saying the rosary in front of enormous crowds in India, where no one had a clue as to what he was doing, but they all joined in anyway," Loretta said. "He was somehow irresistible."

Actress Jane Wyatt agrees. "I first saw Father Peyton one morning at St. Victor's church," she says. "He was a big gangly guy, a poor speaker, and he invited the congregation to come back that night, to hear his plans to start a Catholic radio show. I remember thinking that he was never going to succeed."

Although she rarely went out at night alone, that evening she announced she was going back to St. Victor's. "Didn't you just go to church this morning?" her then non-Catholic husband asked.

"Yes, but I'm afraid no one will show up for this poor priest, and he'll be so disappointed."

Jane needn't have worried. The crowd at St. Victor's was so large that she barely found standing room in the back. Father Peyton's crusade had begun.

During this time, Georgie had decided to give the movies another try. She tested for a part at MGM with Mickey Rooney, and got it. Then the studio postponed the movie. The young Mexican actor who had fallen in love with Georgie's face several years ago, had been dividing his time between the New York stage and making movies in Mexico. When Sally's husband, director Norman Foster, went to Mexico in search of someone to play the part of a bullfighter, he found and hired the young man, whose name was Ricardo Montalban. Sally was charmed by him, and thought Georgie might be too. When she suggested they meet, Ricardo wasn't very enthusiastic. After all, he'd carried that picture of his dream girl in his mind for so long.

Eventually he accepted Polly Ann's invitation to visit. The women took Ricardo to a luncheon where they knew Georgie would be. When Ricardo saw Georgie, he was stunned. It was her, his dream girl! "My heart leaped," Ricardo recalls. "For me, this was it."

Twenty-year-old Georgie evidently felt the same way, for two weeks later, the couple eloped to Tijuana. (They were later married at St. Paul's church in Westwood, with all the trimmings.) Georgie's brief movie career had ended, by her own decision. The Montalbans would go on to have four children, and a rich, loving life together, neither ever regretting the choice they made.

Despite the busyness of her life, Loretta had still not come to terms with being fired. "I'd heard of other stars losing their contracts because they wouldn't have abortions, and I wondered if it might be the end of me too." But God apparently had other plans. After a period out of work after Peter's birth, Loretta signed to do *The Stranger* with Orson Welles. It was one of her best roles, and landed her on the cover of *Life* magazine. Obviously, her popularity had not waned, and perhaps freelancing was the answer. She could pick her own material, and not be subjected to the kind of demands that studio bosses made.

Tom left the service and Armed Forces Radio Network, but returned to New York and resumed his job with Young and Rubicam. He commuted for the next eight months, and if Loretta had assumed they would regain their former closeness, she was wrong. Sometimes she sensed that he too would change the situation if only he could, but he was as mystified as she. One day he phoned Loretta to tell her that he was in a continuing argument with the chairman of the board. He had received offers from other agencies, but none was acceptable. He sounded tired and irritable.

"Oh Tom, don't fight any more, with anybody," she pleaded. "Just come home here with us."

Tom did. He worked in the Los Angeles branch of Young and Rubicam for the next few months. Then, inexplicably, he quit. His decision would prove to be a major mistake in his professional world, and ultimately in his marriage.

PART FIVE

∼

A Real Class Act

It was Christmas week, circa 1980, and I was a paramedic in Tulsa, Oklahoma. A holiday party was being held for police, fire department, emergency medical personnel and media representatives at a local eatery. Rumors had circulated that the actress Loretta Young would make an appearance because her son Christopher Lewis was a TV anchor here. Of course, most of us scoffed at the very notion. Why would THE Loretta Young appear at what was obviously far less than a Hollywood A-List event?

Boy, were we wrong! About an hour or so into the festivities, magic happened. It's trite, but true—the doors opened and in swept this stunning woman. She was gracious, she was funny, she was class beyond compare. She looked like a movie star, and acted like the lady next door. To this day, I remember it—her standing at the bar and literally holding court. She would ask what you did, and then proceed to tell you about an experience she'd had with whatever specialty you were in. She was wonderfully funny, and her laughter was from the gut and sincere. And you just knew she was talking right to you. I still remember the plaid tweed suit she wore with this scarf thrown across her shoulder. I fell in love right there with this bright, and, at times, bawdily funny lady.

When the time came for her to leave, we all just spontaneously stood up and cheered her out the door. It was a real class act.

—Chris,
a fan from the Loretta Young website

Part 5 photo—Loretta backstage at the Academy Awards
with Frederick Marsh after he presented her with the
Best Actress Award, 1948 (photo on preceding page).

The Farmer's Daughter

When I saw you in The Farmer's Daughter, *I wondered
if that Swedish accent was real. . . . (Later) I realized
that the accent was fake, but the actress wasn't.*

—Courtney, age 16, Fan mail, 1999

While Loretta was working on (ironically) *The Perfect Marriage*,
Dore Schary visited her on the set. Schary, a former writer-
producer at Metro-Goldwyn-Mayer, was now the production chief
of Vanguard Pictures, run by David Selznick, Myron's brother.
Selznick wished to do *The Farmer's Daughter* as his next project.
The movie, originally a Finnish play titled "Katie for Congress,"
is about an effervescent Swedish-born girl who works as a maid
for a United States congressman and his family, and eventually
becomes a congresswoman herself. The starring role had been
offered to Ingrid Bergman, a genuine Swede, but she had turned
it down. Several other starlets had been considered, including
the skater Sonia Henie from Norway. Dore Schary had been

sure from the beginning that Loretta was right for the role. But Selznick and others had disagreed. Now, with the rest of the players cast, time was growing short, and Schary was given the green light.

As they spoke on the set, Loretta expressed doubts about her ability to master a Swedish accent. "I could do southern," she suggested to Schary. "My mother still has a trace of it, and I'm used to it." No, said Schary. It was an essential part of the story that Katie is foreign born; Swedish would be better.

Further, Schary had a solution: he would assign Ruth Roberts to coach Loretta. Ruth was Swedish, but had no accent. She had originally taught English to Swedish immigrants in Minnesota, and because her brother, George Seaton, was a Hollywood director (*Miracle on 34th Street* among other hits), Selznick had hired her to help Ingrid Bergman lose her Swedish inflection. ("We always said Ruth took away Ingrid's accent, and gave it to me," Loretta recalled).

Loretta finally agreed because despite her concern she loved the role. Katie was a departure from the glamorous women she usually portrayed but, in many ways, was just like her— determined, headstrong, fiercely principled. The movie also had a patriotic theme, and took a strong stance against prejudice, values Loretta appreciated.

Ruth got tapes of a Swedish friend speaking in English, and Loretta played them repeatedly for the next six weeks. "I was frustrated because no matter how hard I tried, I couldn't get it," Loretta said. "But after a while I got used to the rhythm of the speech, very gentle, very up and down. Ruth kept encouraging me, and finally we felt I was ready." Loretta also dyed her hair blond, and wore four-foot-long pin-on braids, wound around her ears. With her rustic clothes, she looked every inch the farm girl.

She and Tom were also thrilled to learn that Loretta was expecting another baby. Schary may not have been quite as pleased, since pregnancies among the stars often led to delays in production, but he knew how much the Lewises wanted a large family, and offered his congratulations.

Filming began, and Ruth Roberts proved even more valuable than expected, Loretta said. "We'd do a scene, the director would yell, 'Cut!,' I'd think it was fine, but Ruth would stop, and whisper to me: 'Go a little deeper, say this word softly.' I'd ask for another take, follow her directions on these small touches, and we were all surprised at how well they worked. If she hadn't been a woman in that era, she could have been a director, and a superb one, at that."

Dore Schary was immensely pleased with the dailies, and told Loretta that if she kept going like this, he believed she could win an Academy Award for the role. Loretta laughed. Nothing could be less probable in her mind. But the movie had brought her a new and invaluable friend—Ruth Roberts. "Special people seemed to pop up whenever I needed help or encouragement, whether in my professional or private lives," Loretta said. "It was no coincidence."

When Loretta was almost four months pregnant, she lost the baby. She and Tom were heartsick. As Schary had anticipated, he did have to shut down production for about two weeks while Loretta recovered, but even when she returned, she was depressed. Finally, "Tom and I were able to say to God, 'Well, if it's Your will, okay. We'll trust that You have something better in mind.' It was then that the pain of disappointment stopped." Later, Loretta began to think of the child as "my little angel in heaven."

The Farmer's Daughter was released in spring, 1947, to wide acclaim. Moviegoers loved it and so did the critics. Loretta was singled out for much praise, which was unusual since reviewers tended to dismiss her. Delighted, she started work on *The Bishop's Wife,* another immensely charming movie featuring Cary Grant and her old pal David Niven. Both men were fun to have around.

Cary was a natural athlete, who entertained everyone by walking on his hands between takes, and enjoyed skating in the movie's winter scene. (Non-athletic Loretta, of course, used a double.) "Cary is probably the only leading man I didn't fall in love with," Loretta recalls. "But we were good friends. He was always searching for answers about faith and religion—we had some good talks." *The Bishop's Wife* was released to strong box office receipts in December, 1947. (In 1996, *Bishop* was redone as *The Preacher's Wife,* starring Whitney Houston and Denzel Washington.)

Two winners in a row! How could Loretta have doubted God's hand in her career? She often wondered. She had thought, when she was blacklisted, that her acting days were over. But nothing could have prepared her for the next step. One morning, she and Tom were having brunch with Irene Dunne and her husband when the phone rang. It was Dore Schary. "Do you remember me telling you that you could win the Academy Award for Katie?" he asked Loretta.

"How could I forget?" she laughed.

"Well, you're one step closer. You've been nominated for best actress."

Loretta was thunderstruck, especially as Schary read her the list of the other nominees. How could this be? Joan Crawford for *Possessed,* Susan Hayward for *Smash-Up,* Dorothy McGuire for *Gentlemen's Agreement,* and one of her best friends, Rosalind Russell, for *Mourning Becomes Electra.* It was unbelievably wonderful for Rosalind, who usually did light-hearted parts, and had really struggled through this role, a heavy Eugene O'Neil saga. Once, after Sunday Mass, Loretta had asked her how it was going.

"Loretta," Roz had answered through gritted teeth, "all the director says to me is 'Hate him!" (the leading man). "Hate him!

HATE HIM MORE!' I swear, if he says that to me again, I'm going to kill him!"

The women had laughed together. They, along with Irene Dunne, were often dubbed "The Three Nuns" by people in the industry, due to their Catholic faith and careful choice of parts, and they understood each other well. But if Katie had been a departure for Loretta, Rosalind had also stepped outside her niche. The two women had already celebrated Roz's Golden Globe award for *Electra,* which was usually a ticket to the Oscar. In addition, Roz had been nominated Best Actress last year for *Sister Kenny,* and had lost. She was the sure winner, Loretta decided.

In those years, after the nominees were announced, the *Daily Variety* held a straw poll. Rosalind won it by a wide margin, thus confirming Loretta's views. (Loretta finished fifth, out of five.) But Roz was not convinced she was a shoo-in. On the morning of the awards, she phoned Loretta. "Nervous?" she asked.

"Not really. I'm just happy to be one of the five, and wear this beautiful Adrian dress."

"Loretta, my mother is getting out of her sickbed to come with us tonight and watch me win," Roz told her. "But God and I know who's the real winner. So when you get the Oscar, I want you to unscrew it and throw half of it to me!"

"Don't be an idiot," Loretta said fondly. "You deserve it, and you're going to win it. I'll see you tonight."

Loretta wasn't placating her friend. She was so sure she would not be chosen that she had discouraged everyone in the family from attending the ceremony. Judy would be allowed to stay up late and listen to it on the radio. And Georgie and Ricardo had insisted on coming, because they felt someone ought to be around to console Loretta. But since the Montalbans' seats were way in the back, Tom would be the only family member nearby, and that's just the way Loretta wanted it. (Original plans had called for the Lewises to attend with Dore Schary and his wife but, at the last minute, Miriam Schary got the flu, and Dore didn't want to leave her. Instead, he gave his tickets to some good friends, who would sit with Loretta and Tom.) Loretta's only concession to a possible win was the preparation of an acceptance speech, which she had asked Tom to write. "I was so used to following scripts that I felt uneasy talking extemporaneously at an event like this, especially if I bawled and looked unprofessional," she said. "So I told Tom how I felt, and he wrote it, and I memorized it. Then I forgot it."

Now the limousine sped through the Hollywood streets. Loretta was excited and nervous, but enjoying every minute. "Our driver happened to pass the Deluxe Theater, where we boarding house kids had gone to all those Saturday matinees." It seemed like a hundred years ago. Who could have imagined her life now?

The awards were given at the huge Shrine Auditorium, which seated about 6000 people, and the stage seemed to go on forever. It was darkened except for lights following those who walked across it, and there were great white, tiered shelves holding the statues, grouped around a 30-foot Oscar. Today, the Best Picture award closes the ceremony, but in those days, it was presented third-to-last, followed by the Best Leading Actor award, and finally, the Best Leading Actress.

"We had sat through the whole event, and amazingly, every *Daily Variety* poll winner had also won the actual award," Loretta said. "There was no suspense remaining for the final two Oscars." As predicted, Ronald Coleman won the Best Actor award. Then it was the women's turn. People began gathering their coats. Rosalind Russell, then on to the parties. . . .

Frederic March stepped to the microphone, and announced the final award. "And the winner is . . ." he opened the envelope, "Loretta Young for *The Farmer's Daughter!*"

The entire audience gasped. Then Georgie, from somewhere in the back, yelled, "Oh-h-h, Gretch!" The auditorium erupted in astonished applause.

Tom pushed Loretta out of her chair. "Go get it! Go get it!" He laughed. She flew up the stage stairs in absolute shock. Was this a dream? Had she done it? And where was Roz?

By the time she got to the stage, however, she could see Roz. She was standing, leading the applause. Loretta was overwhelmed. And what had she been planning to say? Her mind was a blank. "Holy Spirit, help me!" she prayed. And suddenly, the words were there.

"The Academy Awards has always been a spectator sport for me," she began as the clapping died away. "But tonight I dressed for the stage, just in case!" Everyone laughed. "And as for you," Loretta held up Oscar, "at long last!" She kissed it, said "good night, and God bless you," and walked in a daze off the stage.

Jean Hersholt, the Academy president, was standing in the wings with his arms out. "Oh, Jean!" she gasped, "isn't this wonderful?"

"Loretta, thank God for you." He hugged her. "You probably saved the Academy! You're the only winner who didn't finish first in the poll!" (Loretta didn't know what he meant, but later it was explained to her: Would the awards ever again have been considered suspenseful, or even honest, if winners were all but announced ahead of time? That was the last year the *Daily Variety* took its poll.)

Loretta bolted to the phone backstage, and immediately dialed Gladys' number. "Mama!" she cried, "It's Gretch! I won!"

"That's nice, dear," a sleepy Gladys answered. "What did you win?" Gladys had never been impressed with the Academy Awards, considering them just another public relations ploy. It would be years before she recognized the significance of her daughter's achievement.

There were so many reporters waiting for Loretta backstage (the studio had not even made up a biography on her) that by the time she posed for the last photo, and answered the last question, the auditorium had emptied, and the streets were practically deserted. Tom and Loretta came outside to discover that their limousine was gone, probably grabbed by another group. "I remember looking up at the buildings across the street from the auditorium, still clutching my Oscar, while Tom went to find a cab," she said. "I was in a fog, but a woman hung out her window and shouted congratulations to me. It was marvelous."

They went on to Ciro's for the studio party. Each studio had its own table, and since Roz and Loretta's movies had both been made at the same studio, they were to sit together. But where was Roz? The luster of Loretta's evening would be dimmed forever if her friend had decided to skip the party. Oh, dear. She noticed the waiters quickly changing the card at the winner place setting from "Rosalind Russell" to "Loretta Young." How embarrassing! Everyone seemed to be watching her or the entrance, waiting for the two women to meet.

All of a sudden, a stir went through the room. Roz and Freddie had appeared at the door. It seemed to take them forever to work their way through the crowd, but they were coming straight to her and Tom, and Roz was smiling. At last! The two women embraced. "If I couldn't have won, thank God it was you!" Roz whispered.

"And that," Loretta said years later, "was Roz."

Loretta and Tom got home at dawn, to a stack of congratulatory messages. Amid them was one from Sister Marina, her first-grade teacher. Sister had sent blessings from her infirmary sick bed to a favorite pupil, one who now obviously had her own secretary! (And a Catholic husband too.) Just a few hours later, Loretta's entire extended family—Mama, siblings, nephews and nieces—arrived for a gala breakfast.

The Academy Awards ceremony had been a major event for Loretta. But no one who knew her well was surprised when, the following weekend she avoided the limelight and went off to her annual religious retreat at Marymount. God was there for asking, but also for thanking and praising. And she needed a quiet place where she could think.

She was especially worried about the deteriorating relationship between Tom and Judy. Although he had once treated his stepdaughter with great affection, Loretta had noticed a change the moment Christopher was born, even more pronounced when Peter arrived so soon afterward. His sons were now Tom's focus, and when he did cross paths with Judy, he was critical of her activities, her grades, her friends. Part of the difficulty was that Tom was unemployed, with time on his hands, thus able to get involved in everything that went on in the household. While the boys loved having a Mr. Mom, Judy longed for privacy and freedom.

"I talked about the situation to Tom first," Loretta said. "Then I talked to Judy. As gently as I could, I suggested he'd get over it as soon the boys grew up a little. Judy tried hard to believe me, but in time we both knew I was wrong."

Loretta felt guilty. If she wasn't gone so much, maybe she could calm the troubled waters. But her Oscar had made her a "hot commodity"—she and Tom (along with the Hopes, Robert and Betty Montgomery, and several others) had even been invited to the wedding of the future Queen Elizabeth of England and Prince Philip! One can only imagine Loretta's awe at her own achievements. She, a fatherless boarding house girl, was now not only the most famous actress in America, but traveling to London for a Royal Command Performance of *The Bishop's*

Wife as part of the wedding festivities. Understandable that, in the midst of the excitement, she found herself uttering the mantra of the busy woman: *God, please show me how to handle it all.*

Come to the Stable

To handle yourself, use your head. To handle others, use your heart.

—Anonymous

By now Loretta was filming another good script, *Rachel and the Stranger,* on location in Oregon. Pals Robert Mitchum and William Holden co-starred. Loretta rented a small house in a middle class neighborhood for her quarters, and one Saturday night, she invited the cast over. To her surprise, Bob and Bill drank a bottle-and-a-half of whiskey between them and were, of course, roaring drunk. Loretta let it go, the first time. But when it happened again, she felt she needed to speak up. "You two are going to rot your stomachs!" she scolded them. "And what will happen to your wonderful talents then?"

William Holden was very gracious. He agreed that Loretta was right, and thanked her for her concern. Bob Mitchum had a different response.

"Thin," he told her, "you worry too much. I've been on my own for most of my life, and I can take care of myself." ("Thin" was Bob's nickname for her.)

It must have been true because neither man was ever rumored to have a drinking problem. As Loretta concluded later, they just liked to play.

In 1949, Daryll Zanuck offered Loretta a script through her agent, Bert. Loretta didn't have the same trepidation about working with him this time—since she was freelancing, she didn't have to say "yes" to his demands. And when she read the script, titled *Mother was a Freshman,* she refused. "It's a nothing picture," she told Bert, "but Daryll has a script I would love to do." It had been years since she had read Clare Boothe Luce's *Come to the Stable,* but she had never forgotten it.

Dutifully, Bert took the message to Zanuck, and received a typical response: "Tell Loretta to stop trying to run my studio!"

The two were back to their usual stalemate, but this time Zanuck blinked first. After thinking about it, he phoned Bert. "Zanuck says if you'll do *Mother is a Freshman* first—and he'll do it in color—then he'll let you do *Come to the Stable,*" Bert reported.

"But I don't want. . . ."

"Loretta, all he's doing is offering you two pictures instead of one!" Bert was using that tone of voice again. And, as usual, she was being argumentative—just a hazard of the trade where Zanuck was concerned. But when she signed her contract for *Stable,* she insisted she have approval of the final script.

Clare had originally written the script for Irene Dunne and Loretta, but Irene was working on another project, so the casting director reversed roles: Loretta would portray Sister Margaret, the Mother Superior (many of her peers declared it perfect type-casting), and Celeste Holm was cast as her companion (Celeste has recently been seen as the grandmother in the television series, *Promised Land.*) The script would be slightly updated to include references to World War Two. "While preparing, I realized that I would be the only Catholic on the set, the only person who knew anything about nuns," Loretta recalled. "Celeste, I think, was a Lutheran, the directors were Jewish and our leading man was an avowed atheist. It was going to be interesting."

The first skirmish came when Loretta learned that producer Sam Engel, a good friend of hers, had hired humorist Dorothy Parker to do rewrites. "Sam, I love Dorothy Parker's work—I think her *Big Blonde* is a masterpiece—but I don't think she knows much about nuns," Loretta pointed out. "And why would we need a major rewrite anyway? Clare's pretty good, you know." (Interestingly, *The Big Blonde* protested a social system that offered no place for a woman to develop her potential. Many critics felt it was a forerunner of the women's movement.)

"Loretta, you're going to love it," Sam assured her.

"Maybe, but remember, I have script approval."

"How could I forget?"

Weeks later, Sam came into the commissary. "Loretta, you'll be pleased. Dorothy Parker didn't like the project, so we got someone else."

"Okay, but remember, I've got. . . ."

"Approval. I know."

On Friday of the weekend before shooting began, Loretta finally received the revised script. She almost had a panic attack. "The story was now about two stingy, crabby, arguing old maids, who cheated everyone—it was almost slapstick." Loretta asked Tom to read the script, just to make sure she wasn't crazy.

Tom did. "You have script approval," he pointed out. "Why don't you call Sam and remind him?"

The next day, Loretta phoned. Her call was forwarded to the sauna room, where the bigwigs relaxed, enjoyed massages and often held story conferences. When Sam picked up the extension, Loretta started talking right away. "Sam, don't say a word, and smile. It's Loretta, and there is no way I'm doing this picture."

There was a long pause. She could almost see the blood draining from his face, while he attempted to appear casual so his peers wouldn't sense trouble. "Loretta, could you meet me in my office in twenty minutes?"

"Just let me do the original script, Sam."

"I can't. What would I tell Zanuck?" Sam had spent a great deal of money on revisions.

Loretta sighed. "Well, look, Gene Tierney just got home from New York. We're the same size, and she'd be fine in the role. Ask her."

"No," Sam said. "You are Sister Margaret."

"Think a little more about it," Loretta urged. "And don't forget, you and your wife are coming to our house for dinner tonight—eight o'clock sharp." Sam hung up.

At eight-fifteen the Engels were in the Lewises' living room, and Sam was as downcast as before. "Loretta, you're an albatross around my neck!" he groaned.

"I'm sorry, Sam. Did you call Zanuck?"

"Not yet."

Loretta had hosted cheerier dinners, but she never for a moment considered backing down. The original script was perfect, and Clare deserved her loyalty.

Sam phoned her on Sunday night, the evening before filming would begin. "I talked to Daryll," he reported grimly. "He said we'll postpone everything for a week to get reorganized."

"And the script?" She was breathless.

"We'll use the original."

Hallelujah!

Shooting began, amid more skirmishes. "In one scene, the two nuns go to the top of a hill, kneel and plant a little medal,"

Loretta said. During their first take, Loretta realized that Celeste, behind her, had been sitting back on her heels instead of kneeling upright.

"That's a beautiful composition," Director Henry Kosta enthused. "It's a perfect take."

"No nun in her right mind would kneel that way," Loretta pointed out. "We'll have to do it over." Kosta rolled his eyes, and called for Take Two. This time, Celeste knelt straight up, and everything was perfect.

~

Later, after the movie was finished and Loretta was working on *Key to the City,* she received a call from Sam Engel. "Something went wrong with the sound on that scene on the hill," he told her. "We'll send a car during your lunch hour if you will come over here and re-dub just one line."

Loretta agreed. But when they played the scene, she was stunned. It was the original take, where Celeste was lounging on her heels! Had director Kosta deliberately inserted his preferred cut, or had it been an innocent mistake? It didn't matter. The take's sound had been damaged. Another "God-incidence?"

"Sam," Loretta told him sweetly, "I'm not going to dub this scene. See if you can find Take Two."

Sam and the cutter shrugged. Loretta came back the next day, and they had located it. "Take Two was the one that appeared in the movie," she said. "That's how the Lord watches out for even these little things."

~

At another point during the story, Celeste was supposed to give each of the gangsters a Catholic medal. The scene itself was amusing, but Celeste (whose character was French) decided to add some extra flair by handing out each medal with a bounce and wink. After the second take, Loretta noticed it and again stopped the filming. "Loretta, what now?" the long-suffering director barked.

Loretta explained to Celeste that a real nun would not be flirting with the gangsters. Celeste was surprised. "I thought it gave Sister a little bit of 'frenchiness'," she pointed out. It did, Loretta assured her. The wrong kind!

The scene was shot the way Loretta requested.

"These were all minor points, but everything had to be credible," Loretta said. "Because if you didn't believe they were real nuns, you wouldn't have believed anything else about the picture, especially their faith in God that Clare had written about so beautifully."

Other events were of note during the making of *Stable*. For example, anyone who has ever worked in the movie or television industry knows that profanity on the set is part of the experience. As a novice, Loretta had had no choice but to ignore the language, especially since it was so deeply ingrained, not only in the cast, but among the usually all-male crew. But it always bothered her, especially words that blasphemed God. "I could live with the four-letter words—that just shows that people have a limited vocabulary," she said. "But blasphemy is intrinsically evil, and it always depressed me."

The atmosphere on this set, for some reason, seemed especially offensive. "Here we were, presenting a spiritual story, some of us playing priests or nuns, and in between rehearsals or takes, all this swearing floating around. It got so distracting that it started to show in my face and manner."

Since filming *The Farmer's Daughter*, Loretta had become close friends with Ruth Roberts. Now the two conferred. "What if I started charging a fine for each bad word?" Loretta asked.

"I can't imagine anyone being pleased about that," Ruth mused. "But maybe if the money went to a worthy cause . . ."

"St. Anne's Maternity Home!" Loretta brightened. Sister Winifred always needed help. The next day Loretta brought a box to the set and announced the plan. "One quarter each time anyone takes the Lord's name in vain."

The fifty or sixty crew members and actors were less than enchanted. In fact, for the next few days, the expletives seemed to increase, augmented by mutters of "Miss Goody Two-Shoes . . ." and "Why doesn't she just mind her own business?" Tired of trying to keep track of what everyone owed, Loretta assigned one of the crew members to the task, and went on with her work.

The fines totaled hundreds of dollars. But eventually, the atmosphere on the set calmed. By the time filming ended, only one man, a burly electrician, was still objecting strenuously. "You're interfering with my right to free speech," he thundered at Loretta on more than one occasion, "and I resent it."

"But Bill," she tried to explain, "look how much we collected for the St. Anne's home for Unwed Mothers."

"I don't care," he retorted. "Nobody's going to tell me how to talk!"

Fortunately, Bill was not assigned to Loretta's next picture because, as word of the Swear Box had gotten around, she decided to make it a fixture on her sets. There were more grumbles as additional people learned of the new rule. One rumor claimed that actor Robert Mitchum would throw several bills in the box each morning, declaring, "That ought to cover me for the day!"

Not so, said Loretta. "Bob Mitchum, contrary to his screen image, was one of the nicest, most sensitive, well-spoken and decent gentlemen in Hollywood." Mitchum had a beautiful voice and often, between takes, could be heard singing his favorite hymn, *Were You There When They Crucified My Lord?* "He and his wife Dorothy had married when both were teenagers, they lived a long life together and he died in her arms. He would never have insulted any woman."

Jerry Lewis? Well. . . . Hoping to tease her, he stopped by the set one day, waving a twenty-dollar bill. He stuffed it in the Swear Box, then sent forth a stream of obscenities.

"Jerry, you just lost twenty dollars," Loretta smiled. "Four-letter words are free!"

Eventually, Loretta and Bill the electrician were again assigned to the same set. His complaints were going to make the atmosphere difficult, she realized. But she wouldn't abandon the Swear Box, no matter how obnoxious Bill became! The cast had thrown her a birthday party, and along with the cake and candy boxes, there was a bouquet of fragrant red roses. She opened the card.

"Dear Miss Young," it read, "these flowers are from my wife and three daughters. For many years, they have complained about my profanity. But I never realized how bad it was until you started that crazy Swear Box. Because of you, I have cleaned up my mouth, and we all just wanted to say thanks." It was signed, "Bill."

Mother Was a Freshman, the movie that Daryll Zanuck had wanted Loretta to do, turned out to be "a nice little picture that no one remembers." *Come to the Stable,* however, was a huge hit, at a time when movie revenues were dropping due to a new invention called television. The role of Sister Margaret also brought Loretta a second Academy Award nomination, although she did not win. "Things aren't easy when you're fighting for what you think is right," Loretta once pointed out. "You've got to persevere. This movie took six years to work out, but to me, it was well worth it." She had learned, once again, that God is never late.

Life with the Lewises

To families everywhere, in the hope that your home will be a happy one,
with the conviction that simple prayer will keep it that way. . . .

—THEME, FAMILY THEATER OF THE AIR

In addition to movies, Loretta was also involved in Father Peyton's newest radio project, the launching of Family Theater of the Air. The star-studded rosary broadcasts had been successful, but they were aimed largely at Catholics. Believing that all families needed spiritual encouragement, Father had decided to launch inspiring non-sectarian dramas. By now he knew Hollywood's best writers and actors, and was hopeful they would cooperate.

The first Sunday night show aired on February 13, 1947. Titled "Flight from Home," it starred Loretta, James Stewart and Don Ameche. Many actors volunteered, even those who were not Catholic. Gary Cooper, Lucille Ball, Bob Hope, Henry Fonda, Jack Benny, Jimmy Durante, Charleton Heston, Raymond Burr—the list went on. Script writers tackled moral problems of the day, the lives of courageous people, even Bible stories. One of Loretta's favorite roles was as Mary Magdalene for an Easter show, with Jeff Chandler as Christ.

Although Father Peyton was often out on Rosary Crusades around the world (similar to the Reverend Billy Graham, he gathered crowds in the millions in cities from Manila to Bombay to Johannesburg), the show was in capable hands, and continued on radio until 1969, winning many awards. It then went into television, and is still producing documentaries and dramas for TV specials, syndication and cable. At Family Theater's 50th anniversary banquet in 1997, both Loretta and Jane Wyatt were honored for "saying 'yes' to the powerful influence that their acting could bring to the lives of thousands," and to Loretta, "for sharing Father Peyton's vision, and using her stature to help him recruit other stars. . . ." It was a bittersweet gathering, as Patrick Peyton had died in 1992. But through his work in media, his evangelization continues.

Father Peyton may eventually be declared a saint by the Catholic Church. In summer, 1999, a representative from Rome came to Loretta's house, and she gave testimony about him to help begin the process.

In 1949, actress Ingrid Bergman created the scandal of the decade when she abandoned her marriage and her daughter, went to Italy and vowed to wed her lover, a still-married Italian film-maker. Because the situation was so public (even her letters to her husband had been published in newspapers), shock waves were everywhere, especially in Hollywood. Certainly, Bergman had violated her contract's morals clause. And when Joseph Breen, director of the Production Code Administration, informed Bergman that she must deny the rumors in order to save her career, she refused, stating that she was never coming back to Hollywood. For years afterward, she worked only in Europe.

About this time, Loretta signed with Metro-Goldwyn-Mayer for a picture. Unfortunately, when she read the script, she was very uncomfortable with it. "It glamorized the mistress situation," she explained, "which wasn't as prevalent as it is today. I didn't want to appear to condone adultery." So she told the production manager at Metro that at this stage in her career, she shouldn't have to do anything she didn't want to. "And this script just goes against my spiritual grain."

"We're not a Sunday school here," he objected.

How could she persuade him? Inspiration struck. "You know, even the Breen office agrees with me. They said I shouldn't do it!"

"They did?" Mindful of the Breen office's current clout and publicity over the Bergman situation, the manager hedged. "Well, let me think about it."

Oh, no. Loretta hadn't planned on his hesitation. She had spoken far too soon, and now she would have to pay the penalty.

The next day she returned to the manager's office. He didn't look happy. "Loretta, you didn't send that script to the Breen office. They never heard of it, did they?" Embarrassed at such a dumb ploy, she shook her head wordlessly. "But you're that determined to get out of this role?" A nod. "Then the only way, I think, is to go right to the top, and talk to Mayer."

Louis B. Mayer. His daughters, Irene and Edie, were her friends, but she had never met this imposing mogul, who had a reputation for ruthlessness and fierce temper tantrums. Well, she would have to do it. Within ten minutes, she found herself in his enormous office, frightened to death. "What seems to be the trouble?" he boomed at her from behind his desk.

"I find this script immoral," she said shakily. "I don't want to do it."

Mayer must have been startled. Few underlings had the nerve to argue with him. Even fewer objected to anything on moral grounds. For a moment, he said nothing, and the two stared at each other. "Mr. Mayer, have you read this script?" Loretta finally asked.

"Yes." If anything, he looked fiercer. The eruption was imminent.

"Well, if your daughters, Irene and Edie, were actresses, would you want either of them to play this role?" There. She had said it.

Mayer thought, for what seemed forever. Then he stood. "No, I wouldn't. And you don't have to, either." He put his arm around her, and walked her to the door. Loretta never understood his response. But from that moment, they became fast friends, and remained so until his death.

Again, it had been hazardous to stand up for her beliefs. Yet, if she had to be known as the Iron Butterfly, the risk was worth it.

God did seem to keep a protective hand on her. One night, Tom and Loretta went to a formal party in Beverly Hills at the home of Arthur Rubenstein, the concert pianist. Loretta and her friends often loaned jewelry to each other—Barbara Stanwyck and Loretta had similar taste and were frequent exchangers. (Barbara had dubbed Loretta Attila the Nun.) But on that evening, since Loretta's dress was brilliant, she wore only her own diamond cross, small earrings and her wedding ring. Irene Mayer Selznick was one of the guests (her husband David had just divorced her), and Loretta was delighted to see her. They hugged, then Loretta noticed Irene's incredible pear-shaped diamond bracelet. "Irene!" she exclaimed, "it's exquisite!"

"Yes," Irene smiled sadly. "It's my consolation prize from David." The two women looked at each other, blinked back tears, and hugged again. "Here!" Irene impulsively slid the bracelet off her wrist. "You wear it tonight!"

Loretta showed off the bracelet to everyone, pretending it was hers. By the end of the evening she had forgotten she was wearing it. The Lewises made the rounds, saying goodbye to everyone (Loretta even kissed Irene, who had also forgotten the jewelry), got into their car and started down the driveway. Suddenly Tom stopped. "You're still wearing Irene's bracelet!" he told Loretta. "We should go back and give it to her."

"Oh, Tom, it's so late, and we'll have to say goodbye to everyone all over again," Loretta yawned. "Why don't I just send it over to her in the morning? That's what Barbara and I always do."

"No," Tom announced. "You can stay in the car. But I'd feel better if Irene had her bracelet tonight." He pulled the car back up the driveway, took the bracelet and went in. When he returned, Loretta was almost asleep.

The next morning Loretta and Tom were awakened by the housekeeper dashing down the hall, her face ashen. "Mrs. Lewis!" she shouted. "We were robbed last night!"

"What? Are the children all right?"

"Everyone's fine. I went to open the sitting room windows and the screen had been cut. Someone climbed up the trellis. Look in the fur closet, look in your jewelry drawer. . . ."

It must have been a professional. Every piece of Loretta's real jewelry was gone, though the artificial pieces were still left. Her two best furs were also taken. The Lewises would later discover their insurance company's secretary had forgotten to add Loretta's furs and newest jewelry to their policy. It was a dead loss.

Except . . . what would have happened if Tom hadn't insisted on returning Irene's stunning bracelet? "I never would have been able to explain that away," Loretta said. "It would really have been awkward for everyone."

The Lewises soon learned that a young charming man had visited their housekeeper the previous week, posing as a real estate agent who Tom had asked to inspect the house for a possible sale. The unsuspecting housekeeper had shown him around the premises (including the burglar alarm and safe!), so it was no wonder that the theft proceeded so smoothly.

As the year wore on, other area households were hit. The burglar was so clever that, during a party at Frank Capra's home, his wife Lou came upstairs, saw a young handsome man in black tie going into a bedroom, and assumed he was one of her guests. "I'll be right down," he called to her, then grabbed his loot and climbed out the bedroom window!

Eventually, the burglar was turned in by his girlfriend, stood trial and was convicted. In his statement to the press, he said, "The only one I felt bad about robbing was Loretta Young. I always thought she was nice. But she didn't have much, anyway!" Loretta had learned another lesson. Although she continued to lend her possessions, she never again borrowed.

Judy graduated from eighth grade, and went off to her first experience at summer camp. Loretta was worried about her. She had told Judy that she was adopted, and assumed that would suffice. (Many families in the '30s, '40s and '50s kept adoption a secret; sometimes, children only discovered the truth when finding a birth certificate after their parents' death. Of course, Judy's adoption had been public knowledge, so there would have been no chance to hide it.) But now Judy was asking questions about her "real" parents. So far, Loretta had pleaded ignorance, but would Judy pursue it? She had always been an agreeable child, but adolescence can herald many clashes between mother and daughter.

Tom sat on various corporate boards and did some investing, but was still not actively employed. One day, Loretta arrived home to the news that Tom had sold their house. "Tom, why?" she asked. Without even consulting her?

"If anything happened to you, Loretta, I couldn't keep it up," he explained.

"But nothing's going to happen to me. And where will we go? We're a little spoiled now, you know—not just any house will do."

"I'll take care of it," Tom assured her

And he did. Tom had discovered the Doheny Estate, located on a hill looking down on San Fernando Valley. The main house had been built in the 1920s at a cost of $4 million, and boasted 55 rooms. Its two tennis courts, huge swimming pool and five hundred acres of lawn and ranch were shared by the tenants in the thirty-eight-room "guest house." The Lewises were now those tenants. Loretta was puzzled. Why had Tom decided to rent, rather than buy? And when Judy returned from camp to discover that she did not live in the Carolwood house anymore, she was traumatized. The Doheny Estate was beautiful, but so isolated that she couldn't get around to see her friends.

Loretta hesitated to force the issue. Tom rarely explained financial matters to her, and she was sure she wouldn't have understood anyway. Instead, she fell back on her usual response: Put a Smile on Your Face and Ignore It. She would need all her energy for her next challenge, a role in *Key to the City,* with Clark Gable.

Although the two had no doubt met at an occasional party, they traveled in different social circles, and by now had little in common; Clark was married to his fourth wife, and drank heavily. However, people would again comment on the screen electricity between the two after the movie was made. ("Clark was the only one Loretta allowed to kiss her the way he did," one observer mentioned.) But, at least on the set, the two treated each other cordially, and avoided all personal discussions. Clark's contract allowed him to leave each day at 5 p.m. (ostensibly to drink and party) while Loretta had to stay until six or later, so there was little opportunity for after-hours socializing. In addition, Loretta had an inordinate amount of visitors to the *Key* set, including her brother-in-law and of all people, Gladys. Perhaps the family was providing some silent support, just in case she became vulnerable again?

One hot day, while playing a scene at the top of a hill, Loretta fainted. Clark carried her to the hastily-summoned ambulance, and she was taken to Queen of Angels hospital. There she discovered that she was pregnant. Within a short time, she miscarried.

The crew on *Key* sent her a photo of everyone involved in the movie, along with a huge sign saying, "Come back. All is forgiven!" It was meant to make her smile, but Loretta was devastated at the loss. A second little angel in heaven. Her arms ached for it.

When she finished *Key,* Tom had another project in mind. He had discovered a radio script titled "Cause for Alarm," and wanted to produce it as a movie. He had thought to hire Judy Garland in the lead role, but Dore Shary wanted Loretta. It was Tom's first job since the war ended, as well as their first time working together, and Loretta wanted nothing to come between them. They had some clashes on the set—Tom yelled at her in front of others, which was hard for her to take. But the end result was positive—the suspenseful film was finished in a record-breaking two weeks, and some critics acclaimed it as her best performance to date.

One day Loretta received a call from an Internal Revenue Service agent. "I just had an appointment with your mother, and I'm confused," he told her.

"Oh well, Mama confuses a lot of people," Loretta laughed. "Just talk the truth to her."

"That's just it. We started an audit on your mother, and found a list of antiques she sold. According to us, she owes back taxes of over $300,000 on these profits, but she says she doesn't."

"Mr. Belzer was very scrupulous," Loretta argued. "And if my mother says she doesn't owe it, believe me, she doesn't. If you take her to court, she'll make you look foolish because she doesn't know how to lie."

"Yes, she seems so above board," the agent agreed. "It's a puzzle."

Loretta agreed to ask Jack and her sisters about the situation. Maybe they knew something she didn't. However, the usual financial disinterest had continued among her siblings. No one had ever talked to an IRS agent about anything, and no one wanted to. About six months later, Loretta went to pick Gladys up for an appointment. "Before we leave, dear," Gladys announced, "I want to make lunch for these young men."

"What men?" Loretta asked.

"Four IRS agents. They've been here for weeks, looking through my accounts." Since Gladys didn't know what they were doing, or what any of the myriad of paperwork meant, she was just going about her business.

"For weeks?" Loretta was astonished. She had assumed the problem was solved eons ago. She went into the dining room where the four agents had spread piles of papers all over the table, along with scraps that Loretta recognized as Gladys' "bills." "Can someone show me this list, or whatever you say shows that Mama hasn't been paying taxes?" she asked.

One of the men reached wearily into a stack, and pulled out a five- or six-paged yellow list. Loretta began to read it in her usual painstaking manner, then laughed. "That looks like Aunt Carly's writing," she said. "Show it to my mother, will you?"

The men did. Gladys gasped. "It is Carly's list!"

"Who's Carly?" the agents wanted to know.

Loretta and Gladys explained. Aunt Carly, the sister who had taken Gladys and her four children in all those difficult years ago, had been living with her now-married daughter Carlene, Loretta's childhood companion. One day, Carlene had called Gladys. "Something's wrong with Mama," she said. Gladys had gone right over.

Carly seemed confused and miserable. "I can't remember things," she told Gladys. "I don't like living here."

"Well then, you'll just come home with me," Gladys had decided.

Loretta remembered the situation very well. Aunt Carly had been depressed, so to keep her busy, Gladys had given her a "special job." "I want you to take this yellow pad and go into the basement and inventory everything that's in there," she instructed her sister. Carly, who knew nothing about antiques, had done so, itemizing everything in the basement, and making up her own prices. "One clear bottle, $9,000 . . . one blue candle holder, $2,250. . . ." No figure bore any resemblance to reality.

Loretta's aunt had stayed for about a year and a half, while Gladys nurtured her and got her over her difficulties. During that time, Carly had filled several sheets of yellow paper with strange prices, the papers Loretta was now holding, presumably representing two years of profit upon which taxes had never been paid. How were they going to explain Aunt Carly to the IRS?

The whole thing must have sounded deranged, because ultimately the IRS district superintendent got involved. He even instructed Gladys not to continue feeding the men, as it might be construed as a bribe. "It ended up that they couldn't prove anything, and the superintendent apologized to Gladys, and said they knew she was an honest woman," Loretta says. Gladys shrugged, said they were only doing their jobs, promised to get organized—and continued to keep her records in the same way.

Sometimes I took my nap in Mom's big bed, and when I woke up, she was usually sitting at her dressing table, getting ready to go out. Her music box played a tune I liked, so she would wind it up for me again and again. Those were shining moments. When I grew up, I wrote a song for her, with a melody like the music box.

—PETER LEWIS

During this time, Judy and Tom's animosity was growing. According to Judy, her stepfather complained about the amount of clothes she owned (once throwing everything from her closet onto the floor), picked up the telephone extension during her conversations, and left critical notes for her. When he occasionally drank too much, he would ground her for minimal or imagined offenses. Judy was dating Russell Hughes, a young man seven years older than she, but by all accounts she seems to have been a well-behaved teenager, so Tom's hostility was puzzling.

Loretta wondered if he resented Judy because he had surmised the truth about her origins. Amazingly, he and Loretta had still never discussed the subject; Tom seemed to have accepted the adoption story completely. Or, since he obviously wanted a high-profile wife, he was willing to leave certain areas untouched. Loretta stood up for Judy frequently and undid Tom's punishments ("really, most of our arguments were about her") but tension pervaded the household. At a time when she was strongly supporting the prayer goals of the Family Theater, Loretta felt like a hypocrite.

According to Tom, their difficulties were Loretta's fault. She spent far too much time working, and not nearly enough as a wife and mother. If she really cared about the family, she would re-order her priorities.

Although they rarely discussed Tom's lack of a job—it was far too touchy a subject—Loretta considered it the source of his increasing discontent. Unemployment, she believed, was harder on a man than a woman. But in light of his specific complaints about her long hours, she began to examine her conscience. Was Tom right?

She was scheduled for a publicity trip to New York. When it was over, Loretta decided to come back alone by train. During those three quiet days, she would think everything through, and pray about what to do.

When she arrived home, she had made her decision. "Tom," she told him, "you are right. Nothing should come before our family, not my work, not anything."

"What do you mean?" Tom asked.

"Just this," Loretta told him. "I'm going to give up my career, and be Mrs. Tom Lewis. Judy will be going to college soon, and will probably want to stay here . . . but you can take a job anywhere in the whole world, wherever you want to go, and the boys and I will come with you." There! She had done it, and she hoped he understood that she really meant it, that quitting would be a wrench but far less painful than the breakup of her family.

Tom looked startled. "I . . . see."

During the next few months, Loretta waited for him to announce his new job, and where they would be relocating. She waited in vain. When she eventually began accepting scripts again, Tom never grumbled. But he didn't find a job either. It was an uneasy truce, and Loretta had again misread a man she loved. How could she turn him back into the person she had married? *He only sees the trying,* she reminded herself.

Despite her confusion, there was occasionally a little "hug from heaven" sent her way. One day, she picked up six-year-old Peter and seven-year-old Chris from their ballroom dancing class, held in a studio on a busy Benedict Canyon highway. The boys hated class, because they had to dress up and learn manners. When it was over each week, they couldn't wait to get out. "Chris had stopped behind us, and Pete and I were walking to the car, parked along the highway," said Loretta. Pete suddenly dashed ahead.

"Pete, come back!" There were cars whizzing alongside them. Loretta broke into a run. "Pete, stop!"

Instead, the six-year-old ran into the street as a car bore down on him. "Dear God, help, help!" Loretta screamed.

With a screech of brakes, the car stopped, inches from Pete. He was frozen in fright as Loretta grabbed him. "I thought you were playing, Mom," he said, tears streaming. The driver of the car sped away.

Loretta didn't know whether to hug Pete or kill him. Then another thought intruded. How strange that the car had been able to stop so quickly. There had been other vehicles following closely behind it too, yet no one had crashed. She whispered a prayer of thanks. Surely Pete's guardian angel had intervened, to keep them all from more heartache.

She wasn't the only one who believed in angels. Her friend Bishop Sheen had one who "miraculously" cleaned his blackboards during his television lectures. "Life is Worth Living," had debuted in 1951, a half-hour show on which the bishop, with chalk in hand and humorous asides, lectured about the purpose of life and humankind's relationship with a loving, caring God. Originally programmed in what was considered a "dead spot" (against the popular "Milton Berle Show"), Bishop Sheen's audience soon swelled to an estimated 30 million people, on 123 television stations in the United States alone, along with 300 radio stations and numerous short wave radios tuning in. Interestingly, Sheen never scripted his shows. He would arrive at the television studio about a half-hour before air time, pace back and forth in thought, and then go on, live.

Bishop Sheen would be on television, in one venue or another, for the next fifteen years, often dubbed "the conscience of the nation." He received thousands of letters every day, from people of all faiths, inspiring the Reverend Billy Graham to call him "the greatest communicator of the twentieth century." Loretta was inordinately proud of his success, and thrilled that she had been the one to suggest that Pat Frawley's company sponsor the show.

Goodbye, Movies

For I know well the plans
I have in mind for you,
says the Lord,
plans for your welfare, not for woe;
plans to give you a future full of hope.

—JEREMIAH 29:11

That same year, finally realizing that real estate was a sound investment, Tom purchased a townhouse for his family, and other properties on Flores in West Hollywood. He invested in a small resort hotel, the Ojai Valley Inn, later to become a country club, and also began to build a house in Ojai. One day, he brought Loretta and the children to the construction site. "This is mine," he told Loretta. "I want us to use it on weekends and during school vacations. At other times, the Ojai Inn will rent it out." Loretta was stunned. Another house? Why hadn't Tom talked it over with her?

"This house is yours too, like everything else we have," Tom was continuing. "That is, if you, not your mother, decorate it and make it into a home for our family. Otherwise, it's mine, and I'll rent it out." Tom's relationship with Gladys had been cordial, but never close and Loretta was uncomfortably aware of that. She could see why he wanted her to take charge of this house herself. But the whole situation offended her. Why hadn't he asked? Where was she going to get the time? And why did he presume that anything they owned was just his?

On the other hand, the idea had possibilities. Life in Ojai would be far simpler than the Doheny Estate's guesthouse. Perhaps they would grow closer here. She agreed.

Gladys had been in Europe, and returned far earlier than expected. Since the Flores townhouse needed work—and since Tom wished to avoid ruffled feelings—he belatedly asked Gladys to take on that job. By now, Gladys had done houses and apartments for many clients, including producer Jerry Wald, Lauren Bacall and Humphrey Bogart, Freddie de Cordova, producer of the Johnny Carson Show, actress Leslie Caron, and agent Swifty LaZarr, but she agreed to "squeeze" Tom and Loretta into her schedule. They packed up, left the guesthouse, and moved temporarily to a leased beachhouse on the ocean in Santa Monica. Friends were bewildered at the Lewises' endless relocating, but by now they also knew that Loretta and Tom were struggling to find each other again. Whatever works, everyone agreed.

In addition to her marriage, Loretta was doing a lot of thinking about her career. Hollywood had completely changed since she had begun working. The people who created the film business were dying off, being replaced with Wall Street types more concerned with the bottom line than art. A general coarseness pervaded many movies, as tabloids screeched provocative headlines about stars' personal lives. It made her tired—and sad. Despite her beauty, she was almost forty, and her days of portraying ingenues were over. What now?

She and Tom had noticed all the television antennas popping up on people's houses. This was a new technology, with wide possibilities. "One night we all started to watch a television show together and it was dreadful, dark, and very scary—the kids were crying," Loretta said. "I thought, well, they ought to be able to do something better with television than that." What about a show featuring her?

Loretta was strongly advised by movie executives to abandon thoughts of television. Louis B. Mayer was the first to phone. "If you get into TV," he warned, "you'll never be offered another movie script."

"Well," Loretta pointed out, "I know you consider television The Enemy. But I don't. I've got a purpose, you see. I've already received an Academy Award, and made a lot of money for the studios and enough for me too. Now I want to try television because I can control the product." An idea had been growing: If she could get one wholesome and positive idea into the mainstream of life each week, it would be worth any amount of work and risk.

"At the expense of your motion picture career?" David Selznick asked her, incredulous.

There she went again, swimming against the tide. But since when was it easy to lead a principled life?

"If my movie career is over," she told Selznick, "so be it."

PART SIX

~

The Tears of a Lady

I never knew Loretta Young, the Movie Star. I only knew Loretta Young, my friend. When I met her, her acting career was long over. She phoned me out of the blue one day to congratulate me on the tape I directed about Medjugorje, Yugoslavia, called "Beyond the Fields." She said it changed her life.

"How could it change your life?" I asked her. "You've won every award, you've been everywhere and you have everything."

"You don't understand," she answered. "What you did gave all of that other stuff meaning."

To tell you the truth, I didn't know what she meant. But I did appreciate it. Loretta was like that, quick to tell you how important you were, eager to make you feel like you were the most important person in the world. . . .

She could laugh at herself at the drop of a hat but could, at the same time, be profoundly caring about the feelings of those around her. One evening, I was a little depressed. "What's wrong, dear?" she asked.

I honestly don't remember what was getting me down, but I do remember one thing about that night. Loretta talked to me for a few minutes, then took my hands and placed them in hers, and asked me to shut my eyes. She then began praying for me. But then she went silent, stopping mid-sentence during the prayer. I thought she may have just been taking a dramatic pause, so I waited. But there was nothing. Finally, I opened my eyes and found Loretta crying. When she saw that I saw her, she smiled and finished the prayer through tears.

Whatever I was going through, Loretta had accepted it as her own, she had felt that pain and had, miraculously lifted it from me. To this very day, I can't remember what had gotten me down, but I do remember the compassion, the respect, and the tears of a lady who recognized someone else's hurt, and sought to heal it. That was the Loretta Young I knew.

—Jack Sacco
Michelangelo Films,
Beverly Hills, California

Part 6 photo—Loretta in the role of a singer,
"The Loretta Young Show" (photo on preceding page).

See You Next Week?

*Whenever my mother got a new dress, which was seldom, she would
entertain us kids by sweeping through the doorway of the kitchen and
announcing with a twirl, her hand holding the hem of the dress,
"Hello, I'm Loretta Young." We always loved it when she did that.*

—A FAN ON LORETTA'S WEBSITE

Loretta had one final movie to do, with John Forsythe at Universal:
It Happens Every Thursday. ("A bit of a nothing," was her
assessment.) Then, another "coincidence" occurred. Loretta and
Tom had produced a half-hour pilot film for a television series, just
as Procter and Gamble was looking for one to sponsor. P&G was
the first to view the pilot, and they bought it the following day,
for $30,000 per week. That was to cover all expenses and salaries,
including Loretta's salary of $1,500 per week, a steep reduction
from her lucrative movie contracts. (Tom took no salary.)

For this, Loretta would star in 39 half-hour episodes each
year, the equivalent of thirteen full-length movies. Procter and
Gamble had the right to broadcast each episode once. After
that, ownership reverted to the corporation, Lewislor
Enterprises, Inc., which Tom and Loretta had hastily formed.
Each held 49 percent of the stock, with 2 percent going to their

accountant, Robert Shewalter. Loretta and Tom plunged into work, to get a backlog of programs filmed before fall.

"It was a new medium, and we all felt like pioneers," Loretta says. "But I had worked with the best, and I knew where to start. First, I went to Norbert Brodine, one of the top photographers in the business. I told him we didn't have much money, maybe $2,000 a week tops, but he took it." (Brodine was a coup; when Loretta saw the first dailies, she murmured, "I didn't know cameras could do that.")

The program's original set director came right from Metro-Goldwyn-Mayer. (Later in the series, Gladys would decorate the sets with her antiques, and furniture from her rented basements.) Twentieth Century's costume director told Loretta to borrow anything she needed from wardrobe until she could afford to hire some designers. (In one show, "The Portrait," she rented Deborah Kerr's dance dress from *The King and I.*) Loretta's brother-in-law, director Norman Foster came on board, and her sister Sally emerged from retirement to play a few roles that were perfect for her.

A new face also emerged, Norman Brokaw, today the chairman of the board of the William Morris Agency, the nation's top talent agency, then a young man who had been assigned to represent Loretta. It was the beginning of a lifelong friendship—Loretta loved him. And, although Norman was initially interested in her as a talent, he says today that "as a kid from the mailroom, I learned from Loretta what class and dignity was all about. She dressed beautifully, behaved beautifully— perhaps her only equal today might be Camille Cosby."

By the time filming started, about fifty people were involved—actors, wardrobe, publicity, stand-in, hairdresser. . . . And Loretta ran a tight ship. "Tom wasn't familiar with movie-making, so he had no concept of how much time could be wasted if people lollygagged around," she says. "But time was money, so we rehearsed on Monday and Tuesday, and filmed on

Wednesday, Thursday and Friday. People were amazed at how efficient the set was." (Helen Ferguson, Loretta's assistant, also posted a No Visitors sign to keep Loretta from chatting with everyone who wanted to stop in and wish her luck.) Loretta and Tom were very aware that working together risked their relationship. The two weeks on *Cause For Alarm* hadn't really brought them closer, despite their hopes. But they would work it out.

Loretta had one other reservation. At the beginning of the first season, she asked for a meeting with the Procter and Gamble board. "You know," she told the men, "if my show becomes successful, you're going to get negative mail about me because of my religious convictions. I hope you understand that I won't compromise my principles."

The board members waved away her concerns. Television was a new medium, and there was rarely any controversy. Who would be offended by a dramatic anthology starring one of Hollywood's squeaky-cleanest stars?

That summer, Judy graduated from high school, and became engaged to Russell Hughes. Loretta was adamant: her daughter was too young to get married. She insisted that Judy attend a finishing school in New York for one year. If she still felt the same about Russ, Loretta would agree to their marriage. It was a typical mother-daughter stalemate, with angry feelings on both sides. Judy eventually capitulated.

Judy had barely left for New York when the show was launched (September 20, 1953). Tom and a writer had originally titled the series "Letters to Loretta." Using their format, the show opened with Loretta sitting at her dressing table, reading fan mail. A letter would pose a question, and then the show would begin. Each half-hour presented a lesson for a better life.

Loretta wasn't comfortable with the show's beginning. "I felt that an anthology should give me the chance to play characters young and old, pretty and ugly," she says. "I wanted to be at my best in the beginning, wearing beautiful clothes on a beautiful set, then introduce the story and become the leading character."

The first few shows aired, and some critics were not kind, labeling "Letters" "treacle" and "a disappointment." (One wrote, "I have just seen Loretta Young's television show. It is so bland it won't last a week." Loretta saved the review, and at the end of her show's nine-year reign, the crew gave a party and invited this particular critic. "We blew up the review to the size of the wall in our director's office—and when he saw it, he laughed and said, 'Well, you can't be right every time!' ")

Ratings were passable, but Loretta felt that was due more to the audience's kindness than to the show's strength. She and Tom met with the Procter and Gamble board members, who didn't like the opening either. They decided to change the title to "The Loretta Young Show," written in a signature across the screen. Loretta would glide through a door on the set, wearing a glamorous dress, to introduce the show. She would then play the lead role, and return at the end to deliver a "thought for the evening," something patriotic, character-building or spiritual. (Both the Bible and Bartlett's Quotations were to be extensively utilized.) The show would end with Loretta smiling into the camera, tilting her head and asking, "See you next week?"

During the filming of the first "new" sequence, Loretta emerged through the door as planned. The young Hungarian woman who designed the gown Loretta wore, began to pout. "What's the matter, Marusia?" Loretta asked.

Marusia explained that the back of this dress was actually as dazzling as the front, yet no viewer would be able to see it. Loretta, the enduring clothes-lover, understood. She came through the door again, this time swirling in an almost-complete pirouette as the skirts flew out around her. Marusia smiled in delight—people would now see her entire creation. Loretta didn't know it yet, but her airy entrance had just become her trademark, every bit as memorable as Carol Burnett tugging her ear, or Dinah Shore's sign-off kiss. (Comedians would satirize the entrance unmercifully; in Carol Burnett's takeoffs, the door stuck or her dress got caught in it. Later, Loretta herself occasionally entered a room at a party by spinning through the doorway, in a good-natured parody of herself.) The changes were incorporated on the thirteenth show, and fans loved them. Ratings climbed.

Contrary to public assumption, Loretta didn't own all the dresses she wore for her grand entrance. Hollywood designers made a gown for her each week, in exchange for a credit line (called a "single card") at the end of the show. If Loretta wanted to keep a dress for her personal use, she could. "Some seasons I took one, sometimes six or eight," she said. "It wasn't fair to a designer to take a lot, even though I could have done so. I had enough clothes because I also had to dress myself for the parts I played. The show didn't have a wardrobe department, so I used my closet, and borrowed from my sisters." The designers' challenges were formidable: they couldn't rely on color since television was in black and white, and few textures could be appreciated via film the way they looked up close. Many, especially Jean Louis, made tiny waists and full skirts "Loretta's look," and women tuned in, sometimes just to view the dress of the week. At forty, Loretta was still a perfect size six, due in part to her three-packs-a-day cigarette habit. She never exercised—as Tom commented, "Loretta wouldn't walk across a room if she could get a ride."

Letters began arriving by the cartons. The makeshift fan mail department consisted of two young women who read everything, and culled the most complimentary letters for Loretta to see. One day Loretta visited their cubbyhole. "Do you ever get critical letters about the show, or me?" she asked.

The girls squirmed. "Well, . . . sometimes."

"Those are the ones I want to see," Loretta insisted. "They'll help us more." And so they did. On one occasion, for example, Loretta wore a strapless dress. "It was fine photographed from a distance," she recalled. "But when the camera came in for a close-up, it looked as if I was nude. People objected, so we were careful not to let that happen again."

Petty? Perhaps. But Loretta felt such feedback was critical in establishing credibility and shaping the show's weekly "lesson." However, she did not permit the audience to determine everything. Once, she portrayed a wife who, with her husband, celebrated an event by drinking an entire bottle of champagne. The following week she was deluged by angry letters from the Women's Christian Temperance Organization. She was hurt and angry. "There's nothing immoral about alcohol if it's not misused," she insisted. "These people have missed the whole point."

Tom, she felt, was also missing the point. Although Loretta starred in most of the shows, Tom commissioned some scripts casting her in bit parts, just background for a child star or leading man. It was not what she'd had in mind when she pushed for her show, and the acting challenges inherent in playing a different character each week. They also clashed on production points. For example, Loretta had never read *Aladdin's Lamp,* so when a teleplay involved a magic lamp purchased from Mr. Aladdin, Loretta thought any lamp would do. Tom said no. They argued, and Loretta won . . . until the next day when, obviously chastened, she admitted her mistake to the cast. "I think he was used to dealing with men, and didn't treat me as an equal partner," she said. "But although I would have spoken up anywhere else, I usually let a conflict go."

In March, 1954, shooting for the first season ended. Loretta's migraine attacks were increasing, and the family retired to the house in Ojai to enjoy a supposed two-month hiatus (actually, pre-production meetings began in May.) To their joy, the show was not only picked up for a second season, it collected awards. "Our director received a $10,000 prize, and he had never directed anything before this!" she said. The costumes garnered honors too, primarily due to Jean Louis and his protégé,

Above: Another award for St. Anne's. Loretta and her mother, Gladys, are showing it to Sister Mary Winifred (far left), founder of the home, and her assistant, Sister Mary Thomasine.

Below: Jean Louis (left) and James Galanos, two of Hollywood's top fashion designers, meet Loretta at a charity event benefiting St. Anne's Maternity Home. Some forty-five years later, she and Jean would marry.

Loretta starred with Cary Grant in *The Bishop's Wife*. Here they are shown at a luncheon.

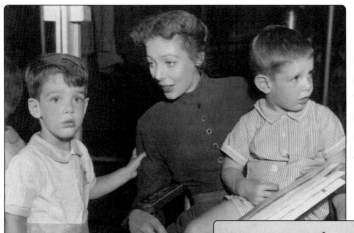

Chris, 3, and Peter, 2, visiting Mom on the set of *Rachel and the Stranger.*

Chris, 6, and Peter, 5, on their way to a party. Loretta hand-sewed Chris' "Lucifer the Cat" costume, and borrowed Pete's from the wardrobe at Twentieth Century.

Judy, Peter, Loretta, and Christopher. Shortly after this photo was taken, the boys went to visit their father in New York and decided to stay.

Dolores Hope, Josie Wayne and Loretta at the St. Anne's board meeting.

Tom Lewis, Loretta, Sylvia Ashley and gossip columnist Louella Parsons on the set of *Cause for Alarm,* which Tom produced in 1951.

Loretta, Bishop Ed McCarthy and Sister Mary Rose, head of the Phoenix Project.

A still from her television series, "The Loretta Young Show."

Loretta and her mother, Gladys, on the set of "The Loretta Young Show."

Peter and Chris all grown up.

Ruth Roberts, who taught Loretta her Swedish accent for her role in *The Farmer's Daughter,* and later, Loretta's story editor on the TV series.

Meeting Cary Grant again, along with other admirers, in 1980.

Loretta greets President Reagan at a White House dinner.

Loretta presents the Academy Award for Best Picture to *Chariots of Fire* in 1981. The envelope is on the podium.

Loretta made it back from her first trip to Medjugorje, Yugoslavia, in time to accept an award presented by Sidney Poitier, broken foot and all.

In 1988, the Young sisters attend an award dinner together. From left: Sally, Polly Ann, Loretta, and Georgie.

Working at the
street shelter in
Los Angeles.

With director Mervyn
LeRoy, who gave Loretta
her first part.

Jimmy Stewart
came to Loretta's
79th birthday
party in 1992.

Loretta Young publicity shot
sent to fans around the world.

newcomer James Galanos, who had lent Loretta clothes from the Metro-Goldwyn-Mayer closet. Loretta's popularity exceeded anything she had known in the movie industry. She was television's First Lady. Even better, she was in control. After a lifetime of taking orders from directors, she was developing a sense of power, and it felt good.

The second season shooting began in June, and the show's reputation for elegance caused production costs to grow. Whenever there was a special effect, a piece of furniture, something to be rented that the budget couldn't cover, Loretta would tell the production people to "Take it out of my salary." (The accountant gave her $20 a week, and she never had time to spend it.) She usually worked late, then drove a long distance back to the Santa Monica beach house, where more dilemmas awaited. Her mother still hadn't finished the Flores house, and was way over budget. If irritations had arisen between her and Tom on the set, it was her job to smooth his ruffled feelings. (Hollywood women in those days were liberated in many ways, but the need to placate one's husband as compensation for holding a job still persisted.) The boys also needed attention—they were growing up quickly.

Judy had left school abruptly earlier in the year, but Loretta had persuaded her to return and finish. Now she was home, and she wanted to marry Russ. The extended Young family was still unimpressed with Russ and his presumed limited potential, and discouraged the wedding. Eventually, the young couple broke up, and Judy later married another man. "That was one of my biggest blunders," Loretta later admitted. "Judy should have married Russ. I was under a lot of pressure with my work and marriage, and I didn't want her to make the same mistake I made when I was seventeen. And, to my mother and sisters, no man would have been good enough for Judy. But we were wrong."

During this time, Loretta had an unexpected and sad reunion with Mae Murray, Aunt Maetzie. "I hadn't been in touch with her for years," Loretta said. "All of a sudden, she phoned. She said she was staying at the Roosevelt Hotel, and wanted to visit me." Loretta sent a car to the Roosevelt.

"Mae arrived in the same type of black dress, black hat, little mittens, a rosebud mouth—just like I remembered her," Loretta said. "She had always been a little spacey, but now she was very vague about where she had been living, what she was doing." After small talk, Maetzie got to the point. She had some friends in need. Could she borrow five thousand dollars for them?

Loretta didn't hesitate. That would be fine. She would call the office, have a check ready, and the car would stop there on Mae's way back. "Give me your number at the Roosevelt," she said. "I'd like to get together with you again."

"Why don't I call you?" Mae suggested. The women hugged. Something was not quite right about this, Loretta thought, but what else should she do?

Later, the driver reported to Loretta. "I let that lady off at the Roosevelt," he said. "But she looked so uncertain when she got out of the car, that I went around the block and followed her. She didn't go into the hotel. She walked a few blocks to a little house, and went inside."

He had gotten the address. Loretta sent someone there to see if Mae was having a problem. She also called the Roosevelt hotel. Mae wasn't at either place, and according to the people in the little house, she never had been. Loretta tried some other avenues, to no avail. She never heard anything about Mae again until her death in 1965.

"There was a story that, like me, she had been pressured to get an abortion or she would never work again," Loretta said. "She had refused, her husband had taken the child and her money, and left her destitute. It's something else I'll regret forever. Had I known how stricken she was, I would have arranged something. There were still plenty of people around who knew her, and would have helped."

Health Crisis

*I believe that if I want faith, I have to go
after it and pray for it and work at it.*

—MARIA SHRIVER

In February, 1955, Loretta completed the show's second season. Her weight had slipped to a hundred pounds (she was never a big eater and often, at work, had to be reminded of mealtimes), and her cigarette habit was now at four packs a day. Migraine headaches were constant, and she had recently turned down not only an eighth term as President of St. Anne's Foundation, but all volunteer work. Worse, the rift between herself and Tom was widening. He had tired of playing second fiddle at work and in public (once, at an Elsa Maxwell dinner party, he had insisted they leave immediately because Loretta had been placed at a more prestigious table than he), and he resented being called "Mr. Young."

"Tom and I never argued at home about the show," Loretta said. "But it was affecting our personal life. If you have two strong egos involved in anything, it becomes a contest, even though one or both might not even realize it." Reluctantly, they decided that putting some space between them was their only chance to revive the closeness they had shared. One of them would have to leave the show.

Procter and Gamble made the decision for them: "We bought the Loretta Young show, and that's what we want," the executives declared. Tom could develop scripts for other shows. But the shows never materialized. Instead, Tom became a fulltime parent to Christopher and Peter.

Although Judy had frequently visited Loretta on the set of her pictures, Tom had never permitted the boys to do so, or to watch their mother's movies. As he told Loretta, "it would confuse them to see you with another man." "We all understood that Mom had to work," Christopher recalls. "Her time with us was golden, but when she wasn't there, it was okay too."

Now her hours would only lengthen, since she was not only the star of the show but also its executive producer and part owner. As third year production plans began, the network asked if she'd like to make the series in color. How much extra would it cost? About $5,000 a week, she was told. "I had two houses to run and couldn't imagine how I would pay that," she said, "but I should have borrowed the money because it would have made the clothes more interesting, and the stories more current."

In March, 1955, Loretta received an Emmy for Best Actress in a Continuing Series, the first star ever to have won both an Oscar and an Emmy. (She would win again in '57 and '59, along with a Golden Mike from the American Legion; a Silver Globe from the Foreign Press Association; *TV Guide*'s "Most Popular Female Personality;" *TV Mirror*'s "Star of the Year" for six consecutive years; the Cannes Film Festival's Grand Prix, the first ever awarded to an American television show; several Best-Dressed and Most Cooperative awards, and many others.) Her statuette display was definitely growing. One day, Pete brought home a new friend, and the boy stared at the awards. "Who do those belong to?" he asked.

Pete shrugged. "My mom."

"Wow," the friend said in awe. "She must be some athlete!"

In April, for Easter week, Loretta, Tom and the boys, and Georgiana and her children, went to the Ojai house. Ricardo would join them soon, and Loretta was looking forward to collapsing for the entire hiatus. On Easter Saturday, she and Georgie were shopping when Loretta doubled over in pain.

"What's wrong?" Georgie asked in alarm.

"Nothing. This happens every month," Loretta said through gritted teeth. "It'll go away in a minute." Georgie half-dragged her to the car, and sped back to the house.

The pain did not go away. Since they had no family physician in Ojai, Tom called a gynecologist who came to the house. The doctor gave Loretta a few pills, suggested a hot water bottle and a nap. After he'd left, Loretta discovered that the tablets were only sleeping pills. Georgie was angry about it, and complained to Tom.

Tom assumed Loretta was overreacting, but as the night wore on and Loretta continued to fight the pain, Georgie grew more and more concerned. She sat by Loretta's bed, and by five A.M. she had had enough. She went into the living room and confronted Tom. "If you don't get an ambulance here in five minutes," she demanded, "I'm going to call Ricardo, and ask him to bring a doctor!" Belatedly, Tom called the paramedics. By eight A.M. on Easter morning, Loretta had been admitted to St. John's hospital in Oxnard.

Although Loretta insisted that her condition was linked to her ovulation, no one originally paid much attention. For ten days she received antibiotics to cure what was assumed to be an infection. However, the penicillin did not work. Nor was her pain being caused by anything tests could uncover. Loretta's family sent specialists to her; the physician on her case visited her every day, but continued to be puzzled. Exploratory surgery might have been in order, but in Loretta's exhausted and frail state, an operation was too dangerous. Loretta had always feared physical pain. Now it would become her constant companion. She was terrified.

And what about the show? Shooting for the third season was due to start in June. "We'll close it," Tom announced to Norman Brokaw, Loretta's agent. "Loretta can't work anymore, and even when she recovers, it's going to be too much of a strain to continue. We'll take the two years, and sell them into syndication."

Norman Brokaw was not at all sure that Loretta would want to relinquish her show, especially without being consulted. He told Loretta of Tom's decision, and she was appalled. Despite her weakness and pain, she called a meeting in her hospital room, declaring herself in complete control of Lewislor (with her shares and the accountant's, they could out-vote Tom), and that the contract for next season should remain. But how?

Brokaw came up with the perfect solution. He checked with some of Loretta's friends, and suggested they fill in as guest hosts and actors until she was well. Loretta was deeply touched by his protective kindness. "Let's do it," she told him. "But don't let anyone come through my special door until I can open it again!"

Thus, when shooting began for "The Loretta Young Show's" third season, Barbara Stanwyck, Rosalind Russell, Claudette Colbert, Irene Dunne, Ann Sothern, Merle Oberon, Joan Fontaine, Joseph Cotton, Van Johnson and, of course, brother-in-law Ricardo Montalban substituted for her. The famous door did remain closed, but at the end of each show, the host would smile into the camera, and say, "Good night, Loretta," reminding the audience that, indeed, the woman they had grown to love each Sunday evening would return. (Another suggestion from Brokaw.)

Loretta was grateful for their loyalty, and moved to tears when she needed blood transfusions, and almost the entire crew volunteered. But there were days when death would have been preferable to the existence she was enduring. Doctors now knew that an ovarian cyst had burst, sending infection throughout her lower intestines. The pain in her stomach was excruciating, and she could stay on morphine for only a brief time lest she become an addict. Limited to intravenous feedings, her weight sank to 82 pounds. She developed severe bedsores until her godson, Michael Wayne, saw them and brought in a sheepskin for her to lie on. (Apparently the lanolin in sheepskin has a medicinal effect.) "I cried almost all the time," she said. "It hurt so much, and I told everyone so."

One night, Loretta had a severe spasm, and she moaned. Sister Mary Rose Christy, a Sister of Mercy and head of the nursing staff, came in, bent over the bed and took Loretta's hand. "Loretta," she said softly, "look at me."

"Oh, Sister," Loretta wept, "it hurts."

"I know. But you've been looking at that crucifix on the wall for all this time. Do you believe that He suffered all that and died for you?"

"Of course, I do."

"Well then, can't you endure this for Him?"

"I-I guess so. . . ."

"You know, Loretta," Sister went on, "you shouldn't waste suffering when it comes. This affliction could save your soul for all eternity. Or your husband's or your children's." She kissed Loretta on the forehead. "Think about it, honey."

It was a new way of looking at her hardship. Of course, she could suffer for Jesus. "It didn't make the hurting any less," Loretta said, "but it gave me a more positive way to think of it." Through the dark days that followed, she clung to the hope that this torment had a purpose, that God allows difficult moments so they might give birth to greater good. In her weakened condition, she had no way of knowing that she was building inner strength for difficulties which lay ahead. She knew only that, somehow, she was letting go and letting God.

Sister Mary Rose began sleeping in the room next door to Loretta, and one evening she brought in a woman gynecologist, Dr. Dorothy Chess, herself pregnant, who seemed far more sympathetic than the male staff. Gently, the doctor probed her stomach, and suddenly Loretta felt the pain recede just slightly. Was there hope after all? She had felt herself doomed to hurt this way until she died.

As she found out later, Dr. Chess had to argue with almost every male physician on staff before she obtained permission to perform a partial hysterectomy on Loretta; they were certain she wouldn't survive the procedure. But on June 29, Dr. Chess prevailed. And although it took several more weeks, eventually Loretta began to recover.

During her hospitalization, Tom had invited his sister, Ruth, and her niece to come and stay with the family at Ojai. One day, Dr. Chess came into her room. "Mrs. Lewis," she announced, "your car and driver are out front, and you're going to put on your prettiest robe and go home to Ojai."

"Oh, I can't," Loretta protested. Although she and her sister-in-law had always been friendly, Loretta had no desire to go home to guests and responsibilities. Despite the long months of inactivity, she was exhausted.

Dr. Chess had summed up Loretta's marital problems accurately. "Yes you can," she said softly. "Or you never will." She beckoned to a young nurse.

"I'm going home with you, Mrs. Lewis," the nurse smiled.

Loretta succumbed. Apparently this had all been arranged. By Tom, perhaps? But when they arrived at the Ojai house, Tom was not in front to greet her. Later, when the nurse put Loretta to bed, they both heard voices floating across the back yard. Tom was telling his sister, Ruth, what a difficult time he was having, because Loretta was either ill or working long hours. Ruth was commiserating. Loretta felt like weeping.

After three days of overhearing Tom's complaints, the nurse came into Loretta's room. "Mrs. Lewis, you're never going to get well here," she said bluntly. "I have to leave you, but I'd feel better if you went to your other house."

"I know," Loretta said, dejected. She summoned Miss Coney, the housekeeper, and explained that she, Chris and Pete would be returning to the Flores house. (Judy was living there and working on her mother's show; however, she was considering moving to New York.) Miss Coney took charge, packed up Loretta and the boys, and supervised the move.

A few days later, Tom phoned Miss Coney. "Aren't you coming back?" he asked. "Someone has to be here in Ojai to cook for Ruth and me."

"Who will cook for Mrs. Lewis?" Miss Coney asked.

"Well . . . maybe we'll come home too," Tom answered.

They did. Eventually, Tom's relatives went home, and by September, Loretta was well enough to appear at the dedication of the new wing at St. Anne's Maternity Hospital. Finally, in October, the moment she'd hoped for, arrived. After 18 weeks offstage, she walked triumphantly through her "special door" onto the set of the Loretta Young show, cast and crew cheering. (Loretta burst into grateful tears, and the entrance had to be re-shot.) "They were like family—so considerate and kind to me," she says. She was even able to appear in the last several episodes of the season. Her television life had been resurrected. If only her personal life could follow suit.

End of a Dream

*I tried but I didn't make it. I still think people should
try as hard as they can to keep a marriage going.*

—LORETTA YOUNG

When shooting began for the fourth season of "The Loretta
Young Show," Tom was still at home all day, and Loretta was
virtually living at the studio, where Gladys had designed a small
suite for her. When she came home on the weekends, Tom would
take the boys to Ojai, ostensibly to give Loretta some peace.
("Mom was particularly sensitive to noise," Christopher recalls,
"and we always had friends around—it could have been a zoo if
Dad hadn't intervened.") Yet Loretta and Tom's relationship was
definitely in its last stages. Carter Hermann, Polly's husband,
approached Loretta. "Would it help things if Tom were
working?" Carter asked.

"I certainly think so," Loretta said. "He seems so unhappy
without anything to do."

"I have a friend in New York who wants to offer Tom an
advertising job," Carter went on, "but he wants to be sure you
approve. After all, Tom would be on the other coast."

"Well, Tom commuted when we were dating," Loretta pointed out. "Oh, tell your friend to at least ask Tom, and let him decide."

Carter did. Tom seemed pleased with the offer. "But before he accepted it, he wanted me to sign a document that he and his lawyer had drawn up," she recalled. "As he explained it, the paper said we were deciding that everything either one of us owned before our marriage and during our marriage was a business arrangement, and had nothing to do with a husband-and-wife alimony, in case of divorce.

"I didn't understand it. We weren't getting a divorce—it had never been an option for us. So I showed it to our business manager, and he told me not to sign it, that I would be signing away half of everything I had before our marriage and during our marriage, including the television show." She told Tom what the business manager had said.

But Tom was determined. "It took him three months, but he eventually persuaded me to sign it. Then he went to New York to take the new job." (It seems incredible that Loretta would blithely sign away half of all the assets she had ever owned; however, one must remember that she had little understanding or regard for money. Also, she was still hoping that her marriage would survive, and if she could placate Tom with her signature, it might have been a powerful motive.)

As Easter, 1957, approached, Loretta had an opportunity to go to Europe with her friend Jane Sharp to see Pope Pius XII, Padre Pio, and stigmatist Teresa Neumann, three of the most famous Catholics in the world. However, she did not want to leave during the boys' vacation unless Tom was in California with them.

"Go ahead," Tom assured her. "Don't pass up this trip—I'll come out and stay with them." And he did.

The trip was impressive, but also unsettling. Both Padre Pio and Teresa Neumann had the same brief and simple message for

Loretta: "You are to go on with what you're doing." No promises, no reassurances, no real answers from heaven's messengers. Yet didn't she know by now that we must sometimes walk by faith, and not by sight?

She arrived home feeling unusually tired. Jane also seemed ill. Perhaps they had contracted the flu in Europe. Instead, it was hepatitis, and both women immediately took to their beds. By the time the school year ended, Loretta was still weak, but work on the show's next season had to begin. Tom came to California to pick up their sons, according to the informal "commuter agreement" he and Loretta had made. Chris, now 12, and Peter, 11, would spend the first month of summer with Tom in New York, and the second month at camp. During August they would accompany Loretta and some of her family to Honolulu.

But events did not follow the plan. At the end of June, Tom refused to send the boys to camp, or back to Loretta. Shocked, she flew to New York to confront him.

Tom brought the boys with him to the meeting. "Tom," Loretta pleaded, "this isn't fair. We agreed that Chris and Pete would come back to me for August, before school starts."

"No," Tom informed her, "the boys and I have decided that they'd rather stay in New York permanently. So I've enrolled them here at St. David's prep."

Loretta looked at her sons. "Is this what you want?" she asked, incredulous.

"Yeah," said Christopher. "I want to stay with Dad." Although his answer stung, it was not unexpected. Chris and his father had always been close.

"And you, Peter?" Peter shrugged, eyes down. Loretta sensed he did not at all want to stay in New York, but he was crazy about his dad and big brother, and wouldn't say anything to offend them.

Although Loretta left her sons with their father to avoid an emotional tug-of-war, she had not capitulated. She flew back to her sickbed, hired an attorney and asked her good friend Cardinal James McIntyre, the bishop of Los Angeles, to intercede for her with Tom. Cardinal McIntyre informed Tom that, for the good of the family, he and the boys should return to California. Tom refused.

Slowly, Loretta's health returned. Despite appearing in all the episodes of the show's fourth season, she visited New York frequently on weekends, to see her sons and try to change the arrangement. Occasionally, she stayed with Georgie and Ricardo who had an apartment in town, at times she stayed in Tom's apartment in the Waldorf Astoria or with Judy, who was now working in New York. Loretta had strenuously objected to Judy leaving California, but since Judy was dating a man Loretta liked, Joseph Tinney, she finally accepted the move. The press, of course, was aware of the difficulties in the Lewis marriage, and often approached her, but Loretta refused to grant any interviews. As always, she was cautious about causing scandal, and chose "No comment" as her best response.

Christopher adjusted well to life with his father. He liked New York and looked forward to traveling through Europe. But during one stay, Loretta discovered that Pete was seeing a psychiatrist. She accompanied him to his appointment. "What seems to be wrong?" she asked the doctor.

"Pete isn't very happy," the doctor told her.

"I know. But there's nothing wrong with Pete. It's his mother and his father," Loretta pointed out. "We should be coming to you, not this little boy. He just wants to be home with both of us."

"Well," the doctor pointed out, "I've called Mr. Lewis several times, but he hasn't come in."

That evening, she challenged Tom. "It's wrong for Peter to be so unhappy. If we can't make things work the way we used to, at least let's go for counseling."

Tom refused, and Loretta returned to California in despair. Later, she received a surreptitious phone call from Pete, asking to come to California. "I arranged a ticket, and he slipped out of the house without Tom knowing about it," she recalls. But when Pete arrived in California, he spent the next week talking to his father on the phone. Tom flew to California, and Loretta had another psychiatrist waiting. The three of them sat down to discuss the situation.

"Frankly," the doctor said, "one of you needs to let go. This child wants to please you both, but you're pulling him apart." He turned to Tom. "Are you willing to let him stay here?"

"Absolutely not," Tom was firm. "He's my son, and he belongs with his brother and me."

The psychiatrist looked at Loretta. "What about you?"

Loretta's heart sank. "Would it be best for Pete?" she asked.

The doctor paused. "I think it would," he said gently.

No child should ever be forced to choose between parents. And given her work schedule . . . "All right," she said softly. "He'll go back to New York."

The moment Pete had settled in again, Tom sent word through his lawyer to Loretta's lawyer. She would no longer be permitted to stay in the Lewis apartment during her trips east.

It was a petty move, but Loretta refused to curtail her visits with her sons. Instead, when in town, she stayed with friends. Bishop Sheen also met with Tom and Loretta on more than one occasion. "God wants you two to be together," he would insist. But perhaps Loretta and Tom no longer knew how to break through the fences they had both built.

In March, 1958, Georgie and Ricardo hosted an engagement lunch for Judy and her fiancee, Joseph Tinney, at a New York restaurant. Judy was exceptionally nervous; she would say later that she felt "pressured" into marrying Joe. The guest list included Tom and the boys, of course, and all three were expected at the wedding as well. Tom would be giving the bride away. But on the morning of the luncheon, the world learned that Tom Lewis had filed a suit against his wife and Robert Shewalter for "dishonesty and mismanagement," asking that Lewislor Productions be dissolved. Georgie was furious. She phoned Tom.

"Tom," she told him firmly, "I saw the newspapers this morning, and I'm calling to say that I don't want to see you at the luncheon. I expect to see the boys, but not you."

"You won't see any of us, Georgie," Tom announced.

"And I suppose you won't be at the wedding either?"

"If we're not welcome today, we're not welcome anytime."

"I didn't mean the boys, Tom," Georgie pointed out. "I just mean you."

But war had been declared. The following month, the Lewislor attorneys countersued. And on June 21, Judy and Joe married in Beverly Hills—without Tom. Judy was secretly relieved, and asked her godfather, Carter Hermann, to walk her down the aisle. (Her brothers did not attend, and according to her, were never told that they had been invited to the wedding.) Loretta was distressed although she managed to remain serene, at least on the outside, as her family and friends rallied around in silent support. But if she hadn't previously admitted that her marriage had fallen apart, she certainly knew it now.

Surely, she could have been a happily-married woman; she'd had the love and the determination. But when things faltered, she had turned to the one outlet which had never failed her— acting. From here on, she would be blamed by many for choosing work over family when, in fact, her career might have provided the comfort and control she was finding nowhere else.

Despite her misery, she sensed God's quiet presence. One dawn, as her chauffeur drove her down the driveway, she spotted a little Mexican man on a ladder, picking avocados from trees near her gate, and dropping them in a basket. Her trees! As the chauffeur drove past, she met the man's eyes, shook her head and wiggled her finger at him. He looked back, mouthing, "No?"

"No," she echoed firmly.

The car swung into the traffic and suddenly, remorse filled her. What was she doing, telling a poor man that he couldn't pick her fruit? How dare she be so selfish? *Whatever you do to the least of My children* . . . "Carl!" she called the driver. "Can you swing around the block and take me back home?"

"Yes, Miss." Carl turned the car down the next street, and circled back. Loretta had a clear view of the sidewalk on both sides, the locked gates of the driveways. No one was out this early. No one, but the little Mexican man. She would invite him in, empty her shelves. The car circled onto her street, and she gasped in surprise. No ladder, no heavy fruit-laden basket, no Mexican man. Nothing but a deserted avenue.

Where had he gone? How could he have disappeared so quickly, if he'd had to carry both a ladder and a basket of avocados? And if he hadn't taken the basket with him, where was it?

Later, Loretta learned that the trees actually belonged to the city, but because her gardener took care of them, she had wrongly assumed they were hers. Thus, the Mexican man had the right to pick the fruit, after all. Despite watching for him, she never saw him again, and "It haunts me to this day," she says. "Why would I do that to someone?"

Perhaps her personal problems were overwhelming her sense of judgment, her usual warm generosity. Or, perhaps the episode should be looked at in another context. Even if she had unintentionally chased him away, a guardian angel never goes very far.

During one show hiatus, Loretta was ordered into the hospital for a forgotten malady. Loretta always took advantage of hospital stays as mini-vacations, and no visitors were allowed. One day, a nurse popped in to inform Loretta that a Father Hiss wanted to see her. "I don't know any Father Hiss," she said. "Please make my excuses."

The nurse gave her a look. This was a Catholic hospital and no one turned a priest away. Loretta attempted to explain. "The only Hiss I ever knew was Marty Hiss, in eighth grade. I had a crush on him, but he did not return the compliment."

The nurse laughed. "I'll give Father your message." She left, and returned quickly. "He says he is Marty."

After all these years! Loretta couldn't believe it.

Father Marty Hiss had just returned to California, read in the newspaper that she was ill and come to see her. He strode into her room, laughing. "You'll never make it, Marty!" she told him.

The two enjoyed a fun-filled afternoon, and Loretta eventually introduced Father to her whole family. Interestingly, each of the Youngs had been trying for many years to convert Carter Hermann's mother to Catholicism. Mrs. Hermann simply wasn't interested. But a few years after Father Marty surfaced, the Youngs all received unexpected invitations to Mrs. Hermann's baptism. How had this happened, and who had converted her? None other than Father Marty, who was visiting neighbors one day, and received a warm welcome from Mrs. Hermann because she had heard of him through Loretta.

"The longer I live, the smaller the world becomes," Loretta said. Father Marty came back into her life at the right time, bringing laughter and faith—just what she needed.

Lourdes

To those who believe, no explanation is necessary.
To those who do not believe, no explanation is possible.

—Franz Werfel, The Song of Bernadette

Each year, Catholics—actors, crew, writers—in the movie industry attended an annual Communion breakfast. In 1958, the breakfast was held shortly after Judy's wedding, and the speaker was Cardinal James McIntyre. During his talk, the cardinal said he believed that director Cecil B. DeMille was the greatest apostle in the motion picture business. DeMille wasn't Catholic, but, because many of his movies involved Biblical epics, such as *King of Kings, The Ten Commandments, Sign of the Cross* and others, he opened the doors of faith to many. "He spends his entire talent and time trying to prove the existence of God, and a person who lives that way is certain to be blessed," said the cardinal.

Loretta was in the audience. "He's right," she thought, remembering *The Crusades*. Cecil B. DeMille had done great good. And her television show reached far more viewers than his movies. "What can I do on my show to prove the existence of God?" she wondered. "Maybe something involving miracles? What about Lourdes?"

Loretta asked her producer and writers for a script on Lourdes, a shrine in France where, exactly one hundred years ago, a peasant girl named Bernadette Soubirous had witnessed several apparitions of Mary, the Mother of Jesus, as well as the emerging of a spring of healing waters. The circumstances surrounding the apparitions had been the subject of a novel and a motion picture in the '40s, winning an Academy Award for actress Jennifer Jones. (*The Song of Bernadette* is still shown frequently on television, especially during the Easter and Christmas seasons.)

Loretta's writers produced a script in which Loretta's character, suffering from a brain tumor, visits Lourdes and receives a healing. "I sent it to the Cardinal to see if he had anything to add," Loretta said. "His assistant called a few days later."

"Loretta, the script is excellent," the priest said. "But does the star have to be cured?"

"What do you mean?"

"Well, the real miracle of Lourdes is that no one comes away empty-handed. Either they're converted or they amend their lives or they're uplifted in some way. Not everyone receives physical healing, but that doesn't diminish the blessings of this holy place."

"I see." Loretta hadn't considered that. She returned the script to the writers, and the second draft, "The Road," was flawless. Her character, now a cynical agnostic, would see someone else receive a healing, and experience a rebirth of her own faith. The only stumbling block was getting the story from paper to film.

The crew could go to Paris, then on to Lourdes during the three-month summer hiatus, Loretta decided. And since there was no extra budget for this extra show, she would borrow the money to produce it, and bring her friend, Ruth Roberts, along to help with everything. Plans were progressing when Loretta learned she had received the award that year for television's Most Important Female Personality. How delightful—first an Emmy and now this honor! A board member from Procter and Gamble wanted to come to California to lunch with her before she left for France. No doubt, Loretta thought, he was coming to express his congratulations for the awards and high ratings her show continued to pile up.

To her consternation, his visit was anything but upbeat. "Letters are coming in demanding 'that religious nut' be taken off the air," he told Loretta. "The board has had a meeting and we'd like you to tone down your moral standards, and stop doing shows involving priests and nuns, and. . . ."

Loretta listened to the conditions quietly, despite a sharp stab of hurt and disbelief. Finally, she asked, "Is that all?"

"Yes."

"Well," she sighed, "I can't, and I won't. That's not why I gave up my movie career and got into television. So, remind the board that I warned them about this several years ago. And tell them I'm on my way to Lourdes to make a picture about a miracle—which I'm sure they'll all hate."

"But Loretta, we have to pay attention to letters."

"I know you do. And even though you have no right to it, if Procter and Gamble won't have me as I am, I'll let you out of your contract."

"You'll what?"

Loretta showed him out. She still had packing to do before she left for France.

$\sim$

She had been in her Paris hotel only about three hours when the phone rang. It was her agent. "Loretta," he said slowly, "Brace yourself. Procter and Gamble has cancelled your contract."

Loretta's heart seemed to stop. They had actually done it. And here she was, halfway around the world, committed to making a film with borrowed money, a film that now might never be shown.

She wept all night. How could they, especially given the awards her show had won? Should she have bent her principles to satisfy the board? No. She wiped her eyes. She had chosen her path years ago, and whether it was wise in the eyes of the world could make no difference. God was the only One she had to please. To everyone else—no comment.

She felt more optimistic the next morning. And she almost wept again—this time with joy—when her agent called. "I've found two new sponsors," he announced. "Would you accept Listerine?"

"Oh yes—provided I won't be known as the Bad Breath Girl!"

"And Toni, the hair products."

Two sponsors instead of one! It was a miracle—the first of several waiting for her in France.

One day, as Loretta, Ruth and the others had lunch in Lourdes, Loretta noticed two nuns at a table across the room. As they got up and came her way, one spoke to her. "Loretta, don't you remember me?"

Loretta was startled. It was Mother Gabrielle, a Dominican nun from a monastery near Los Angeles where Loretta often went for retreats. Mother was accompanied by a little nun from India. Everyone laughed at the coincidence of them meeting on another continent, and Mother Gabrielle explained that she and her companion were returning from India, where they were planning to open a new convent, and had stopped to visit Lourdes. They would travel to Paris next morning, and then on to America. Most certainly, the entire monastery would pray for the success of the Lourdes film.

When the nuns had gone, Loretta had an unmistakable urge to give them some money. Although she contributed to many charitable organizations, convents were not among them; she'd always assumed the orders that ran them were solvent. But this instinct was strong. How much should she give them? She looked in her purse. How much did she have? Who could tell—it was all in foreign currency. She went to the front desk for an envelope, and put all the cash she had inside. "Be sure Mother Gabrielle gets this," she admonished the concierge.

"But, of course," he assured her. It was the last she heard or thought about it.

After she returned to California, however, her sister Sally popped in one day. "I'm absolutely fascinated about this story concerning you and Mother Gabrielle," she told Loretta.

"What story?" Loretta asked.

Sally had just attended a retreat at the monastery. "Mother Gabrielle said that she and her companion were going from India to Paris, and they were so close to Lourdes that both wanted to see it," Sally explained. "But they had no extra money, not one dollar, for bus tickets or hotels there."

Loretta started to get a funny feeling.

"So Mother made a nine-hour novena to Our Lady," Polly went on. "Then she cashed in their tickets to America, took the money and blithely bought two bus tickets to Lourdes."

"But then they wouldn't have had enough left to re-purchase the airline tickets to America," Loretta pointed out.

"Exactly. The morning you met them at Lourdes, they had no idea how they were going to do that. They would be stranded in Paris when they returned there. And then you left them an envelope, with the exact amount of money they needed. Not a dime more—or less!"

The blessings continued to flow. . . .

Rudy Matee was a French motion picture director with whom Loretta had once worked. She knew he was earning about $150,000 per picture at that time. But before leaving for France, she had tracked him down. "Rudy," she'd asked, "how would you like to earn $1,500 for about nine days work on a project of mine?"

He had laughed. "What is it about?" he asked.

Loretta explained, and to her utter amazement, Rudy agreed. Since he knew where to find actors and crew, he also took on all the hiring—about 37 people, including an assistant director, George Lauteniere. Rudy also journeyed to Lourdes to choose locations. When Loretta arrived, the company worked in Paris the first day, then went to Lourdes where they worked a second day.

Then Loretta lost her voice.

It had never happened before. And there was no reason for it, no virus going around, no bad weather or injury. She was in almost every scene, so no work could be done without her. For six days production halted while Loretta sat in her room. A physician came every few hours, squirted something down her throat, and warned her against getting excited. Nothing worked. "God," she prayed, "I came to Lourdes to try to prove your existence, and You let this happen to me?" Maybe she wasn't supposed to do the project? However, it was a little late to change plans now.

Loretta's voice returned on day seven, and everyone worked for three more days. Then she lost it again, and production ceased. The on-again, off-again schedule continued for 29 days, twenty more than the loan had been planned to cover. Loretta was able to double the financing but, realistically, it would take her years to pay off a debt of several hundred thousand dollars. Yet, for some reason, she felt everything had been worth it. Even a wild thunderstorm on their last evening in

Lourdes didn't dampen her spirits. The film was going to be beautiful.

On the final day in Paris, the assistant director, George Lauteniere, invited Loretta and a few others to have dinner with him and his wife on a boat cruising the Seine. After dinner he asked to speak with Loretta privately. The two went up on deck.

"I must tell you this before you leave," he said. "When Mr. Matee hired me, I hadn't worked in over a year. My wife is a top Givenchy model here, but she was getting tired of supporting me.

"I was thrilled to get your script—until I read it. Then I went home and said to my wife, 'I can't do this. It's one of those religious things. And there's nothing to do in Lourdes—no bars, no nightclubs or movies.'"

"My wife didn't care. She demanded that I take the job. So I came."

Then Loretta had lost her voice. The first time he had thought he would go mad with boredom as he and the others waited for her recovery. The next time was even worse. When the second week passed, he had gone to Rudy Matee. "I'll find a substitute assistant director for you," he'd told Rudy, "but I have to go home, now. The religion here is driving me crazy."

Rudy had looked at George. "If you leave this place, I will personally see to it that you never work anywhere in this industry again."

George's jaw dropped. Rudy could do it, he knew. There was no alternative but to stay.

"The last night, there was a loud thunderstorm, and I couldn't leave. Do you remember?" George asked. Loretta nodded.

"I grabbed my jacket in a fit of rage and went out to walk in the rain," he went on. Although he didn't realize it, George was following the Way of the Cross, a commemoration of the journey

Jesus had made to Golgotha, marked by life-sized statues and scenes along a hill. As he reached the top, a great flash of lightning illuminated the cross itself, with Jesus' image hanging upon it.

"I looked at Him, and something broke inside me," George whispered. "I began to cry, falling into the mud beneath the cross. I sobbed and sobbed—I just couldn't stop.

"Finally, I struggled down the hill." He looked at Loretta. "Today, my wife and I went to Mass and confession—for the first time in nine years. I attribute it to you and your script."

So that was why she had lost her voice, and production had been delayed for so long! Further, it answered a question she had just begun to wonder about: Here she had been at a shrine known for healings. Why hadn't she drunk the blessed water and asked God for a healing of her throat? It had never occurred to her to do so.

Now, looking into his glowing face, Loretta beamed. "You're an expensive conversion, George."

He smiled back. "But worth it, yes?"

Yes!

~

About ten years later, Loretta had a chance to visit Paris again, and she contacted George Lauteniere. Yes, he and his wife were still faithful Catholics, he assured her. Moreover, they now had two beautiful children. And in some marvelous quirk of timing, his career had absolutely taken off since he had worked on the Lourdes project, in fact, he was one of Europe's most sought-after directors.

"Isn't it amazing?" he asked.

Not so amazing, she thought. Not if you get out of the way, and watch God work.

~

There was more to come. Loretta and Ruth hand-carried the film across the ocean and all the way to Los Angeles, and they were glad to see Loretta's business manager waiting as the flight arrived. "Loretta," he began, "you must be the luckiest person alive."

"Really? Why?"

"Did you realize that you were the only person on that crew to be insured?" he went on.

"I guess I didn't pay too much attention. What does that mean?"

"It means that, because you were ill, your insurance company is going to pay the entire second loan."

~

Loretta and the producers went immediately to work, cutting, editing and adding music to "The Road." When it was finished, she invited her entire crew, as well as the president of the Toni Corporation, one of her new sponsors, to preview the film. It had turned out beautifully, she thought, and was the perfect piece to start the season. There was just one very large problem. It was an hour long, and her show was only a half-hour. And dividing the film into two weekly episodes would sacrifice much of its impact.

After the preview, several people went out to dinner. Loretta turned to the Toni president, and flashed him her most charming smile. "You know, I've always wondered why Toni didn't send Rosalind Russell and me diamond bracelets after all the great publicity we got for you last year."

The president looked startled. "Excuse me?"

Loretta told him of the annual Hollywood photographers' ball, in which movie stars came in costume. "Roz and I had originally decided to dress as Dewey and Truman," she explained, "but our husbands put a stop to that. Later, Roz suggested we go as the Toni twins." (The Toni twins were two identical models, one having a Toni home permanent and the other a salon version. Which twin has the Toni? asked the commercial.) The women had rented black wigs, black feather boas, long black cigarette holders and striped gowns; they had won first prize and their photograph had been seen all over the world. "And no gift for all that publicity?" Loretta now teased.

The Toni president was chuckling. "You did deserve it," he admitted. "But I wasn't the president then. This is my first year." Of course, he would ask for the second half-hour for her show— it was the least he could do, considering the Toni twins. . . . The company's board of directors agreed to buy it. "The Road" opened Loretta's fifth season, and was a smashing success.

And for several Christmases thereafter, the Toni president sent her a small diamond.

～

The final shoe on this project dropped after "The Road" was broadcast. "Isn't it odd, Mama?" Loretta mused to Gladys. "I've never been that close to the Blessed Mother, yet I felt compelled to film this story—and look at all the blessings that came from it."

Gladys was frowning. "What do you mean, you've never been that close to the Blessed Mother?"

"Just that. I haven't. Oh, she's darling, of course, but I usually just go straight to God."

"Gretch, didn't I ever tell you what happened when I was pregnant with you?"

"No, Mama, I don't think so."

The words came tumbling out—the young, worried woman, another child on the way, the abortion offer, her decision. Only then did Loretta learn that, all those years ago, she had been dedicated, consecrated, to the Mother of the Lord. "So many good things have come to you through her—I'm sure of it," Gladys explained. "I wish more women realized that Mary can take care of everything."

Loretta still wasn't saying a daily rosary. But she would now.

End of the Show

I do not try to dance better than anyone else.
I only try to dance better than myself.

—MIKHAIL BARYSHNIKOV

Grant Withers committed suicide on Good Friday, 1959. Although Loretta had not seen him in many years, she had been aware of his life's downhill spiral, and was saddened by the news. But there was not much time to mourn. Just a few days later, Loretta, now president of Lewislor, was nominated for the sixth time in a row for an Emmy, and won her third statue. In addition, the show was nominated as Best Continuing Series. By now, Loretta had played an amazing range of characters—a Japanese wife, a Swedish servant (with accent and braids similar to her Academy Award role), an Indian Maharani, nuns, a gangster's girl, a waitress. . . . And the mini-morality plays had touched just about every subject. One of her favorites was "Forbidden Guests," about a career woman facing the end of her life, who is trying to tell her imaginary children why she never had them. Another venture, "The Accused," dealt with the sale of pornography to minors, and Representative John Saylor of Pennsylvania read a congratulatory mention of the script into the Congressional Record. Loretta had also hired many actors, known and unknown, who would go on to develop good careers, including Eddie Albert, Hume Cronyn, Barbara Hale, and Cloris Leachman. The show had proven to be an amazing vehicle.

NBC purchased 176 installments for daytime reruns, just in case people had missed it the first time around. Before signing the contract, Loretta inserted a clause stating that, in re-runs or foreign markets, her trademark entrance through ·the door would be cut out. Always aware of fashion, she knew those beautiful gowns would eventually become dated, and she didn't want her audience wondering why she was so out-of-style. The "clause" actually ran three pages, but NBC agreed to it. When the re-runs began, Loretta was simply shown in a close-up, announcing the show.

Because of the document she'd signed for Tom a few years ago, two million dollars, half of the syndication purchase price, went to him. Still, her share would cover the Lourdes production, and allow her to catch up financially.

"What you really ought to do," her accountant frequently pointed out, "is to stop working, since half of everything you earn for the rest of your life will go to Tom." What a mistake signing that paper had been! Not only had it failed to revive their marriage, Loretta had even ended up buying back furniture from Tom which had been in her family since her childhood! But work was security, and she wanted to take the show as far as it would go.

She had also agreed to co-author a book about her philosophy of life. The book, *Things I Had to Learn,* was published in 1961. It sold well, but most critics regarded it as treacle.

Unfortunately, the show's days were numbered. Loretta always believed that it was canceled after its seventh season because sponsors were becoming irritated with her spiritual message. The sponsors claimed that, because of the daily reruns, her Sunday ratings were dropping. Whatever the reason, in 1961, she tried another format, "The New Loretta Young Show," featuring her in a recurring role as a widowed mother of seven children. It lasted just a year. For the first time in her life, Loretta faced a blank canvas.

There were personal bright spots, of course. Judy had a baby girl, making Loretta a proud grandmother. ("Whatever you do in life," Loretta wrote to her daughter, "you will never accomplish more than giving birth.") And fourteen-year-old Peter had come back to live with Loretta, with Tom's permission. He had hated school, and apparently missed his mother more than any of them had anticipated. Back in California, Pete had some rough times adjusting to life without his father and brother, but Loretta took him to Honolulu with Jane Sharp and her son, Tommy. "We all fell into this restful, peaceful environment," she says. "And I think Pete began to heal." But where was the healing for her?

Shortly after her show finished its eighth and final season, Loretta attended a party in Los Angeles, and met an English artist, Sir Simon Elwes. Sir Simon was best known for a portrait he had done of the young Queen Elizabeth, but he had also painted other luminaries, and his works were rumored to sell for as much as $25,000. At that time, however, Loretta knew little about Sir Simon, although she saw him almost daily at morning Mass. She had noticed that he had a physical disability, for when he limped up the aisle to receive communion, he dragged his right side.

Sir Simon quickly explained his handicap. "I suffered a stroke two years ago," he told Loretta. "My right hand, the one I painted with, was left almost completely useless."

"How awful!" It was hard to imagine how anyone would cope with such a tragedy.

"Yes, it was. I lay in bed for almost two years, feeling sorry for myself. Then one day my wife came in and said, 'Simon, I'm going to leave you unless you go out to your studio, and let your left hand teach your right hand how to paint again'."

Loretta was fascinated. "And did you?" she asked.

"In a manner of speaking. I have to dab now, instead of stroking—my technique has changed. But I am ready to accept commissions again. As a matter of fact, I'd like to paint you."

"Oh, I don't think so." Loretta wouldn't spend money on such a frivolous purchase, nor time on endless sittings. In addition, both her personal and professional lives were in shreds. Wouldn't a sensitive artist pick up those emotions, and transfer them to canvas? Would people guess that, despite the Bible verses and hopeful mottoes she had presented to the world, she herself was broken and bereft? Because she didn't want to reveal her real objections, she voiced the first thought that came into her mind. "You know, I've never liked the candy box paintings people do of me. They're just too sweet."

"What makes you think I'd paint like that?" Sir Simon demanded. "That's a bit insulting, isn't it?"

Now she had hurt his feelings! "Honestly," she blurted, "I've only seen one portrait that I really love. It hangs in the front hall of a house in New York, a painting of a friend of mine. It looks like she's actually stepping out of the picture. . . ."

"With a lace handkerchief in her hand?"

"Why, yes." Loretta was astonished. "You've seen it too?"

Sir Simon smiled. "I painted it."

It seemed an amazing coincidence. In fact, the following day Loretta phoned her New York friend to verify his statement. "It's true," her friend said. "But, of course, that was before his stroke. Who knows what the poor man will be able to do now?"

Loretta found herself thinking about Sir Simon. Would he ever return to his profession? When she phoned her hostess to thank her for the party, the two women talked it over. "I really wish you would let him paint you," the hostess told Loretta. "He needs to get his confidence back."

"Maybe I could arrange time for the sittings," Loretta mused. "But buying it. . . ."

"Oh, I'm sure he just wants it as a sample, to get some commissions," Loretta's friend pointed out. "Let me check with him."

And that was how, a few weeks later, Loretta found herself posing for Sir Simon. She wore a colorful dress and a favorite white peacock pin, and sat demurely on a small stool in the living room of her home. But the project was difficult for both of them. Simon's new dabbing technique often frustrated him. He painted a ring on—off—on Loretta's folded hands, then off and on again. And her concern about Simon sensing her emotional state had been well founded. Occasionally, she would look at the canvas and see disturbing images: her eyes, shiny with unshed tears, her spine, ramrod straight with tension. "Simon, don't paint that," she would sometimes plead, looking at the day's results.

"I paint what I see," he would respond. Only Judy seemed excited by it all. She dropped in frequently to check the oil's progress.

In about six weeks, it was done. Simon carried the portrait away, to Judy's chagrin. "I never got to see the finished product!" she complained to her mother. Loretta had mixed emotions about the project. She felt that God had brought her and Sir Simon together for a reason, perhaps to re-start his life, and she was happy to cooperate in the Plan. But she was not so pleased that a vulnerable time in her life had been revealed for anyone to see. When the painting was finally hung in a British museum, she was relieved and determined to forget about it.

~

Over the next two decades Sir Simon painted many famous people. After he died, sometime around 1980, a collection of his portraits came to a New York gallery for exhibition and sale. Loretta's was among them. Loretta called Judy, now in New York, to tell her about it, since Judy had never seen the completed work.

Judy went immediately to the gallery. That evening, she phoned. "Mom, you'll never guess. The gallery owner used to live next door to us on Carolwood! She and I played together."

"Amazing! And what did you think of the painting?"

"It's beautiful. But someone already bought it."

Loretta was surprised at her disappointment. The painting, yes, had exposed a painful part of her life, but she had managed to hold on, and ultimately survive. The raging anguish of that time had dulled to an occasional ache, and life held promise again. Perhaps, after all, it would have been comforting to have a visual reminder.

Sometime later, Judy dragged a huge carton through the front door. It took only a moment for Loretta to realize what her daughter had done. "I thought you said it was sold!" she cried.

"It was. I bought it," Judy grinned. "Mortgaged my salary to get it. But it's only yours on loan, Mom."

"I understand, Judy. I'll write it into the will." She was staring again at the glistening eyes, the determined set of the jaw. Who was this fragile woman in her late-forties, holding on so tightly? Hadn't she yet realized that God could heal all wounds?

In desperation, you turn to Something bigger than yourself, she thought, and He makes everything pass. She looked around for the perfect place to hang the painting.

PART SEVEN

The Perfect Stranger

My husband Otra and I were on vacation in Palm Springs in the fall of 1999, and had stopped in a jewelry store that sold Swarovski Australian crystal. I try to buy a piece as a souvenir of each trip, but it's expensive and hard to find.

As we entered the store, I noticed a well-dressed elderly woman at the counter, admiring a ring on her finger. I smiled at her and said "hi." We chatted a bit, and she showed me the ring. It had several rows of crystal on a wide golden band. "Isn't it lovely?" she asked. "And excellent quality too—my husband, Mr. Louis, was a designer, and I know about jewelry." She looked at Otra. "You ought to buy this for your wife—it's perfect for her."

Otra gulped. The ring was rather pricey, and he knew I was going to buy some crystal if I could.

The lady noticed our hesitation. "Tell you what—if you want it, I'll pay half the cost," she said, and gave the ring to the jeweler. "Put it on my bill," she told him. Obviously, she was a regular customer.

We were amazed. Nobody does anything like that for a perfect stranger! I reached out for her, and when we hugged, something went through me, like a wave of heat or love . . . like something almost spiritual. "Can I do anything to repay you?" I asked, still stunned.

"Pray for me, for nine days," she said, and left the store.

We bought the ring—how could we not?—along with a little crystal heron. The next day we went back to ask the jeweler if I could send Mrs. Louis a "thank you" note through him. "Didn't you recognize her?" he asked us. "That was Loretta Young, the actress."

I'm not old enough to remember her movies or TV shows, but when we began sharing the story—on the plane going home, and with our friends and family—many people knew of her. A lot of them cried when they saw my ring. The whole episode seemed like a movie itself. I won't forget, and I do pray for her—every day.

—Valerie Smith,
Irvington, New Jersey

Part 7 photo—In Medjugorje with her
husband, Jean Louis (photo on preceding page).

Around the World

Hold a true friend with both your hands.

—NIGERIAN PROVERB

Loretta slept "for about a year." She was exhausted to her very bones, and couldn't seem to sleep enough. When she wasn't sleeping, she made caftans and beaded sweaters for her friends. And she read voraciously, catching up on every book she had earlier set aside. Loretta had also heard of a newly defined learning disability: dyslexia. People who had it, she discovered, were often intuitive, with excellent memories and speaking abilities, but had difficulty reading. The symptoms matched her own. By now, she had learned to compensate, and could read as quickly as anyone, but it was nice to put a name to her earlier problem. If she had ever felt less intelligent than others, she knew better now.

One day Gladys gave her some advice: "You know, Gretch, you think the whole world is a sound stage, and it isn't. There are things out there you never imagined, and you ought to go and take a look for yourself."

Travel? Well, why not? After a stint at Purdue University, Pete was traveling with a band, and there was no reason why she shouldn't go. But not alone. Loretta was used to traveling with entourages, but perhaps Josie Wayne would be her companion. Josie agreed.

On the morning they were to leave for the Orient, Loretta arrived at the airport with 24 suitcases. Josie had 23. Since the studios had always taken care of the luggage, Loretta was shocked when she had to pay an enormous amount in overweight costs. (This time, however, she didn't label her boxes. Once, on a trip to England, Loretta had, at the last minute, written "FURS" in huge letters on one of her crates as it stood on the loading dock. She was surprised when it never arrived in England.)

Globe-trotting itself was also a rude awakening. Loretta was used to having a maid, who packed, unpacked, ironed, and hovered around. So, of course, she asked the hotels to have one on hand for her. "I honestly thought that's the way everyone traveled," she laughed. Not surprisingly, the baggage diminished as clothes were misplaced or given away.

The tour began in Taiwan and Quemoy, off the mainland of China. Ruth Roberts was now working there, and had told Loretta that unless one is a guest of the government, one would not be permitted to see anything of note. "So think about it," Ruth had warned Loretta. "Are you doing anything important?"

Being a movie star didn't "count," Loretta said, because in China, if you make your living on your feet, you're considered lower-class. She had written that book. . . .

"Great!" Ruth said. Journalists were always official guests. And Josie could be Loretta's "writing assistant."

"When you enter the country, you have a government host who arranges everything for you," Loretta said. "Josie and I were assigned a general, as well as a priest and a reporter from *The Stars and Stripes* newspaper. Ruth came along too. We wanted to see it all, but especially the leprosarium in Taipai."

"Surely there are more interesting places to go," the general objected.

"A friend specifically asked me to visit," Loretta explained.

The friend was Bishop Sheen. He had been terrified the first time he met a leper. But God was in that leper, Sheen realized, God suffering for His children. The bishop had taken the afflicted man's hand, buried his face in it, and prayed that he could overcome his fear. Later, he found a leper on the streets of New York, brought him home, gave him food and medicine and paid for his care until he, the bishop, was reassigned. Now, he had instructed Loretta to visit the leper colony in Taipai, and to wear her prettiest dress in respect for the patients. She was ready.

The general relented, and "we went to a beautiful compound, with a big wall around it," Loretta recalled. "There were little gardens, miniature bungalows, a tiny jail painted blue and white—it was almost like a Disney set. We were told there were seven religions represented there, and each group had built its own church. There were no workers from outside. The people, about seven thousand of them, all took care of one another."

In the first bungalow, young men wore nothing but shorts. Sores were evident on their exposed skin. They stood when the general entered, but as the women followed, they turned away. (There was a television set in the room and since Loretta's show was now seen all over the world, it was likely they recognized her.) "They are embarrassed," someone explained. Loretta went to one man facing a corner, and touched him on the back. Then she put her arms around him. He started to tremble, but never turned around. Quietly she whispered to him.

In another area, large tubs held medicated oil. The patients put their aching limbs into the mixture for temporary relief. Loretta dipped her hand in the oil too. Everyone seemed shocked, yet moved. Somehow they understood that although she had not experienced their misfortunes, she understood pain and was telling them so.

"We stayed there all day, visiting people, hugging them," she said. "I've never seen a community like it, no hatred, no selfishness, no bitterness. I thought it might not be so bad, living like this." Although they later attended a festival hosted by General Chiang KaiShek, the leprosarium was Loretta's most memorable visit.

Loretta and Josie continued on to Japan, Hawaii, then India. Newspaper reporters and photographers met them at every stop. "We were supposed to be in India for two weeks, but I couldn't cope with the poverty in New Delhi," she recalled. "You could give everything that you had away, and the beggars would still need more. I told Josie we had to leave."

"Not until we've seen the Taj Mahal," Josie protested.

"Well, . . ." Loretta relented. They hired a car and a Sikh driver. "As we traveled, we saw women getting water at wells, cows dragging carts—it seemed as if we were back in biblical days. Then, another car came along, and our drivers spoke to each other." Suddenly, their driver turned around, and went back the way he had come.

"What's going on?" the women asked.

"I will tell you later," the man promised.

But would he? The women grew uneasy. They were very vulnerable, they realized, out in a primitive countryside with no protection, no language skills. They began to pray. Soon their driver turned again. "We are going to the Taj Mahal by this road instead," he explained. "That driver told me that a bus had gone through the small village we were approaching. It had hit a child and kept on going. The villagers were killing everyone passing through. I did not think we should go there." *Thank you, God, for keeping your hand on us.*

Early the next morning, Loretta and Josie were scheduled to watch a session of Parliament. "How about tomorrow afternoon?" Loretta asked their guide. "I like to sleep late."

The guide agreed. The following morning, thousands of Indians stormed Parliament, and in the melee, many were killed or injured. The women had missed all the violence. *Thank you again, God.*

After India, they went to Thailand, where they were also guests of the government, their host being Prince Pano. The Prince and his entourage (including photographers) met them at the airfield, and Loretta found him charming. "He owned motion picture studios and theaters, and his wife, whom he met when she was thirteen, had starred in some movies before their marriage," Loretta says. "He also owned fabric stores, so we had a lot in common." The people of Thailand seemed to love Prince Pano—apparently the men in his lineage had died out (his father was the King, in *Anna and the King*). At the age of seven, his grandmother had started preparing him to rule.

"They took us to the palace, which was closed to everyone but the royal family," Loretta said. "It wasn't the kind of palace one would expect. It had golden stairs and was up on stilts (so you could mount an elephant from the first floor), and one huge room—you cooked in one corner, ate in another, slept in the third corner and ran the country from the last." The royal couple also introduced their daughter, a three-year-old with no fingers, and an infant son missing a limb. The children were thalidomide babies whom they had adopted.

Prince Pano was a balm to Loretta's sore soul. "You are a Vesuvius—you are still erupting!" he told her one evening. She hoped she could return to this beautiful land someday. Unfortunately, it would be torn to shreds during the Vietnam War.

From there the women were going to Iran, but once again, they ran into a snag at the airport. Although they had been leaving belongings behind, each flight on Pan American still charged high overweight fees. Now the ticket agent informed Loretta that she owed another $900. It was four in the morning

(Loretta was always comatose at that hour), and she had had enough. "We have been traveling forever, and every time we get off your airplanes, someone puts a big Pan Am bag on my arm and I end up doing an unpaid commercial for you," she snapped. "I'm not going to pay you any more overweight."

"You have to pay it," the agent said.

"No, we won't!" Loretta was warming up. "And if we get off in Iran and the luggage isn't there, I'm going to sue your airlines, and I'm going to win!"

"But madam . . ."

"Call the manager!"

"He's asleep."

"Wake him up!"

The sleepy manager arrived. "But madame . . ."

"Raisa Fala, a friend of the Shah, is going to meet us," Loretta told him, name-dropping with a vengeance. "They are giving us a dinner. I think they will be unhappy if our luggage does not arrive." The women flew to Iran, leaving a bewildered manager.

"Maybe it was unfair, maybe I was just tired, but I thought it should be a quid pro quo," she says. After two uneasy days, their luggage did arrive in Iran. Afterward, no PanAm reservationist ever charged them overweight again.

Eventually, Loretta and Josie arrived back in California. It had been an incredible experience, one that they would never forget. But for Loretta, it was time to decide what she was going to do with the rest of her life.

Going It Alone

Preach always. When necessary, use words.

—St Francis of Assisi

Even after almost three years away from television, Loretta had no inkling that her film career had virtually ended. "Offers still came in, but nothing worth getting up early for," she said. "Most were evil or weird characters. I would ask Norman Brokaw, 'Why do you send these things to me?' And he would say, 'You should see the stuff we don't send you.'" But God would know what was right for her. If she was meant to work again, He would send her the script.

Never one to be idle in His cause, Loretta also took Jane Wyman under her wing. The actress was divorcing her fourth husband, and one day she asked Loretta, given her problems and disappointments, why she still seemed so happy. "I guess it's God, and my confidence in Him," Loretta answered. "Maybe that's what's missing in your life."

Jane was open to any suggestions. Soon she was taking instructions to become a Catholic. (Just recently, she sponsored another young convert.)

One day Loretta slipped into St. Victor's church for a quick prayer. She noticed someone kneeling ahead of her, up at the communion rail. It was Jane Wyatt Ward, and she was weeping. Loretta was surprised—Jane was always such a sunny person. What could have happened? Worried, she slipped out before Jane discovered her presence.

The women later met at a party. Loretta admitted that she had seen Jane in church. "I hope you're okay," she said. "Can I help?"

"I don't think anyone can help," Jane explained slowly. "It's our son, Michael. He's had some kind of . . . breakdown."

Michael Ward had always been a brilliant boy, especially in music. Now, at the age of twenty, he had inexplicably fallen apart, and the doctors seemed unable to help him. Jane and her husband had no recourse but to watch their son suffer. They were devastated, and so was Loretta.

The following Sunday, Loretta met the Wards at church. "You're Michael, aren't you?" she asked the young man. He nodded. Loretta invited him to get in her car and visit for a while.

Neither knew that something good would come out of their meeting.

Pete was on the road. Chris was attending the University of Southern California's school of film study. She had seen Chris frequently during trips to New York, and their relationship was good. He and Tom now lived together in an apartment near the USC campus. Judy had finished a role on Broadway, and was acting in a soap opera in New York, while juggling her role of mother to little Maria. She would eventually divorce her husband.

In February 1966, Loretta started writing a column for the Catholic News Service, syndicated to diocesan newspapers around the country. The column answered questions from teenagers. She also met some New Yorkers who wanted to start a chain of Loretta Young bridal salons, so she decided to live there for a while. Gladys decorated an apartment in Central Park south for her. The bridal salon idea fizzled, but a similar concept involving charm schools was more successful. "We opened at least ten franchises before the lovely lady who ran it died, and I pulled out," Loretta said.

In 1968 Loretta moved back to Hollywood. It had been ten years since she and Tom had lived together. But Tom had always been a reasonable man, and she felt certain he would agree to exchange and reorganize their property arrangements, now that their lives had both changed so much. When she contacted him about it, however, he became so furious that Loretta decided it was the last straw. She filed for a civil divorce. She was fully aware that this changed nothing in the eyes of the Catholic church; she and Tom were still married until death parted them.

Fortunately, Loretta collected friends the way others sought antiques or teddy bears. One of her special pals was Virginia Zamboni whom she had met during a visit to Rome in the '50s. Virginia had had a multi-faceted career, working for the American Red Cross, hostessing at the embassy in Ankara, leading tours for Americans in Rome. She visited Padre Pio often, and brought him jars of American peanut butter, which he loved. Now Virginia had recently moved back to Santa Monica, and she and Loretta deepened their friendship. Other friends also offered comfort. Her life might be lonely at times, but she felt blessed with so many caring people around her.

Lonely, perhaps, but never dull. In 1970, Twentieth Century Fox released a movie, *Myra Breckinridge*, which, given the mores of the times, bordered on being pornographic. Without permission, the producers had taken clips of Loretta from other movies, and used her face and dialogue to create double entendres. They had done the same with other stars, but no one else seemed to mind. Loretta was furious. By the time she'd caught wind of it, six hundred brand new prints of Myra were on their way to movie houses across the country and England. "What can we do?" she asked her lawyers.

They decided to sue for a then-astronomical figure, $10 million, which would surely get Twentieth Century's attention. And, rather than take the case to any court in Hollywood, they went to a judge in Cleveland. Why Cleveland? Earlier, this same judge had ruled that another movie, *I Am Curious Yellow,* was pornographic, according to Cleveland community standards. He might be expected to have more understanding of Loretta's dismay than a Hollywood court.

The judge listened to each side. He then ruled that $1 million be put on his desk immediately. "If the clips of Miss Young are not out of all 600 prints of that film within ten days," he said, "Twentieth Century can add an additional $9 million to the pile." Within ten days all the prints had been re-edited, and re-issued without Loretta's clips. Loretta held out until she was reassured that the master or "vault" prints had also been edited.

Around that same time, Loretta got involved in hospice work at the Los Angeles Veteran's Administration hospital. Her sister Sally, always involved in a project, suggested she help. "Sure," Loretta agreed. "What do I have to do?"

The first step was being trained. Hospice was a new concept—giving patients whatever they needed, in order to make the dying process more comfortable (for example, people who were dying of lung diseases such as cancer or emphysema still were permitted to smoke, and doctors could relieve pain with whatever drugs were necessary). Loretta's job was to be a friendly visitor for a few hours each week.

Word got around the hospital. Soon Loretta was getting mobbed at the elevator by patients not in hospice. "They'd line up to meet me as I stepped out," she recalled. Instead of passing them, she would oblige the patients with talk and autograph-signing. By the time she got to the hospice wing, she was already keyed up. Then she would spend several hours with dying people, listening to the heartbreak of their inconsolable families.

The hospice director was not happy about the extra conversations. "Loretta, there is only so much one person can do," she pointed out several times. "Just tell the men at the elevator that you are here for hospice."

Loretta couldn't. The men's faces reminded her of the beggars surrounding them in New Delhi. So much need and sadness, all around her.

"I got extremely close to several families, and I grieved when their loved ones died," she remembered. "One woman was there every day from 8:00 A.M. to 8:00 P.M., so I started coming in at extra times, to give her a break. We both happened to be at his bedside when the man died." But, although this patient had surely gone to heaven, there were so many still waiting. Loretta kept accepting more hours.

"Then, one morning about a year after I started, I got to the hospital door and I literally couldn't open it. It was as if an invisible barrier stood between me and the entrance." Loretta started to tremble. Maybe she was coming down with some illness. She went home, phoned the director and told her she wouldn't be in.

The following week, the same thing happened. She must be having some kind of breakdown. Why could she go through any door except that one? She went home and called the director again.

"Loretta, I could have predicted this," the woman told her. "Don't you remember me telling you that you would burn out unless you do just what's asked of you, and no more?"

"Yes, but. . . ."

"I know everyone in the hospital wants to see you, but if you spread yourself too thin, you won't have enough to give to anyone."

She was not invincible after all, Loretta realized. And why should she be? Was it a strange combination of love and guilt that pushed her this way? She had been given so much—had she made the most of it? She might never know the answers, but she decided to take some time off from hospice.

Between her legal battles with Tom and the *Myra Breckinridge* flap, Loretta had had her fill of lawyers and courtrooms. But when Mary Coney, Loretta's housekeeper, went home to England for a visit, she phoned Loretta, bursting with excitement. "Oh, Mrs. Lewis, it's so nice to see you on English television, twirling through the door again!"

"Are you sure, Mary?" Loretta was shocked. According to the clause she'd inserted into the NBC re-runs contract, her pirouette and introduction were to have been eliminated. "Would you watch it again next week, and phone me?"

Mary did. Sure enough, for six years, Loretta's shows had been seen throughout Europe with her wearing dated gowns. Another lawsuit. This time she collected over $500,000 from NBC.

Loretta had still not given up the idea of franchising her name in some way. While she was working in hospice, Patrick Frawley, now the chairman of the Board of the Schick Corporation asked if she would lend her name and expertise to a new line of women's cosmetics. This was something she knew about! Not only had she heated eyelash wax since her teen years, she had also developed a method to warm skin cream and other lotions, just because they felt so soothing. Now dermatologists had caught up to her, finding that warmth is good for the face.

Pat Frawley put Loretta in charge of the Loretta Young Division of Schick, where the first line of "Warm 'N Creamy" products were introduced at the end of 1972. Loretta, who had barely attended high school, now sat in an executive's chair, looking every inch the polished professional. As he had done right along, designer Jean Louis kept her in clothes, this time more tailored for her new corporate image.

Loretta did not have to be in New York all the time, and this was fortunate, for there was another job awaiting her. Sister Mary Rose Christy, the nun Loretta had met in the hospital when she almost died, had undergone back surgery and needed rest. This was a problem, since Sister Mary Rose didn't understand the concept of "rest." Instead, she transferred to a hospital her order of sisters ran in Phoenix, and decided to launch a program for needy children. She recruited some local volunteers for after-school tutoring, mentoring, and just Being There. And, of course, she tapped Loretta to become a member of the fledgling Board of Directors. "Sister, I don't live in Phoenix," Loretta pointed out the obvious.

"It's a quick ride." Sister brushed her objections aside. "And I need you to find me a wealthy benefactor so we can buy a house. After-school programs are fine, but we really need some group homes. It's important to rescue these kids before they ruin their lives."

Loretta was familiar with Sister Mary Rose's formidable mindset, so she abandoned argument, and went to Phoenix for what was to be a temporary visit. A donor gave the women a two-bedroom trailer, which they set up as an office. Days turned into months, as Loretta attempted to raise funds for the project, and rouse enthusiasm among the wealthier residents in the area, between trips to New York or California. The nuns arranged an apartment for her in the hospital, but she took her meals with them and attempted to keep the prayer schedule and other disciplinary rules. This arrangement was not exactly orthodox, but who was around to object? It was an unexpectedly peaceful time, and she enjoyed the comforting routine.

Her old life, however, continued to collide with her new. On one occasion Henry Fonda's wife called Loretta. "Henry is coming to Phoenix with a funny play—can we get together for dinner?" she asked.

"Oh, it will be wonderful to see you both!" Loretta enthused. "I'll get extra tickets and bring some friends, and we'll all go out to supper afterwards." She had never heard of this play, but everyone loved comedy.

Loretta invited Sister Mary Rose and four others, including one shy young novice who, Loretta was willing to bet, had never attended a play in her life. All were mad with excitement over watching and meeting one of Hollywood's great stars!

Henry called her when he got into town. "I'm looking forward to seeing you and your friends tonight," he told Loretta. "By the way, do I know any of them?"

"I don't think so, Henry. They're all nuns."

There was a silence. Henry cleared his throat. "Loretta, are you sure you want to bring them?"

"Why not? Nuns laugh."

"But. . . ."

"We'll see you tonight!" Loretta hung up.

That night she led her little band of veiled companions down the aisle of the crowded theater to some of the best seats in the house. The curtain rose, a hush descended upon the audience. . . .

And within five minutes, Loretta discovered, to her horror, that every other line in the play contained an obscenity or off-color joke. She glanced carefully at the nuns. The little one looked a bit pale. The others weren't laughing, but they weren't leaving either. One was furiously knitting. "Lord," she murmured, "looks like I've done it again!"

After the play mercifully ended, everyone went backstage, hugged Henry and gathered for a late supper. Conversation was stimulating, and Henry and his wife enjoyed the nuns as much as Loretta had assumed they would. By unspoken agreement, no one mentioned the four-letter words.

The next morning at breakfast in the convent, Loretta took a deep breath. "Well, ladies, I'm sorry to have gotten you into that situation last night," she said. "I wasn't forewarned about the play, and then I wasn't sure if it would be better to stay or go."

Sister Mary Rose spoke for all of them: "It wouldn't have been kind to Henry if we caused a commotion by leaving, dear," she said.

Loretta felt better. Nothing more was mentioned and surely it was only a coincidence that the order's Mother Superior soon arrived for an important meeting and a check-up of the convent's general discipline!

By default, Loretta had become the "wealthy benefactor" Sister Mary Rose sought. She took a mortgage on an old derelict farmhouse, which had only two bathrooms, no glass in any of the windows and electricity far below code. Although her friends thought her insane, she was having it enlarged and remodeled into a group home. "This was typical of Loretta," one says, "jumping into things with her heart in control instead of her head." Slowly, the Loretta Young Home for Children became a reality. There was just one problem: the people who lived nearby.

This was an upscale area (the farmhouse was the only eyesore) and instead of welcoming the children, most residents developed a major case of Not In My Back Yard Syndrome. Funding never materialized. Although the state was willing to subsidize some of the expense, the nuns had expected the rest to come from the community, and it did not. Reluctantly, after all their work, Loretta and Sister Mary Rose eventually decided to give up. Loretta was bewildered. Had she gotten ahead of God again? What had been the point of all of this? And without help from others, what was she going to do about that impractical house, and its big mortgage payments? *God, it's me again.*

About a week later, a stranger phoned. "Mrs. Lewis," she began, "I've been driving past your house ever since you began remodeling, and although I've never seen the inside, I have this—this peculiar feeling that it's supposed to be ours. I know it's going to be a home for needy boys, but I have just made a novena asking that it will someday belong to my family. If you ever decide to sell it, will you let me know?"

Loretta was almost speechless. "I just put the house up for sale."

It was the other woman's turn to be shocked. "Oh! Please don't sell it to anyone else until my husband and I get there!" she screamed and slammed down the receiver.

It was a match made in heaven, for although Loretta had to sell at below her costs, the couple and their eight children moved in immediately, and she felt better about the demise of the original plan. Knowing that God is the Great Recycler and never wastes what someone else can use, she consoled herself by imagining how happy the current residents must be in that special house. And who can tally the words, the hugs, the love spent on destitute, lonely boys, even just for a short time? Saints have been fashioned with less raw material. Loretta left Phoenix permanently, and took up residence in a house in Beverly Hills, on Ambassador Avenue, where she would live for many years.

Sister Mary Rose is still launching projects. Not much about her has changed, except that she wears civilian dress now. (Loretta liked the habit better.) But the shared laughter and love were irreplaceable.

One day in 1975, Loretta received a fan letter from Michael Ward, Jane Wyatt's son. "I didn't expect her to remember me from that day after church," he says, "but she did."

Michael was still depressed. "In fact, the '70s were the most difficult years of my life." He felt frightened and frustrated because he wasn't able to use his extensive talents.

Loretta wrote back. "Keep struggling," she advised. "Each of us has our own road, and we have to find the way ourselves." Michael responded, and soon the two became pen pals.

"We talked about almost everything," Michael remembers. "Loretta was not like a big sister, not newsy or chatty. She was affectionate and philosophical, and offered constructive advice." The two exchanged views on their shared faith, the current culture, politics. . . . "We spoke about Our Lord. I asked her once if she thought He was tender. She said yes, that real men were always tender, like Jimmy Stewart who was a good man, with great compassion." Michael began to realize too that hidden within his difficulties were blessings. "Because I was ill, I didn't have to go to Vietnam," he points out. "I'd had a wonderful education, excellent teachers." Loretta agreed with his dismay over the falling American morality too, and he didn't feel quite so lost.

"When I discovered that Loretta was regularly writing to Michael, I was deeply touched," Jane Wyatt says. "She had so much to do, yet she made time for him."

One day, seven years later, Michael suddenly realized that the correspondence had ended. There was nothing more to say. He had healed during those years, and was ready for a new life. Today, he teaches piano in the Hollywood area, and does volunteer work at convalescent homes for stroke and multiple sclerosis patients. He has saved all of Loretta's letters, and still occasionally reads them.

My dearest Mom,

You have been my role model for grace and beauty (inside and out), and a powerful mentor and guide,

I cannot begin to tell you how much you've meant to me . . . you have made my life so much better, in every way possible.

Your loving daughter in spirit, Linda

On May 29, 1976, Loretta welcomed a daughter-in-law, Linda. She and Chris had met (on her 21st birthday) when Chris was working as a documentary film editor and writer. After the wedding, the couple lived in Ojai, where Chris had a job as a radio disc jockey, and Linda worked in a florist shop. Later, they moved to Tulsa when Chris became a popular entertainment reporter at a TV station there.

Loretta visited them frequently, developing a warm relationship with Linda, who taught her to use a sewing machine (after all her years of hand-sewing). On one trip, she volunteered to prepare dinner. Linda and Chris were surprised—Loretta rarely cooked. But she set about the task, using a recipe Jane Wyman had given her, chicken with sauerkraut. "It was fine that night," Loretta claimed, "even though there was enough for ten people." Leftovers the second night were edible, but less appealing. By the third evening, Chris staged a strike, and the rest went into the garbage. "Linda was so polite and nice, she probably would have eaten the same leftovers for a week," said Loretta.

Since Loretta needed a car in Tulsa, she asked to borrow Linda's Volkswagen. "Mom," Linda cautioned, "it's a stick shift."

"Honey, remember, I learned how to drive on a stick shift; I'm 180 years old!" Loretta reminded her. Linda said no more.

The Volkswagen was a gem but Loretta could not get it into reverse no matter what she did. "I had to drive forward all the time, so when I went into a mall, if the person in front of me wasn't gone, I stayed in the parking lot until they left." It made for some long shopping days, and eventually, Loretta admitted her mistake to Linda. Linda wisely remained mum. Loretta loved her even more.

The Loretta Young Division of Schick had closed, but Pat Frawley was still busy. He asked Loretta to be a guinea pig for a new stop-smoking treatment he developed. Perhaps her high profile would attract others. "But I don't really want to stop," Loretta told his secretary.

"It's not a healthy habit, Mrs. Lewis," the secretary pointed out. (She was talking to someone who never coughed and seemed to have unlimited stamina.) "This won't work unless you're motivated. Can you think of a reason to give up cigarettes?"

Loretta thought. Often she smoked instead of eating, or would take one bite of something, then light up. There were times when she had discovered a cigarette in each hand. Wasn't it time to get rid of her crutches? "Well, I've always wanted to gain ten pounds," she suggested.

"Perfect!"

The stop smoking program was unique, and effective. Smokers brought their cigarettes to the center and while puffing, pressed a button with their arm. The button emitted a little buzz, which gave off a negative reaction, perhaps a minor version of shock treatments. Whatever the mechanism, the therapy worked for a lot of people, including Loretta. At the age of 63, she finally kicked the habit, and soon gained ten pounds.

Loretta followed politics, but was not actively involved. However, she watched Ronald Reagan's move from films to politics with great interest, since she knew the couple well. "One evening during the first presidential campaign, I attended a dinner party at their house," she recalled. "There were about ten of us there, and I remember saying to Nancy that I couldn't understand why anybody, particularly someone of Ronnie's taste and sensitivity, would want to be president of the United States. It's a terrible job. Whatever you do, half the people are going to hate you."

"I don't know why, Loretta," Nancy had answered thoughtfully. "But right now, he wants it more than life itself. And that's good enough for me, and I'll do everything I can to help him get it."

"I expected that of Nancy. She took a lot of mistreatment for him," Loretta said. Eventually, the Reagans went to Washington, and a few months later, Loretta received an invitation to dinner at the White House. She declined in a note, saying simply that she couldn't manage it, but was praying for both of them, and hoped they were doing well.

Loretta hadn't dated since her divorce from Tom. They were still spiritually married, she felt, and dating might give rise to gossip. Often, she appeared in public with a married couple such as Jean Louis, the designer, and his wife, Maggy—"I was famed as a third wheel!" she laughed. Nor did she like to travel long distances by herself, especially to a place as momentous as the White House. But there was no point in explaining any of this; the Reagans now had many dignitaries to entertain, and an old friend from Hollywood would not be missed.

She was mistaken, for a month or so later, she received another invitation from the White House, this time to a party. She declined again. A third invitation arrived. About that time, the Reagans came back to California to a party given for them by Nancy's best friend, Betsy Bloomingdale. Loretta attended, and another close friend of Nancy's approached her. "Nancy is wondering if there is any reason why you don't want to come to Washington and have dinner with them," the friend asked.

Somewhat embarrassed, Loretta explained the situation. Apparently she had inadvertently offended Nancy, and she felt terrible.

But Nancy understood, and sent her an invitation for a state dinner for the Prime Minister of India, Indira Gandhi. "I hope you let me arrange something this time so we can get you here!" she wrote. "Let me know what you need."

Loretta knew a man her sons' age, who lived in the Virginia area. They had been friends for years, having worked on many of the same committees, and he was now dying at home, alone. In his most recent letter to Loretta, he'd mentioned that "the one thing I would love to do before I die is go to a White House dinner. Wouldn't that be marvelous?"

Loretta phoned Nancy. A few moments later, she was talking to her young friend in Virginia. "How would you like to escort me to the White House for dinner?" she asked. There was an incredulous silence on the line. "It's all taken care of," she went on. "You have to send your name in because they'll need to clear you for security reasons. And then I'll come and stay at your house that night."

Plans were made, Jean Louis created a beautiful chiffon dress for Loretta, and she hopped a plane to Washington. A few hours later, she and her wide-eyed escort were walking through the historic building to the grand dining room, where years of history surrounded them. They went through the receiving line, and met amazing people. Loretta had once been at a dinner hosted by Rupert Murdoch and sat next to Henry Kissinger, so she was delighted to see that he and his wife were attending the banquet too. It was an awesome evening.

A few weeks later, the young man called Loretta. He sounded noticeably weaker. "Would you like me to come back and be with you?" Loretta asked gently.

"No," he said. "I don't want you to see me. I just want to say good-bye . . . and thank you for everything."

He died soon after their conversation, and arranged for Loretta to receive his exquisite Meissen bowl of cobalt blue along with cups, saucers and dessert plates. She never used them without the image of his delighted face dancing before her.

Loretta revisited the White House, once escorted by then-Secretary of State George Schultz, and another time attending a dinner for Margaret Thatcher. To her delight, Mr. Denis Thatcher was her dinner partner. "Your wife is an amazing woman," Loretta said. "Is she . . . for real?"

"Oh, yes," he assured her. "My marriage to Margaret is about as perfect as anything could get."

"Really? Why?"

"Because you know exactly where you are with her, twenty-four hours a day. No pussy-footing, no half-truths. . . . It makes life very uncomplicated for both of us."

"It must be wonderful to trust someone that much," Loretta said. "You can say exactly what you think, can't you? You don't have to get mad, or have a quarrel, just be honest."

"Exactly."

Tom and I were never able to do that with each other, she thought, as an unexpected ache encompassed her. It was so sad. *He misunderstood everything I said, and I misunderstood everything he said. Maybe we were acting our parts, instead of living them.*

Angels, Angels Everywhere

Loneliness and the feeling of being uncared
for and unwanted are the greatest poverty.

—MOTHER TERESA

She had met Father Maurice Chase at a charity ball. He was known as The Dollar Priest, because he went to Skid Row at least twice a week to pass out dollars, which he obtained by soliciting the rich and famous. "I really didn't believe this at first—I thought he was just a priest who liked hobnobbing with society people," Loretta said. "So the next time I heard him talking about the people on Skid Row, I challenged him to take me along someday."

"Why, sure." Father looked surprised. None of his donors ever asked to accompany him. "I'll pick you up early next Sunday morning."

"How about after Mass?" Loretta didn't like the sound of "early."

"No, I say Mass down there." She was stuck.

The next Sunday Loretta and Father Chase drove to a tiny double storefront in a poor section of Los Angeles. As they parked, Father said, "Oh, there's Rhonda. She won't talk or even look at anyone, but she comes to me because she wants her dollar." Rhonda was dressed in torn, dirty clothing, pushing a shopping cart. Just as Father predicted, she turned away when she caught sight of Loretta.

One store held a kitchen, the other had beds. The woman in charge, Jill, didn't have a license to stay open all night, so the street women would come in after sleeping at a shelter, and then stay all day at her place, napping, washing their clothes or making phone calls. Father introduced Loretta to everyone. Then he vested, and began to say Mass on a little table near the entrance. Loretta knelt, but only a few others followed suit. The rest continued to sleep, talk or move around aimlessly.

After Mass, there was a meal, and the women gathered around Loretta, asking her questions about her movies. "One darling woman looked Scottish, like a leprechaun with a funny little hat," Loretta said. "'Will you talk to my mother on the phone?' she asked. I said, Of course!"

She called her mother in Santa Monica. "Mama, you'll never believe who's here. Loretta Young!"

Loretta had to get on the phone. "It's all right," she explained to the confused mother. "Your daughter isn't having a delusion. It's me—I'm a friend of Father's."

Loretta was impressed with everything. She began to accompany Father Chase once a week. "I didn't do a thing but talk and listen," she said. "They'd open up like sponges, sopping up any type of attention or kindness. I think every woman can connect with every other woman on some level. We did a lot of laughing." There was only one who wouldn't get involved— Rhonda. Occasionally, Loretta would glance out the storefront window to see her standing on the sidewalk, watching everyone inside. Jill would occasionally take food out to her. But she would not respond. What might have happened to Rhonda, Loretta wondered, that she was so afraid of people? She asked the Blessed Mother to help her reach this woman.

Months passed, and Loretta noticed a change in the women. They seemed more sure of themselves, more determined to make their lives better. Almost all now attended Mass, so many that Father had to set the altar up on the kitchen side of the store. Some had found jobs. Eagerly, they looked forward to Loretta's visits to tell her of their progress. "Only one ever asked me for money," she said, "but I gave money to Father instead of directly to the women—it was easier that way and saved everyone's pride." Only Rhonda continued to ignore her.

One day Loretta and Father drove past Rhonda, and Father honked the horn. Rhonda turned away. "Father, let me out!" Loretta said impulsively. He pulled over, and before Rhonda knew it, Loretta bounded out of the car, and put her arms around her. "I've got you now, and I want you to tell me why you don't like me," Loretta said. Rhonda struggled, but Loretta held on. "I like you, Rhonda," she whispered. How often, she suddenly wondered, was a homeless person hugged?

There was silence. Rhonda quieted. "I like you too," she said in a tiny voice.

Loretta was elated. "Then why do you run away from me all the time?"

"I don't like those others," Rhonda stated emphatically. "They're no good."

"They're just like I am," Loretta protested. But Rhonda had calmed under her touch, and they actually had a conversation. It was enough for the first day.

A month passed. Rhonda began to step into the shelter now and then. People observed her unobtrusively. It was like watching a fawn—if someone breathed too loudly, it would bolt.

Another month passed, and Rhonda was attending Mass with the others, sitting in the back, of course, but there. It was then that Jill announced she had found a real building, where women could live in apartments. Rhonda would be one of the first tenants, because her future looked bright.

The last time Loretta visited Skid Row, the storefronts had been replaced by large public housing buildings. "They were rather cold in comparison to those years we'd spent in the kitchen," she says. But there were more volunteers now, and she was involved in other things. Gradually, she stopped her weekly visits. But she never forgot Rhonda—and the miracle that a simple touch could bring.

Goodbye, Mama

There is a destiny that makes us brothers;
No one goes through life alone.
All that we send into the lives of others
Comes back into our own.

—EDWIN MARKHAM

Gladys had never stopped working. In 1982, as she finished up a home for Patrick Wayne, one of John Wayne's sons, and a ranch in San Francisco, she suffered a slight stroke. "It hardly slowed her down," Loretta recalled. "She finished her four final jobs on paper while she convalesced."

Gladys loved Loretta to drive her around, so she could look at houses and architecture. The only problem now were her unpredictable kidneys. "Mama, we know plenty of people in Beverly Hills," Loretta assured her. "You don't need to worry about that."

One day Loretta and Gladys were sightseeing, when Gladys suddenly required a bathroom. Irene Dunne's home was just ahead. Loretta skidded into the driveway as the butler opened the front door. She whisked Gladys up the stairs, and into the foyer, past Irene, who was just coming out of the library. "Well, Mrs. Belzer, how nice to see you . . ." she began.

"Hello, dear, be right back!" Gladys headed for the powder room.

"Sorry, Irene, your bathroom was the closest," Loretta explained, laughing. The butler had already gotten pie and coffee for Gladys, so the women had a pleasant, though unplanned, visit. "We ended up meeting a lot of our neighbors during those drives," Loretta said.

Gladys' second stroke was more serious, affecting her activity and memory. She moved to Polly Ann's house, along with a nurse, and the other daughters rotated weekends. Once, on Loretta's weekend, she gave Gladys a bath, then lay at the end of her bed, rubbing her feet with lotion. Gladys looked at Loretta. "This is not a very nice thing to say because you've been so good to me, but . . . who are you?"

"Mom, I'm Gretch! One of your daughters!"

"Oh, you couldn't be my daughter. You're too old!"

"You think I'm old?" she was half-laughing, half-crying. "You know that gray-haired lady that walks in and out of here every now and then? That's Polly Ann!"

"Oh no, dear," Gladys protested. "Polly Ann has long black curls. I do them every morning."

"Mama, you did them every morning. . . ." She gathered her mother's frail body into her arms. Gladys lay back, her eyes closed.

A moment later, she opened them. "I just said something stupid, didn't I?"

"Well, Mama. . . ." More laughter. Polly Ann came in, was told the story and joined in the hilarity. It was a joke among the family for weeks afterward. A way to get through the inevitable.

Gladys had a third stroke, and was taken to the hospital in a coma. Loretta was scheduled to give a fund-raising lecture in Chicago. Should she disappoint the audience there, or leave Gladys? Her sisters persuaded her to keep the date. "You've said your good-byes, and Mama might be here for weeks," Polly Ann pointed out.

Loretta flew to Chicago on October 10, 1984. Just before she was introduced, Polly Ann phoned to tell her that Gladys had died. "Although I felt sad, there was a great part of me that was joyful because I knew she was now in heaven," Loretta says. "I went out on the stage, told this large audience what had happened and asked them to pray with me for Mama. They were wonderful about it."

Hollywood people turned out en masse for Gladys' funeral, many of them clients who had become friends. One was fashion designer Gus Tassell, who had originally met Gladys at an antiques auction. "She was always a lady," he recalls, "and always beautiful." Although not a Catholic or even very religious, Gus made a donation to a Catholic seminary in Gladys' name when she died. Over the next years, the seminary kept him on their mailing list, and each year he responded with another donation. By the mid-'90s, Gus estimated that he had probably financed six men to ordination. It's typical of what Gladys inspired.

Around the time of Gladys' death, Loretta was pleased to meet Mother Angelica, the "television nun," as she was then called. Mother had settled her community of sisters in

Birmingham, Alabama, and supported them by writing various pamphlets and tracts. A speaking ministry was next, followed by appearances on Christian television programs. Mother eventually decided that she should launch a Catholic television network. Starting with $200 (and barely knowing how to turn her own set on) she received the first FCC license ever granted a monastic order, in 1981. The Eternal Word Television Network began with four evening hours, seven days a week. It was amazingly successful, and by the time Mother and Loretta met one day for lunch, the network was expanding. "And how am I going to fill all those hours?" Mother wondered aloud.

Loretta was enthralled with the miracles happening at Our Lady of the Angels Monastery, and with this witty down-to-earth nun. Who wouldn't want to be a part of it? "Mother," she mused, "I've got all these television shows. Would you want to broadcast them on your satellite?" Mother thought it was a perfect solution.

However, Loretta had once again led with her heart instead of her head. Other people were involved in the business end of the shows, and when EWTN officials inquired, they were told they would be charged $1,000 per show, a reasonable fee but one that EWTN could not handle. "It was just like Mom to offer the programs, and then remember that she had given control to other people!" son Christopher said.

But although Loretta was temporarily disappointed, she believed later that it was meant to be. "What if Mother Angelica had filled that time with situation comedies or dramatic series, instead of good solid Catholic programming that she finally developed?" Loretta asked later. "The network would have been entirely different, and maybe nowhere near as effective." As usual, God had the last word.

Although scripts were still occasionally coming in, (Norman Brokaw estimates she had already looked at some 150), Loretta now considered herself permanently retired. However, when a script from producer Aaron Spelling arrived, his accompanying letter was so delightful that Loretta relented and signed a contract. "Dark Mansions" was intended as a pilot for a gothic TV series, but although they rewrote and rewrote, the script was still terrible. "I had to tell Aaron I couldn't do it, so Joan Fontaine took over for me. I didn't like to see her doing roles like that—I don't know why she did." Loretta's instincts were right. "Dark Mansions" garnered bad ratings and reviews, and a series never materialized.

In 1987, Loretta was finally offered the perfect script, the lead in an NBC made-for-TV movie titled "Christmas Eve." The story involved a feisty grandmother who gives her wealth away to the homeless, and hires a detective to find her family for one last reunion. The screenplay had been written by an older woman who, Loretta said, "knew how to express things without being sloppy or sentimental."

Although filming was on location in Toronto, and twelve-hour days were the norm, the director and crew allowed her to sleep a little later than everyone else in the mornings. Other than that, she kept up with the pace. And she had lost none of her perfectionist tendencies: every night she looked at her dailies to see if her character was developing onscreen the way she should. "Unless you do," she told the director, "you don't know if the character is alive, dead, or too one-dimensional."

Four months later, Loretta attended the Golden Globe awards, and applauded winners such as Oliver Stone, Marlee Matlin, Sissy Spacek and Bruce Willis. Then the "Best Performance by an Actress in a Television Movie" category was announced. And the winner was . . . Loretta Young!

She received a standing ovation from the crowd as she went in astonishment to the stage to collect her prize. "Miracles do

The Road to Medjugorje

The person who thinks only of himself says prayers of petition.
He who thinks of his neighbor says prayers of intercession.
He who thinks only of loving and serving God
says prayers of abandonment to God's will,
and that is the prayer of the saints.

—*Bishop Fulton J. Sheen*

Tom Lewis never remarried, nor—say friends—did he ever "get over" Loretta. "He would sit on his patio at night with a glass of wine, and talk about her for hours," said one. "At the end, he took responsibility for much of what went wrong in their marriage. He always did say he was a terrible father to Judy." Too little, too late. . . . But during his last years, Tom became a born-again Catholic, traveling the speaking circuit with Kathryn Kuhlman and other evangelists, developing a healing ministry, which must have brought him some measure of spiritual and emotional comfort. He died in 1988, finally severing the bond between himself and Loretta. (According to some sources, Tom left his entire estate to his sister, Ruth.)

Loretta attended Tom's funeral. A week later she received a tape recording about a place called Medjugorje, in then-Yugoslavia. The Blessed Virgin Mary was rumored to be appearing there, and a group of pilgrims was going to see for themselves. Would she like to join them?

Mary. Her heavenly mother. Of course, Loretta was interested. And it seemed right to mark a new beginning in her life with a new experience. Perhaps Peter would accompany her.

Peter had had some rough years with the rock band, and all that the culture included. But he was now married to a young woman Loretta loved, and the father of a three-year-old son and another baby soon to be born. But when Loretta asked him about the trip, she was greeted with silence.

Pete finally answered, "Can I let you know?"

Of course. While waiting, Loretta played the tape again. It had been made by a young man in Birmingham, Alabama, named Jack Sacco, and was very moving. The next day Pete phoned. "Corin told me to go," he reported. "What should I pack?"

The trip to Medjugorje takes about eleven hours, and is not comfortable. Pete, at six feet four, was cramped the entire way, and the foreign plane crew was rude. A bus met them (Vicka, one of the six visionaries, rode along to welcome them and explain what they would encounter) and when they finally arrived in the little village, quarters were rustic. Loretta and Pete boarded with a peasant family, as all the pilgrims did then, in a tiny bedroom, with two thin mattresses, a table and one chair, sharing the bathroom. (In addition, their shower flooded.) "When the apparitions began at Medjugorje in 1981," Loretta explained, "the Communists were furious about the prayers being offered. But then word spread, pilgrims began to arrive, and the government saw . . . money. Families had to give Communists a large percentage of the pittance they charged visitors, since there were no hotels available. But because of the money, the villagers were left alone."

Now, as evening fell, all the fatigue and discomfort evaporated, and a sense of quiet settled over the travelers. As Loretta and Pete strolled the paths, a stranger approached. "If you would like to see Vicka, don't say anything, just follow me," he said. They did. Somehow they knew that strangers were not to be feared in this blessed place.

"We went four blocks to Vicka's actual apartment," Loretta recalled. "The guide left us, and we were the only ones with her. She and Pete played her guitar, and I asked her questions. It was a great treat."

The following day Loretta was buying a statue at one of the outdoor carts. "Look at the sun!" a woman shouted.

Loretta's eyes had been scorched twice by kleig lights, and they became bloodshot very easily. If she stared at bright objects, her eyes would easily burn. "But before I realized what I was doing, I looked right at the sun," she said, "and it started to grow." The pulsating golden orb grew from avocado-size to watermelon-size, changed to red, to green, to white . . . then the communion wafer appeared in the center of it.

"Mom, come on." Peter was calling her.

"Don't you see it, Peter?" she cried, stunned.

"See what?"

But the vision was over. The woman next to her had seen the Blessed Mother in the sun, not a wafer. She and Loretta stared at each other in wonder. They had heard of such things, but had never thought that they would be personally touched.

That night Peter made a confession. "You know, Mom, if I wasn't married, with a child and another on the way, I'd stay here. Everybody likes everybody here."

That's called peace, Loretta realized. "When everybody likes everyone, that's the great commandment. It has to start in your heart. I think that's what Mary wants." Slowly, as she thought about it, the truth grew. Her faith had never been based on sins and punishment, fear of God's judgment, the impossible attempt to live up to His expectations. Now, as a flood of joy seeped through her soul, she understood. It was so simple. Her faith was love.

One evening, as Loretta and Pete attempted to find seats for evening Mass in the crowded church, Pete spotted two small spots on the fifth altar step. It was the perfect spot to see and hear everything. But, after Mass, Loretta went down four steps and missed the fifth, twisting her foot as she fell. Pain shot through her.

Horrified, Pete swung her into his arms, and just then an Indian nun came up. "I'm a physician," she said. "Bring her outside." By now, Loretta's tears were flowing—the pain was intense.

Sister left them for a moment, then returned, carrying what appeared to be a pot of mud and some bandages. She slathered the goop on Loretta's foot, and bound it up with bandages. "This is going to hurt," she said, "but don't take the bandages off. There's no hospital here, not even a first aid station."

"Lean on me, Mom," Pete got Loretta to her feet, but he was almost carrying her. Then they saw a friend from their tour, carrying a broom. "I bought it for the lady at our house," he explained. "She's been sweeping the kitchen with a whiskbroom. You use it as a crutch, and I'll get another." None of them noticed that the nun had disappeared. They never saw her again.

"That night we were supposed to climb Apparition Hill, where Ivan, another of the visionaries, was going to have a visitation," Loretta said. "Usually on that hill there are about 700 people, and it takes people at least a half hour to climb up, since there is no path. People fall on rocks, get bloody knees. . . . I knew I couldn't make it." Loretta sat down on a bench near the bottom of the hill. "Pete, I'll wait here for you."

"But. . . ." Pete saw some of the friends he'd made and, explained the situation. Of course his mother could get up the hill—they'd see to it. One brought a stretcher, and gathered several young men around it. Quickly they put Loretta onto the stretcher, and lifted it.

Loretta looked at the hill. "It was steep and scary," she says, "especially in the dark, and my foot was throbbing. But no one stumbled, and we seemed to sail upward." When they reached the top, it was glorious. There wasn't a sound, and the only light was from the stars. Loretta sat on the ground, busy absorbing everything. Pete took her foot and put it in his lap, so no one would stumble on it. The young visionary, Ivan, knelt, waiting for Mary to come.

Time passed. Loretta's foot continued to ache unmercifully. After a while, a man announced that the Blessed Mother had just left. "She says to tell everyone on this hill that they have received a very special blessing tonight," he said, "and she asks that they pray specifically for peace in their own hearts."

People started the steep descent, and once again Pete and the other men gathered around Loretta's stretcher. An eight-year-old boy was now with them. "I'll help too!" he announced. He took hold of it, and again, the entire group was down the hill in about ten minutes.

Loretta sat up in amazement. "Pete," she cried, "my foot doesn't hurt at all!"

The little boy grinned. "Lady, I said a prayer for you up there!" he told her.

"Thank you, dear," she told him. "It certainly worked."

The next day one of the young men saw Pete again. "Did that stretcher seem heavy to you?" he asked.

"At first it did," Pete agreed. "But then, as we went up. . . ." He stopped. It sounded too strange.

But the other was nodding. "I've carried stretchers up and down that hill before, with a lot more helpers," he said slowly. "It always takes a long time—it's hard, heavy work." He looked at Pete. "They say there are angels here. I wonder."

Loretta was able to get around for the remainder of their stay using the broom as a crutch. And somehow the muddy bandages kept her foot pain-free. She had promised the Hollywood Chapter of the National Conference of Christians and Jews that she would personally accept an award they were giving to her. ("Sidney Poitier was presenting it—and I am crazy about Sidney—so I did not want to miss it"). When she got home, she immediately visited the doctor.

When he removed the bandages, her foot suddenly swelled to twice its normal size. Loretta looked at it, astonished. "That was some sprain!" she said.

"Not a sprain," the doctor looked at her x-rays. "You broke six bones in that foot. There's no way you could have been pain-free all this time."

No way, except for a special blessing from her heavenly mother on the top of a miraculous hill. . . .

"I went to the awards evening wearing a cast, all dressed up, in a wheelchair with balloons on it," she said. "And for the next six weeks, I never had any discomfort."

A few weeks after they had returned from Medjugorje, Peter called Loretta. "Well, Corin and I have a beautiful baby girl," he said.

"Oh, wonderful, Pete. And what is her name?"

"Arwen."

"Arwen? After you just got back from Medjugorje?"

"Arwen Mary, Mom."

"A lovely name, dear."

After her Medjugorje trip, Loretta began to say a fifteen-decade rosary each day, and keep a bread-and-water fast on Wednesdays and Fridays, as Our Lady of Medjugorje has asked. It was easier than she expected, and it wasn't necessary to explain to dinner hosts either, as most people assumed it was dietary or health-related. "Medjugorge solidified everything I'd always hoped and prayed for," she says. "I have visited several shrines but no place has affected me quite as much." Yes, she was still fighting distractions during prayer. But this time—true to form—she hit upon the idea of picturing Mary's clothes during each mystery of the rosary. What did Mary wear during the birth of Christ? The Ascension? Loretta never had problems praying again.

"Loretta," a priest once observed, "is the only person of her age that I have ever met, who keeps trying to be better each day."

Life Goes On

He who sows courtesy reaps friendship,
and he who plants kindness gathers love.

—SAINT BASIL

Judy received her master's degree in clinical psychology, and began to make notes for an autobiography. She and Loretta had a somewhat uneasy relationship by now. Loretta had finally told Judy the circumstances of her birth, and while Judy had understood why secrecy was needed in those years, she saw no reason for it to continue. Why would her birth mother still refuse to acknowledge her in the fullest way possible? It was something Judy longed to hear.

Instead, Loretta had sworn Judy to secrecy about the entire matter. Her stated reason was the same as it had been in 1935—it could create scandal, and there was no need for the public to know about something so personal. Things might have been different if Clark had played a role in Judy's life. But he'd seen her only twice (Judy claimed she met him a third time, at home, when she was about 12 years old—Loretta said no such meeting ever took place) and he had given Loretta no support money, aside from a few hundred dollars for a crib, during Judy's life.

Loretta had given an earlier television interview, in which she was asked about the graphic tell-all books written about Joan Crawford and Bette Davis by their daughters. Could such a thing, the interviewer wondered, ever happen to Loretta?

"Anything can happen to anybody," Loretta said during the interview, "but my daughter is a beautiful, loving girl. If she ever decides to write a book, it's her business and I'm sure it will be a nice book, since we've always been very good friends." Later, Loretta thought perhaps Judy might have interpreted this as encouragement for her book project.

But Loretta had no suspicion that the book would be about Judy's search for her ancestry. When she discovered the truth, the two women had a terrible quarrel, beginning an estrangement that was to last more than 10 years.

During that same period, Loretta agreed to star in another NBC made-for-TV movie, "Lady in a Corner," with Brian Keith. The script seemed designed for Loretta; she played the editor-in-chief of a top fashion magazine being taken over by a sleazy English publisher. With the help of her friends and co-workers, the character managed to raise the purchase price herself, and fall in love with an old flame (Keith) along the way. Loretta seemed even more beautiful in this role than in "Christmas Eve," although she was now 76. After the movie aired, there was talk of creating a series around Loretta's character. It would be a wonderful chance to get back to the one constant in her life, she realized. But did she want to live that demanding schedule all over again? The question became moot, when the network decided not to proceed.

The decision was understandable; another generation was now running the movie and television media, and few of them had heard of her. It was to be expected, but not always easy to take. One day she came out of St. Paul's church in Westwood, just as the parish school was dismissing students. She had parked her

Rolls-Royce nearby, and a nine- or ten-year-old girl was hanging around the car, patting it and draping herself across it as if it were hers. Her classmates were milling around. Loretta watched for a moment, then started toward the scene. "Do you like this car, honey?" she asked.

"Oh!" Startled, the little girl blushed fiercely. Then she dropped her voice. "I told the kids that this car belonged to my aunt, and that she was coming to pick me up today. . . ."

"Oh?" Loretta noticed the group of children watching from a distance. The little girl looked up at her, eyes pleading. *Don't give me away . . .*

"Well," Loretta whispered. "I can play that part. Can you?"

"Really?"

"Of course. Call me Aunt Loretta."

The child slipped into her role. " 'Bye everyone. My Aunt Loretta is here, and I have to go now!" She hopped in the front seat and Loretta went around to the driver's side. As she pulled away, she asked the child where she lived.

"Oh, you don't really have to take me home," the child answered. "Just drop me off in another block."

"Well, as long as I'm driving you, we might as well get you home safely."

As they rode, they chatted about inconsequential things. Mary Jane, the child, kept stealing sideways glances, and finally she asked, "Is your name really Loretta?"

"Yes. Loretta Young."

"Oh," the girl looked disappointed. "I was hoping you were Loretta Lynn."

"Sorry about that! Would it make you feel any better to know that Loretta Lynn was named after me?"

"No!"

"Truly." Loretta Lynn's mother had considered Loretta Young and Claudette Colbert the two most beautiful women in the world.

If her expected baby was a girl, she was going to be named after one of them, but which one? Loretta Lynn's mother had hung pictures of both stars up on the wall of her humble coal miner's shack, trying to decide. A day before the birth, she chose "Loretta." (Loretta Lynn has wondered more than once whether she would have succeeded in country music if her name had been "Claudette.")

Mary Jane had a one-track mind. "Have you ever met her?"

"No, but we've tried to get together a few times. Maybe someday we'll do it."

"Well," Mary Jane's eyes were shining, "if you ever meet her, can you get her autograph for me?"

Loretta laughed. "I'll certainly try," she promised.

Mary Jane went home with an adventure to tell her mother, never knowing who her "Aunt Loretta" really was. (And when Loretta's pals took her to task, she belatedly agreed one should never drive a child home without parental consent. Not only the movie industry had changed.)

On another occasion, Loretta and actress Carol Channing were coming out of a restaurant when a group of young women noticed them. The women stared—at Carol. One finally expressed admiration for a recent play Carol had done.

Carol is surprisingly shy around her fans, and sensitive to others' feelings. She introduced Loretta and attempted to draw her into the group. No one seemed to recognize her.

Later, in the car, Loretta told Carol that such politeness was kind but not necessary. "They weren't old enough to have seen me in anything," she pointed out. "And they were so thrilled to meet you."

"There are forty-year-olds who don't know anything about me," Loretta said later. "Then there are those who watch the classics on television without realizing how old these films are. They believe that I look the same way I did then." Why, she asked, should she disillusion them? After all, she was discovering, anonymity had a certain charm.

PART EIGHT

Last Request

I met Loretta about fourteen years ago, when I gave a retreat at Dolores Hope's house, and she attended. As Loretta did with so many new friends, she kept in touch and offered us the use of her house when we came to California. She collected my tapes and books, and always wanted to talk about them when I saw her (in fact, she often quoted my words back to me!).

Loretta was a deeply religious woman. I'm not sure many people realize that. Struggles in her life had made her a realist, very down to earth in the midst of a make-believe theatrical world. Her faith could be summed up in one phrase: her acceptance of the Divine Will. Whatever happened, she knew that God would be there.

I visited her in her hospital room two weeks before she died. Her doctor was with her when I arrived. Her first words to me were not, "Hello, Father" but "Do I have to have chemotherapy?"

"Do you want it?" I asked.

"Absolutely not!"

"What good will it do for her?" I asked the doctor. He pointed out that she might gain another year or two of life. But at what cost? I could sense that the timing of my visit was fortunate for the doctor. He now had a witness to Loretta's wishes.

"Loretta, are you afraid of dying?" I asked.

"Heck, no! I'm afraid of living!"

As far as I was concerned, she didn't have to say any more. This was a woman who knew where she was going, and what was awaiting her. Who would want to keep her from it? Her last request was granted.

Benedict J. Groeschel, C.F.R.
Director of Spiritual Development,
Archdiocese of New York

Part 8 photo—One of Loretta Young's favorite candid shots, taken in Honolulu, Hawaii (photo on preceding page).

Grow Old Along With Me

If I could find some man who was out of his mind,
I might just marry again. . . .

—LORETTA YOUNG

It was a new decade, the '90s. Loretta's life was as busy as she wanted to make it, filled with house parties and galas. She was still receiving awards and working on fund-raisers too. But when she was home on Ambassador Avenue, she was alone, except for a housekeeper, and there were risks. One evening, as Loretta sat in her bedroom at her sewing machine, she looked down and suddenly saw a pair of man's shoes on the floor. Her eyes traveled upward, across trousers, shirt, to a face disguised by a stocking mask. "Give me all your jewelry!" the burglar demanded.

"It's there, in the drawer," she quavered, her heart pounding. This was the second time she'd been robbed in this house.

The man rifled through bracelets and rings. "Is this all you have?" he growled.

"Well, the last burglar cleaned me out, and I haven't had time to replace the good stuff." Her nerves were settling down. This poor man seemed more frightened than she. "Are you in trouble?" she asked.

He was. For the next few minutes, he explained the family difficulty, which had led him to these desperate measures. Loretta was moved with pity. "Tell you what," she suggested. "I can write you a check, for cash!"

The burglar stared at her through the mesh. "Lady, you must be nuts," he murmured. "But I'll figure out another way. Thanks for listening." He headed, empty-handed, toward the bathroom from where he had obviously entered. "And get yourself a better burglar alarm," he told her. "The one on this window is too easy."

"I'll pray for you," she called after him.

Loretta's friends were not surprised when she related the story. "For years we had been warning her about her own safety," her friend Mary "Gabe" Farrell says. "She would pick up strangers in her car, carry money around to give to people in need—it was just a matter of time before something happened."

Loretta was unconcerned. She had an innocence, and that irrepressible giggle, that seem to disarm most people, and few took advantage of it. God was in charge, she told her friends. After all her struggles, she was arriving at that happy place of "spiritual indifference" where she sought only what He wanted.

And what He wanted was love. When she heard of someone in need, she would ask her attorney or perhaps a close friend such as Mary Farrell or Virginia Zamboni to check the situation out for her, and see what was needed. Once she anonymously paid the cost of an operation for a person who was uninsured. The only time she put people aside was if tourists interrupted her in church—she would quietly ask them to wait until she had finished praying. Even under those circumstances, she was gentle.

She wasn't afraid to widen her perspective either. At first, she had been dumbfounded when Tom became involved with "holy rollers." But as the Catholic Charismatic Renewal gained ground in the United States, Loretta suspended her objections, and attended prayer meetings to see what it was all about. She came to understand that the charisms of healing, tongues, and prophecy were as old as her church, and just another way to worship. (Not that she would ever forsake her rosary!)

Her household continued to accommodate a constant bustle of guests, both old friends and new. Once Loretta agreed to do a rare interview with a *New York Times* reporter, just before the Academy Awards presentation. Syndicated columnist Cal Thomas read the article with great interest while en route to a speaking engagement in Kentucky. "Like many Americans, I had loved Loretta for decades," he says. After checking into his hotel, Cal turned on the television, and one of his favorite Loretta films was showing: *The Bishop's Wife*. "It must be a sign!" he thought. When he returned home, he wrote to Loretta, in care of Norman Brokaw, her agent, and asked for a photo.

Loretta believed in signs too. Two weeks later, a brown envelope, hand addressed, arrived in the mail. "Since you didn't specify whether you wanted an old photo or a recent one," she had written, "I'm sending one of each."

"I can't tell the difference!" Cal wrote back.

It was the beginning of a warm friendship. Cal and his wife eventually met Loretta, and began staying at her home when in southern California. One year she threw a birthday party for him. Jane Wyman attended, and one of his favorite photos is of "being flanked by these two wonderful women at the dinner table."

"Often at night, we would get into deep discussions about God and His Son," Cal says. "Loretta's faith went deeper than the label 'Catholic,' although she was a very devout and sincere Catholic. We often spoke of Jesus and our mutual desire to know Him and represent Him better.

"Sometimes the light from a lamp would caress her face in a special way, and I would see flashes of that youthful brilliance that captivated people for decades," he recalls. "It would nearly take my breath away, not only because of her remarkably-preserved beauty, which was far more than skin-deep, but because I had the privilege of sitting with her in her home."

There are celebrities, and there are stars, he says. Loretta Young was, and always will remain, a star.

Father John Lynch, of the diocese of New York, also stayed up late with Loretta—watching her old movies. "When Father Groeschel and I (and usually another priest) stayed with Loretta, he would go to bed after dinner and we 'young ones' would be treated to Loretta redirecting a film," Father Lynch remembers. "She'd pick it apart—the costume was awful, the lighting worse, this shot should have been held longer . . . she was hilarious. For me, who'd grown up on old movies, it was an enchanting experience." Loretta could be very hard on herself, but "I never heard her say a negative or cruel thing about anyone, in the business or out of it."

Loretta enjoyed the commotion, but it was bittersweet. She was gradually facing the fact that not only had her career ended, so would many of her relationships. This would be a time of great loss. But she had lived through sorrow before, and she could do it again.

In 1991, her longtime friend, Jane Sharp, developed bone cancer. Jane was expected to die quickly, but she lingered for eighteen painful months. Loretta, radiant with good health, decided to spend weekends with Jane, to give her daughter, the primary caretaker, a break.

It was like a spiritual retreat, the women agreed. There in that quiet bedroom, their lives touched again, now on a far deeper level, as they discussed suffering and God and what was going to happen to Jane. Loretta prepared Jane's meals, helped her with the bedpan, brushed her hair. When Jane grew afraid or depressed, Loretta slept on the sofa bed next to her. It was, as Loretta put it, one of the best gifts that God had ever given her.

And Jane must have agreed. On August 30, 1992, she smiled at Loretta, murmured "Gretch," and slipped into a coma. She died the next day, with her children and Loretta at her side.

Another longtime friend had died during this time, Maggy Louis, the wife of Jean, the dress designer. Loretta had been at her side too, and had heard one of her last requests. "Take care of Jean," Maggy had asked her. "Don't let Hollywood swallow him up."

"Don't worry, Maggy," Loretta had reassured her. "I'll keep an eye on him."

Jean Louis, a devout Catholic, had been born in France and come to America when hired by designer Hattie Carnegie. Irene Dunne had fallen in love with his dresses, and he became head Columbia Pictures designer in 1944, dressing Judy Garland, Carol Channing, Doris Day, and others (many stars specifically requested his services in their contracts). His most famous creations included the strapless black satin that Rita Hayworth wore in *Gilda,* (other designers called it "a masterpiece of engineering") and Marilyn Monroe's flesh-toned sequined dress, worn when she sang a breathy "Happy Birthday" to President John F. Kennedy. It sold at auction in 1999 for over one million dollars, setting a new record. Jean also ran a salon in Beverly Hills, dressing private clients such as the Duchess of Windsor. He and Loretta had become friends on the set of her television show, for which he had created fifty-two of her gowns.

People remember Jean with great affection, as a gentle, quiet man. "I met him years ago in New York when I was on the stage," says Jane Wyatt. When Jane got the role of the wife in the acclaimed television series, "Father Knows Best," Jean Louis designed her wardrobe. "My housedresses in one dressing room, then, in the room next door, a sequined gown for Marlene

Dietrich," Jane says. "It was quite a contrast, and we had a lot of laughs about it, especially since Marlene was actually the domestic one—she shopped for the fabric for all her clothes, and loved to cook. She was always eyeing my aprons."

"Jean was kind to his models," says Rosalie Calvert, who worked for him in print layouts and at his salon. "Other designers would yell at you if you gained as much as an ounce. But Jean would say, 'Oh, perhaps the seamstress made this too tight.' He respected your dignity."

"My first impression of Jean Louis was not only his impeccable dress, but his impeccable manners and humility," Cal Thomas recalls. "He was a man of many graces, and of an old school which has largely passed away."

Jean's humble nature masked a brilliant talent. Before retiring, he had been nominated fourteen times for an Oscar, "but he refused to promote himself," Loretta said, "he never even took out an ad as other designers did." Edith Head, a perennial favorite, usually brought home the awards, but the clothes in *Solid Gold Cadillac* (1956) finally won Jean the Oscar most felt was long overdue. He and Maggy were childless, but Jean was devoted to his wife, and now, at her death, friends felt he would be lost.

One morning, Jean's housekeeper phoned Loretta. Jean had come home in a state of confusion from his customary walk. Loretta went immediately to see him. He wasn't sure who she was.

Jean had had a small stroke. He recovered, but Loretta was concerned about him. Gradually, the two began to "date." "It was lovely, since I had known him for what seemed like forever," Loretta said. "We were completely compatible." Jean no doubt knew Loretta very well too—and understood her need to stay in control of her life while still enjoying a man's companionship.

Chris and Linda had begun a company, The Entertainment Group, producing videos and television documentaries. Their work took them around the country, but their home base was now in Palm Springs. Loretta and Jean went to stay with them for a few months. Both were tired of the busyness of the Los Angeles area, and wished for a simpler life. "Almost as a lark, Jean and I went house-hunting, just to see what was available in Palm Springs," Loretta said. "The real estate woman was confused by our names—Lewis and Louis. 'Then, you aren't married?' she asked. Jean and I looked at each other, and realized we had both been thinking the same thing."

Loretta consulted a priest. Would it be appropriate for a couple as old as they to marry? Assured that there would be no barriers, she and Jean went to Los Angeles and applied for a marriage license. (The clerk handed it to them, then grandly announced that, "The state of California compels me to remind you that your union could result in a child." Loretta and Jean could barely keep from laughing. "Even I wouldn't believe in that miracle!" Loretta murmured.) On August 10, 1993, in a quiet ceremony at the Church of the Good Shepherd in Beverly Hills, they wed. Peter Lewis was best man, Georgie Montalban, matron of honor. The bride was 80, the groom 85.

The third time was apparently the charm. Loretta and Jean put their Beverly Hills properties on the market, settled down in Palm Springs and simply enjoyed life. Jean would arise first, dress immaculately and go out for long walks, where neighbors learned to watch for him, and wave. "He and Loretta were very tender with each other," Cal Thomas says, "and there was a quiet communication between them, something understood only by people who have enjoyed a long satisfying relationship. It was clear she was taking care of him, but then, Loretta took care of so many people."

During these years, Loretta narrated two documentaries in an award-winning series titled "American Traditions," produced by her son Christopher. But, for the most part, she had decided that her career and all that it entailed—speaking, traveling, even interviews—was over. She was content, except for one problem:

Some of us, like Bishop Fulton Sheen, are roosters. His dinners began at 6:00 P.M. with the expectation that guests would leave promptly at 7:45. This allowed the good bishop to be in bed by eight so he could arise cheerfully for prayer and meditation each morning at four.

Loretta, of course, was just the opposite, an owl. Thus she had been dismayed after moving to Palm Springs to discover that the latest daily Mass was usually over by seven A.M. Her retirement plans had definitely not included driving to church in the dark, so she searched for a priest willing to say Mass at a slightly more benign hour. Finally, she found one, and was able to arrange a daily fifteen-decade rosary recitation and Mass, beginning at eleven, at a tiny chapel in the Desert Regional Medical Center. It was here that she met several new friends, including Dee Reynolds, a volunteer on the hospice floor.

Loretta had never returned to a regular schedule of hospice volunteering, but she still missed it. When Dee occasionally mentioned a particular AIDS or cancer patient who needed cheering, Loretta was willing to stop by. "We had to be sure not to overwork Loretta," Dee says. "Everyone on the floor wanted to see her." According to Loretta, she did nothing but listen, hold their hands and hug them—but the expressions of joy on their faces told even a casual observer that her presence meant much more.

One December, a woman named Lola was on the list for hospice home visits. She was an independent, bossy and rough-spoken woman who, Dee discovered, was a huge fan of Ricardo Montalban. As Christmas approached, one morning after Mass, Dee made a suggestion to Loretta. "I was wondering if I could give Lola a gift basket, and ask Ricardo to sign the card," she suggested. "Lola would be ecstatic."

"Wonderful! Only I'm sure Ricardo would like to be a real part of it." And she would too, Loretta realized as she drove home. Actually, wasn't it time she stopped giving Georgie and

Ricardo Christmas gifts? Her sister and brother-in-law certainly didn't need anything, and everyone was just going through the motions because of a date on a calendar. Christmas was so much more than that.

By the time she got home, she had decided what to do. She would give a gift basket, in Ricardo's name, to Lola (and find another needy soul for Georgiana's basket). Such gifts would grace many people, and carry out the real meaning of Christmas. She alerted Ricardo, who happily signed the card. She learned from Dee what Lola's favorite items were, and packed a very personal basket. On Christmas Eve, a friend of Loretta's went to Lola's house, rang the doorbell and presented the astonished woman with the beribboned gift, giving no information and quickly slipping away.

It was a wonderful Christmas. Loretta decided that, although she would not banish all gift-giving in the family, she would prefer to give baskets in the names of many people she loved, instead of shopping for them. And so she did.

Note: A week after Christmas, when Dee went to visit Lola, the patient was still on Cloud Nine. Dee tried to act surprised as Lola described the event again and again. "A basket from Ricardo Montalban! Ricardo! How did he know about me?"

Dee casually shrugged. "Maybe an angel arranged everything."

Lola paused and thought. Then she shook her head. "Naw. What kind of angel would bring me cigarettes and wine?" What kind, indeed?

∼

Loretta had never forgotten her experience at Medjugorje, and had been passing out copies of Jack Sacco's audiotape to anyone who was remotely interested. She knew of more than one miracle resulting from a visit to this holy ground, and longed to share the

Medjugorje experience with Jean. But the trip had been rigorous. Could Jean manage it?

Loretta and Jack Sacco had become friends—in fact, Jack was currently house-sitting her home in Beverly Hills, which was still unsold. Jack had made the trip several times, and volunteered to go with Loretta and Jean. They took a more comfortable commercial flight to Germany, spent a day in rest, then flew to Split and boarded the bus to Medjugorje.

The group arrived late at night, and Loretta was relieved to see that improvements to Medjugorje had been made. Their young host family, friends of Jack's, welcomed them with big smiles, and showed them to a private room with bath. Not surprisingly, after the ordeal of the trip, Jean seemed extremely tired, and Loretta was alarmed. "Do you have your rosary?" she asked him. He pulled out his black-and-silver rosary to show her and she noticed the crucifix was missing. "We'll go and buy one tomorrow," she told him. Exhausted, they both fell into bed, too tired to recite the prayers.

The next day, Jean seemed perkier, but Loretta was still concerned. Had she done the right thing by bringing him here? Their tour group spent some time with Vicka, one of the visionaries, and afterward went to a little stand to look for a silver cross for Jean's silver rosary. When Jean took the rosary out of his pocket, however, everyone gasped. The silver chain links had all turned to gold! "I think now that it was Mary's way of reassuring me that Jean would be well cared for, and I didn't need to worry about him," Loretta said. "Abandonment to His will—isn't it thrilling to watch it work?" After Jean died, Loretta used his rosary. One day she noticed that the new cross had turned from the color of silver to gold.

See You in Heaven

The problem with making heroes out of humans is that when they
eventually act like humans, everyone is disappointed.

—*TOUCHED BY AN ANGEL*

Perhaps it was fortunate that Loretta had a restful spiritual period in
Medjugorje, because she would soon hit another low. Judy had
written her book, and to Loretta's chagrin, it detailed conversations
they had had about Clark Gable, conversations Loretta had assumed
would always remain private. One can again argue that Judy had a
right to know her background, and another right to reveal it if she
chose. Many in the Hollywood community also felt that—the secret
now revealed—Loretta should have admitted it and stood by her
daughter, rather than resorting to her usual "no comment."

However, Loretta remained aloof, and the media apparently
respected her decision; although Judy made several television
appearances, no one in the media asked Loretta to comment or
appear. In fact, Loretta told many friends that she did not even
read the book, *Uncommon Knowledge,* all the way through. "I got
to about page 60, and closed it," she said. Wouldn't curiosity
have forced her to finish it? "I suspected that whatever I read
might cause me to become bitter," she explained. "Judy and I
were already estranged and I was sorry about that; if I resented

things she had written—and kept remembering them—it might keep us from ever reuniting. It was better not to know."

And yet she wrote a note to Judy, saying, "I have just finished your book, and I'm stunned. I don't know how you could ever face me, much less say you love me . . ." It isn't know whether Judy ever received this note. But obviously, Loretta was devastated.

No doubt the situation also increased Loretta's recurring guilt over her parenting decisions. If she had not been absent so much, steeped in her own private misery, if she had taken a firmer stand over Tom's fathering of Judy, would Judy have written such a book? But if she had learned anything during her sojourn on earth, it was this: one cannot go back. "You do the best with what you have at the time," she often said, "and then, you let it go."

Years had passed, without communication from Judy. In fact, the entire family had sided with Loretta over *Uncommon Knowledge*. In 1997, Christopher and Linda were producing a television program on the Beverly Hills Hotel, and decided to ask Judy if they could interview her. (Because Loretta and Tom had once owned a percentage of the hotel, Judy had spent time there.) The interview went well, and Judy had dinner with her brother and sister-in-law. Later, Loretta and Judy met for lunch, but they quarreled again and continued the stalemate. Nonetheless, family fence-mending had begun.

Perhaps 1997 was Loretta's most difficult year. Polly Ann died of emphysema shortly after the holidays. In April, Loretta faced another loss—Jean. "Goodbye, my angel," he had told Linda one Saturday evening, blowing her a kiss. Sunday morning, while getting ready for Mass, Loretta noticed him apparently napping under a patio umbrella, wearing a spiffy white suit and waiting patiently for her. She thought it was too hot for him to be outside, and went to "nag" him. . . . It was the paramedics who told her he was gone. "I was joyful because I knew Polly and Jean were ready to face God," Loretta said. "It was a relief to know they were safely home." But it was an enormous loss too; despite their ages, she had hoped for more happy years with Jean. "A little chunk of your heart goes with each person you've loved and lost."

Her siblings, Sally and Jack, were both battling cancer. Soon she would surrender them too. And there was another loss in her life, someone she refused to think about because the anger and pain still ran too deep—her daughter. How would she know if Judy was ill, or in need? What if something happened to her? The barriers between them seemed insurmountable, and yet . . . For the first time in years, Loretta begged God to intervene, to show both women how to forgive. Then Loretta wrote Judy a note.

Judy responded tentatively. A short time later, Sally died, and when Loretta went to the funeral in Los Angeles, Judy was there. This time the two of them grabbed a Montalban grandchild, put her in a car between them (so they would not fight), and talked for a long time.

It was the beginning of the end of the feud. Soon Judy was spending weekends with her mother in Palm Springs. Things were precarious at first, but both women truly longed for healing, and were willing to let God bring it about. One day, Loretta turned to Judy. "Honey, I'm sorry about a lot of things but most of all, that I pushed you to marry Joe Tinney. I know how unhappy you were."

"Mom, it was a long time ago. It's okay."

"I'm still sorry."

"Well, I'm sorry that Grandma pushed you to marry Tom." The two looked at each other. Recovery had begun. Could closeness be far behind? During Loretta's last stint in the hospital, people recall a touching scene—Judy and Loretta watching TV together in silence, holding hands.

Loretta's brother Jack died in 1998, leaving Georgiana the only family member of her generation. Loretta plunged back into charity work. She and Jane Wyman now belonged to St. Louis parish, and the church definitely needed help. Over the next few years, the women refurbished the sanctuary, recarpeted the entire church and contributed heavily to the newly-established food bank. Loretta liked to arrive at 3:30 for the Saturday evening Mass (in order to recite the rosary first) so the pastor learned to race over and unlock the doors before she arrived.

Loretta also continued her voluminous correspondence, the piles on her desk truly constituting a fire hazard. "I guess the mail is like a ministry," she once said, "although it's also fun for me." She was always interested in her fans, and intrigued that, according to the webmasters on her sites, many visitors were young people, just getting acquainted with her old black-and-white films. Her appeal to the young was a welcome surprise. Once, she and Virginia Zamboni went to a sushi bar for dinner, a place they had never been before. They ordered madly, and ran up a fairly large bill. When they went to pay it, however, they saw a sign: "No credit cards accepted."

The women were aghast and embarrassed. "We searched our purses and pockets," Virginia recalls. "We had very little cash." Visions of police stations danced before their eyes. However, two husky young men had noticed their dilemma. One quietly said something to the manager. A moment later, the manager approached them. "Miss Young," he asked, "could you possibly sign an autograph for us?"

He got his autograph—and his money, the next day. How interesting that of all the patrons in the dining room, only the youngest apparently recognized Loretta. She found such happenings very meaningful. "Not everyone lives long enough to be told, 'you made a difference' or 'you kept me from doing something wrong,'" she said. But her type of fan was easily intimate with her, sharing tender parts of a life with no trace of embarrassment. Like a stone thrown into a pond, she created ripples that went much further than she could imagine—and she loved knowing where some of them ended up.

In January, 1999, bowing to the pleas of an editor-friend, she consented to be photographed for an article in *Vanity Fair* on Hollywood's greatest stars. It would be her final shoot. Her photo caused a sensation among readers—the same high cheekbones and astonishing eyes, the hair softly graying surrounding still-flawless skin—could this woman possibly be 86 years old? Loretta waved the comments aside, noting that "today's air-brushing techniques can do wonders," and retreated to her private life. She still enjoyed an occasional dress-up affair, where she "put on my Loretta Young face," but was far more comfortable at home now, her array of awards, including Oscar, resting casually on top of some kitchen cabinets, surrounded by statues of the Blessed Mother, and under the cabinets, photos of Judy, Christopher, and Peter. The blend summed up her life as no words could.

For at last, when she least expected it, she had found peace. There was surface turmoil of course; in a life as large as hers, there would always be. But the inner core, the strength she had pursued for so long, had finally been won. "I know now when I'm Loretta and when I'm Gretchen," she said shortly before her death. "As Loretta, I'm controlled, stricter, alert to even a tone in a person's voice which can compliment or criticize. Gretch is more relaxed. It's easier to laugh, cry, get mad, love, and say exactly what I mean. Maybe that's why my life is more pleasing to me now; I'm not playing those roles."

Nor was she anything but honest with her life's Companion. No fudging, no excuses now—just herself before Him. Things had not always turned out the way she'd hoped. But as she clung to Him, giving Him the knots and threads of her brokenness, He had fashioned a tapestry. Now she knew no other way to pray, except to say, "God, I want to thank you beforehand for everything, good, bad, and indifferent, that's going to happen to me tomorrow—a parking space or cancer. I want to feel, think, say, and do only what You want."

It was the very essence of Love.

POSTSCRIPT

He walks with me and He talks with me,
And He tells me I am His own.

—IN THE GARDEN, *TRADITIONAL HYMN*

When Loretta allowed my wife and me into her world less than a decade ago, we joined an exclusive club whose members were never rivals for her attention and affections, which she gave freely. Instead, we felt ourselves members of a family who enjoyed each other's company because we all enjoyed hers.

—CAL THOMAS,
LOS ANGELES TIMES *SYNDICATE, AUGUST 15, 2000*

Loretta Young defied the years better than any actress I can think of. At a very elegant party in Malibu honoring Rudolf Nureyev and Margot Fonteyn several years ago, Loretta arrived in what seemed a motorcyclist's outfit, except that it was of black sateen, clinging to a form that could not have changed substantially since she was in her teens. It and she were gorgeous.

Nureyev, who caught sight of her as she walked in, slipped upstairs and returned in his own black motorcyclist's outfit, paying homage to a beautiful woman.

—CHARLES CHAMPLIN,
LOS ANGELES TIMES, *AUGUST 14, 2000*

I went to work every day, my pregnancy showing more each month, looking straight ahead, hoping I wouldn't get fired. In those days, it could have happened. No insurance for the baby. No maternity leave. All that was left was shame.

I went to the Blessed Mother for love and understanding, and she gave it. I found St. Anne's Home for Unwed Mothers. And I met Loretta Young. She gave me hope, and showed me the right way to address problems. If she—and St. Anne's—hadn't been there, I don't know what the outcome would have been.

My son is a fine man. I thank God, and Loretta, for him every day.

—NAME WITHHELD

Loretta Young's career was so significant and went on for so long that she's a little like the mythic animal—so big that the description varies, depending on whether the describer saw the head or the tail. . . . It is probable that (she) is just beginning to be appreciated. Her body of work is vast. Her early films are winning her new audiences, and when her television work becomes available, we'll be able, for the first time, to grasp the full breadth of this career.

—MICK LASALLE,
SAN FRANCISCO CHRONICLE, *AUGUST 14, 2000*

I believe that if we have lived our lives fully and well, and have accomplished, at least in part, the things we were put here to do, we will be prepared—mentally, physically and spiritually—for our separation from this world.

—LORETTA YOUNG

He only saw the trying, Gretch. Welcome home.

Resources

Web Sites

www.lorettayoung.com Established by Meredith Leonard in 1998, to add to her main site (www.meredy.com) which features many classic film stars. Loretta's site contains photos, free LY downloads and tribute pages with messages from her fans. "Loretta Young has always been one of my favorite actresses," says Meredy. "Her beauty and genuine charm appealed to me. Her career spanned almost a century, and I think it's a true shame that she was not given lifetime achievement awards while she was alive to enjoy the kudos."

www.apostles.com/lorettayoung.html Established by Bob Hubbard. "Since the 1950s, Loretta has been my favorite actress," says Bob. "When I was ten or eleven, I tried to figure out her age and estimate if she was too old for me to marry." He first considered doing a site for her in 1995 when he was making some others, one for the Padre Pio Foundation, another for Albert Magnus College, where he teaches. He finally did the site in 1998. "Over the past years, I have sent Loretta updates on the site's main pages, and she has responded with very kind and gracious letters," says Bob. "The very facts of Loretta's life—her dedication to producing TV shows and movies that would help people, her charitable work, and most of all, the example of her religious faith—clearly show why she was important."

Videos

The Loretta Young Show:
A boxed set of 7 videos containing 14 half-hour television programs, hosted by her son, film producer, Christopher Lewis. (Approximately 6 hours)
$49.95 + S/H and applicable sales tax

or

Four individual videos, with 2 programs on each $19.95 per video + $5.00 S/H and applicable sales tax.

It's possible that more Loretta Young shows may be made available on video. Stay tuned.

The Great Steamboat Race
A documentary narrated by Loretta Young (50 minutes)
$19.95 + $5.00 S/H
and applicable sales tax

Life Along the Mississippi
A documentary narrated by Loretta Young (50 minutes)
$19.95 + $5.00 S/H and applicable sales tax

To order, phone:
The Entertainment Group
Toll Free 877-337-2100
FAX (865) 681-9031
131 Littlebrook Circle
Rockford, TN 37853-3127
Email: www.theentertainmentgroup.com

Loretta also narrated a series on the mysteries of the rosary titled **The Story of Our Redemption** for **The Family Theatre.** There are three videos, on the Joyful, Sorrowful and Glorious mysteries. The series is $39.95, or $14.95 each.

To order, phone:
Holy Cross Family Ministries
Toll free: 800-299-7729
518 Washington St.
North Easton MA 02356

For more information on Medjugorje:
Medjugorje Magazine,
317 W. Ogden, Westmont, IL 60559. A quarterly. $15 per year, $18 in Canada and Mexico, U.S. dollars only

To contact author Joan Wester Anderson, write P.O. Box 127, Prospect Heights IL 60070
Email:
angelwak@mcs.com or check her web site at http://www.mcs.net/~angelwak/home/html